JOSSEY-BASS TEACHER

Jossey-Bass Teacher provides educators with practical knowledge and tools to create a positive and lifelong impact on student learning. We offer classroom-tested and research-based teaching resources for a variety of grade levels and subject areas. Whether you are an aspiring, new, or veteran teacher, we want to help you make every teaching day your best.

From ready-to-use classroom activities to the latest teaching framework, our value-packed books provide insightful, practical, and comprehensive materials on the topics that matter most to K–12 teachers. We hope to become your trusted source for the best ideas from the most experienced and respected experts in the field.

The Problem with Math Is English

A LANGUAGE-FOCUSED APPROACH TO HELPING ALL STUDENTS DEVELOP A DEEPER UNDERSTANDING OF MATHEMATICS

Concepcion Molina

JOSSEY-BASS
A Wiley Imprint
www.josseybass.com

Published by Jossey-Bass
A Wiley Imprint
One Montgomery Street, Suite 1200, San Francisco, CA 94104-4594—www.josseybass.com

Jossey-Bass books and products are available through most bookstores. To contact Jossey-Bass directly call our Customer Care Department within the U.S. at 800-956-7739, outside the U.S. at 317-572-3986, or fax 317-572-4002.

Wiley publishes in a variety of print and electronic formats and by print-on-demand. Some material included with standard print versions of this book may not be included in e-books or in print-on-demand. If this book refers to media such as a CD or DVD that is not included in the version you purchased, you may download this material at **http://booksupport.wiley.com**. For more information about Wiley products, visit **www.wiley.com**.

Library of Congress Cataloging-in-Publication Data

Molina, Concepcion, 1952-
    The problem with math is English : a language-focused approach to helping all students develop a deeper understanding of mathematics / Concepcion Molina.
        p. cm.
    Includes bibliographical references and index.
    ISBN 978-1-118-09570-6 (pbk.), ISBN 978-1-118-22362-8 (pdf), ISBN 978-1-118-23702-1 (epub), ISBN 978-1-118-26195-8 (mobipocket)
    1. Mathematics—Study and teaching. 2. English language—Study and teaching. 3. Language arts—Correlation with content subjects. I. Title.
    QA135.6.M685 2012
    372.7—dc23

                                                                                    2012011537

Printed in the United States of America
FIRST EDITION
PB Printing   V10018023_031220

ACKNOWLEDGMENTS

This publication would not have been possible without the support, patience and encouragement of family, friends, and workplace colleagues. Sincere appreciation goes to Dr. Victoria Dimock, chief program officer at SEDL, for providing the opportunity and SEDL support necessary for completion of this extensive task. In addition, her support, commitment, and guidance were essential throughout the process. Special recognition is deserved by Joni Wackwitz, SEDL communications specialist, who was instrumental in the editing process. Her thorough review and thoughtful insights resulted in clear communication of the intended messages as well as smooth transitions and connections among topics.

My colleagues at SEDL are the most professional and knowledgeable educators I have ever had the honor of working with, and their support was instrumental in this endeavor as well. Special appreciation is deserved by Dr. Stephen Marble, former program manager and supervisor, for bringing me on board at SEDL and providing the opportunity to grow as a mathematics educator through the design and delivery of professional development for teachers. His guidance, reflective questions, and continued encouragement helped to bring out dormant mathematics knowledge within me that I did not realize existed.

The list of acknowledgments would be inadequate without the inclusion of the educators that helped to shape my future and my life. I was fortunate to have had caring and expert teachers during my 12 years in the Karnes City (Texas) Independent School District. It was their example and dedication that influenced my choice of education as a career. Recognition also goes to the faculty of the College of Education at Texas A&M University for their expertise and guidance during my teacher preparation and certification. Special thanks also to fellow teachers and staff at McAllen High School (McAllen, Texas) where I began my career, as well as fellow faculty at Moody High School (Corpus Christi, Texas) where I spent the majority of my time in the mathematics classroom. In particular, much appreciation to Mr Franciso Moreida, Moody High School mathematics department chair, who helped me grow as a teacher during my 11 years there.

I would be remiss if I did not acknowledge the students that I had the honor of teaching during my years in the mathematics classroom. Quite honestly, I often learned as much from them as they learned from me. Their questions, thinking, and approaches to mathematics expanded my horizons and raised my level of expertise. And their growth and appreciation helped energize me to do more and try harder.

Above all, I give thanks to the Lord Almighty for providing me with the insights, the experiences, the support, and opportunities, as well as the depth of thinking and the perseverance to reach this milestone.

To my wonderful wife, Yolanda, for her understanding and unwavering behind-the-scenes support.

To my immediate family members for their encouragement and patience.

To my SEDL colleagues for their support and guidance during the entire research and writing process.

To my departed siblings whose memories served as the inspiration to fulfill their unrealized potential through my work.

And most of all, to the memory of my parents, Carlos and Luisa Molina, who believed in me and unselfishly sacrificed so that I could avail myself of the educational opportunity they were never afforded.

CONTENTS

Concepcion Molina, EdD, grew up in a small south Texas town. Although born a Texan, he began school knowing very little English because Spanish was the primary language spoken at home. His entire elementary through high school education took place in that small town. He did well and was the first in his family to attend college. But first, he served four years in the U.S. Air Force as an accounting specialist.

After being honorably discharged, he attended Texas A&M University–College Station and graduated with honors with a Bachelor of Science degree in Educational Curriculum and Instruction with teaching certifications in secondary mathematics and Spanish. After graduation, his initial experience in the field of education was as a mathematics teacher at McAllen High School in the Texas Rio Grande valley. He remained for three years and taught Fundamentals of Mathematics, Pre-Algebra, Algebra I, and Geometry.

The next education stop was as a college admissions counselor at Texas A&M University—College Station. In that five-year span, Molina counseled visitors to campus on admissions, housing, and financial aid, represented the university at college nights and career fairs throughout Texas, and helped administer a scholarship program for academically gifted black and Hispanic students. The mathematics classroom beckoned, which led to teaching high school mathematics in Corpus Christi, Texas, for the next 11 years. The classes he taught included Algebra I, Algebra II, Geometry, Trigonometry, and Pre-Calculus. While teaching he earned a Master of Science degree in Educational Administration from Corpus Christi State University.

In 1998 he took on a new challenge by moving to Austin, Texas, to join the Southwest Educational Development Laboratory, a nonprofit educational agency that is now known as SEDL. As a program specialist he used scientifically based research to guide the design, piloting, and delivery of mathematics professional development training to clients in the five-state Southwest Consortium for the Improvement of Mathematics and Science Teaching (SCIMAST) region. In addition, he assisted and led in the planning, design, and delivery of the Consortium's regional forums and state meetings, as well as collaborating with other educational organizations and disseminating information that supported and promoted SCIMAST work. During this stage of his career, he finished the doctoral work that he had begun while still in Corpus Christi. In 2004, he earned an EdD in Educational Leadership from Texas A&M University–Corpus Christi.

When the SCIMAST program ended, Molina became part of SEDL's Texas Comprehensive Center and Southeast Comprehensive Center. As a staff member of both centers, he assisted and supported the state departments of education and their intermediate agencies in their efforts to implement No Child Left Behind (NCLB). Tasks and projects included the planning, design, and delivery of Comprehensive Center regional forums and meetings, assisting states with revision of state content standards, as well as designing and delivering professional development training requested by state agency staff on such topics as mathematics content, high school dropout prevention and high school reform models, systemic school reform, and mathematics instruction for EL students (English learners). This variety of experience and research has led to expertise in mathematics instruction, instructional leadership, teacher quality, professional development, and systemic reform.

ABOUT SEDL

SEDL (www.sedl.org) is a nonprofit education research, development, and dissemination organization based in Austin, Texas. Throughout our 45-year existence, two central ideas have guided our work. The first is one of purpose—serving the educational needs of children in poverty. We believe that a quality education is an essential mechanism for freeing both individuals and society from the ravages and inequities of poverty. The second idea is one of means—bridging the gap between research and practice. We believe a responsive, effective educational system must be grounded in a strong research base that is tightly linked to practice.

SEDL is committed to sustainable research- and experience-based solutions. We work at national, regional, state, and local levels to develop and study approaches to strengthen educational policy and practice. We also provide professional development, technical assistance, and information services tailored to the specific needs of our diverse constituencies, which include educational practitioners, policymakers, families, and other researchers.

Our current efforts address five program areas: improving school performance, strengthening teaching and learning in core content areas, integrating technology into teaching and learning, involving family and community in student learning, and connecting disability research to practice. Work in these areas concentrates on pre-K–16 education and on underserved students, particularly those living in poverty and English language learners. Among our current projects are rigorous scale-up research studies of mathematics and reading interventions, and two technical assistance centers that work intensively with state education agencies to help boost achievement among low-performing schools.

ABOUT THIS BOOK

The goal of this book is to raise readers' mathematics expertise while simultaneously explaining the critical role of language and symbolism in understanding mathematics conceptually. The main body of the text focuses on fundamental mathematical concepts that fall primarily in the algebra and number and operation strands of the mathematics content standards. At the same time, the text explores the relationships between and connections among key mathematics topics to illustrate how a basic understanding of more complex concepts can be developed while teaching fundamental ideas.

SUMMARY OF CONTENT

The journey begins with an investigation of issues related to language and symbolism in mathematics and mathematics instruction. Chapter One provides a sampling of the problems in both the language and math arenas. Chapter Two builds on that start with an in-depth look at why language is so problematic, and Chapter Three extends the conversation with a focus on language-based hurdles that permeate traditional instruction. Chapter Four begins the transition to a mathematics focus by examining the meaning and makeup of conceptual understanding in the math classroom. Next, Chapter Five uses the order of operations to illustrate how language-focused conceptual instruction leads to a deeper understanding than procedure-based traditional instruction. Chapter Six then spotlights the *concept* of multiplication, which transitions the focus from math instruction to math content.

The remaining chapters continue to explore how to help students develop a conceptual understanding of mathematics. Because fractions are such an issue for students—and even some teachers—two chapters are devoted to the topic. Chapter Seven examines the concept of fractions, with a deliberate slant to the language and symbolism involved; and Chapter Eight provides a deep look at the computation of fractions. Chapter Nine has a content focus, with the objective of merging the deep understanding of both concepts and their associated language and symbolism in a way that each bolsters and supports the other. Chapters Ten and Eleven apply all the preceding information by examining what conceptual math instruction looks like in action. Chapter Ten investigates language-focused instructional strategies, such as how fundamental concepts can be used to connect to more advanced topics, and Chapter Eleven focuses on how relationships in mathematics can serve as a powerful strategy for deepening understanding. Finally, Chapter Twelve recommends changes in the U.S. mathematics education system that would enable teachers to implement more effectively many of the ideas in this book.

APPROACH AND PHILOSOPHY

All teachers want their students to do well and to learn as much as possible. In their quest to boost learning, teachers often seek out new lessons and activities to use in their classrooms. Providing such lessons or activities is not the purpose of this book, although teachers are encouraged to use the models and strategies provided with their students. In some ways, creativity is a function of expertise. Rather than just provide activities, the philosophy of this book is to help teachers understand mathematics at a conceptual level so that they can develop their own activities to deepen students' learning. To maximize the book's utility and value, readers should *experience* the mathematics, answering questions or solving problems as they appear in the reading. The intent of these questions and problems is to take readers' content expertise to a higher level as well as to prompt readers to reflect on their personal knowledge of fundamental mathematics.

Through the process of answering questions and solving problems, readers will enhance their level of pedagogical content knowledge. Part of that learning will occur as readers identify the shortcomings in traditional instruction. Another part of that learning will occur as readers work through purposeful problems and activities to explore conceptual-level mathematics from a number of perspectives. The central theme of this text is that with a conceptual understanding of mathematics, teachers are empowered to do the following:

- Identify and understand the nuances and true meanings of mathematical language, symbolism, and visual representation.
- View a mathematical concept from different perspectives.
- Make connections among key concepts which will enhance and leverage the learning of a new topic with the deep understanding of another.
- Provide instruction focused on building a conceptual understanding of mathematics rather than memorizing rules and following procedures.

INTRODUCTION

Mathematics education in the United States has been the focus of a great deal of scrutiny. U.S students continue to perform poorly on state, national, and international math exams and continue to fall behind their global peers in mathematics performance. Although some progress has been made to address these issues, more work is needed. For years, the primary focus of mathematics reform has been on improving classroom instructional practices, and rightfully so. However, the best teaching practices in the world and the most advanced educational technology are of little use if the math content and the communication of that content are not of equal quality. This book focuses on these two often overlooked issues in mathematics education: (1) what we teach and (2) how we communicate it.

JULIAN'S STORY

Julian sits in his first-grade math class. He listens attentively because he enjoys the class and wants to please the teacher. Today is his first exposure to the topic of length, which the teacher refers to as a duration of time. Julian watches closely as the teacher moves the hands of a clock from one position to another and asks questions such as, "How long did it take to drive to grandmother's house?" The lesson is interesting, and Julian feels he understands. But a few weeks later, the teacher says the more common meaning of length is as a measure of distance, such as the length of a table. Then, later in the year, during an English lesson, Julian learns that length can also refer to a piece of some item, such as a length of rope. He is surprised and slightly puzzled by all these different meanings of the word. Things get even more complicated in his math education when Julian learns that if a length is vertical, it is called height, even though the units of measurement remain the same. He scratches his head when he is told his height is 37 inches, but his legs are 16 inches long. Some time later, Julian learns in basic geometry that the sides of a rectangle are called the length and the width. He is given an assignment where he must find the length of the width of a rectangle given the length of the length. Sometimes, Julian gets a little confused.

But mathematics remains Julian's favorite subject. He goes to college and gets certified to be a high school math teacher. To obtain this credential, he has to take calculus and a number of other rigorous mathematics courses. On his first day as a teacher, he walks into his freshman math class feeling confident and well prepared. While reviewing some basics with the class, one of the students asks why we invert and multiply when we divide by a fraction. Julian is at a loss, saddened to realize he does not know despite his level of education. The only answer he has is "That's the rule." The experience eats at him all day. That evening, Julian reflects on his knowledge of mathematics. He is teaching algebra as well as freshman math. Nervously, he wonders, "Do I know enough to teach these classes?" He looks ahead at the content of the algebra textbook. Slowly, he starts to panic at the thought of all the different questions students might ask. "What if someone asks why something to the zero power is 1?" Julian worries. He has no idea of the answer. As a student, he blindly accepted and memorized the various rules and procedures presented—just as his teachers told him to do. The panic turns to fear as he wonders what his response will be if a student asks what a logarithm is, rather than how to convert an equation from exponential to logarithmic form. Shaken and dejected, Julian realizes he does not know mathematics at the level needed to teach it well.

RATIONALE AND PURPOSE

Julian's story is my story. I began grade school knowing very little English. At the time, no bilingual or dual language programs were available, nor were teachers aware of all the EL (English Learner) strategies we have today. With regard to the challenge of learning English and mathematics at the same time, quite simply, I lived it. The inherent issues related to learning a language and academic content simultaneously led me to develop an acute awareness and appreciation of the problems and nuances of language, particularly in mathematics. Many of these problems go unnoticed by math educators. Addressing the neglected issue of language in mathematics and math instruction was a driving force in why I decided to write this book.

In addition to language, I wanted to focus this book on the mathematics content being taught in our education system. The start of my teaching career was a rude awakening regarding the depth of mathematics taught in the U.S. education system. I was a product of that system, and although I had made good grades and was certified to teach math at the secondary level, my initial classroom experiences clearly revealed the lack of depth of my mathematics knowledge. The true test of knowledge is revealed when one must teach it. In my first few years as a teacher, I struggled, but began deepening my knowledge of mathematics, learning more about what concepts were and why things work the way they do. And it was a focus on language that was the bridge in the transition from my being a good student of rules and procedures to a teacher of deep, conceptual mathematics.

In time, I left the classroom and began designing and delivering professional development in mathematics. This work focused primarily on middle schools, but included elementary schools as well. In my professional development sessions, my goal was to improve teachers' math content expertise by simultaneously using and modeling effective instructional practices grounded in research. During this time, I began to really examine the content of mathematics. The combination of teaching advanced math to high school students and fundamental math to elementary and middle school teachers enabled me to see surprising vertical connections across topics and concepts that previously had eluded me. In addition, during this time in my career, I did a doctoral dissertation that focused on the content knowledge of middle school math teachers. The volumes of research on this topic combined with my personal experiences as a student, teacher, and trainer transformed my perspective about what we are teaching and how we are communicating it.

As a compilation of hundreds of "aha" moments that I experienced both as a learner and a teacher, this book aims to improve the math content expertise of the reader. Teaching is a complex endeavor, and subject-matter expertise is only one of the many interrelated components involved. However, a teacher obviously cannot teach what he or she does not know. My dissertation research revealed that many elementary math teachers know the facts and procedures they teach, but have a weak understanding of the conceptual basis behind them—just as I did when I began teaching (Kilpatrick et al., 2001; Molina, 2004). Moreover, the educational system sends teachers the message that if they get good grades in college and get certified to teach, they know the content they need. The result is a teaching force with deficiencies in content expertise—and in many cases, neither teachers nor district and campus leaders even realize the deficiencies exist. As a result, educational reform in mathematics tends to focus on *how* instructors teach and overlooks *what* they teach.

This book uses a unique language-focused perspective to bring to light the deeper content knowledge that math teachers need as well as issues with how teachers communicate that content. The role of language and symbolism in learning and understanding mathematics is generally slighted in the U.S. education system, including K–12 education, teacher preparation and professional development programs, and state standards. Thus, the intersection of these issues leads to a specific focus on the role of language and symbolism in understanding mathematics conceptually.

The term language as used in this book goes far beyond the simplistic idea of vocabulary. Because language and symbolism are an integral part of teaching any mathematics concept, these two topics not only constitute separate chapters but are integrated throughout the text. The National Council of Teachers of Mathematics (NCTM) standards emphasize the importance of communication in mathematics, particularly in students' explanations and justifications of their mathematical thinking. However, in this publication, mathematical language and symbolism are viewed from a content perspective, where each aspect and nuance of mathematical language and symbolism is considered an integral part of the content to be learned. When I was a high school teacher, a sign above my classroom door read, "Se Habla Algebra," meaning "I speak algebra." More broadly interpreted, it states that the language of mathematics is spoken and understood here, which sums up the approach and philosophy of this publication.

WHO BENEFITS FROM THIS BOOK?

The ultimate goal of any educational publication is to improve student learning. To this end, this publication is geared primarily toward K–12 teachers who provide classroom instruction in mathematics, although the bulk of the content focuses on middle school mathematics. The language-focused conceptual mathematics presented in this text should be a new and refreshing approach to novice as well as veteran teachers. Readers who work in the classroom will increase their content knowledge while learning how to address language-based problems in mathematics, which in turn will improve instruction and student learning.

Improving the mathematics content knowledge of current and future teachers is a problem of scale, however. For this reason, a secondary audience for this publication consists of leaders in mathematics education. This group includes, but is not limited to, campus mathematics coaches and specialists, district mathematics coordinators, and state directors of mathematics. For example, this publication should prove valuable to educators who provide technical assistance and professional development to math teachers at the elementary and middle school levels. These leaders can accelerate change and affect a larger audience. Likewise, campus administrators can benefit from this book by seeing the type of conceptual mathematics that students should be learning. With this knowledge, administrators can ensure that teachers know and provide instruction in mathematics at a conceptual level. In addition, university staff in colleges of education can utilize this resource to ensure they produce a future teaching force of content experts.

The Problem with Math Is English (and a Few Other Things)

M any people do not consider English as playing a significant role in math, except in word problems. My hope in the forthcoming pages is to change that perspective. A well-known proverb says that to truly understand another's perspective, you must walk a mile in that person's shoes. Not everyone has experienced the struggle of learning both academic content and a new language at the same time. True, this double burden makes learning mathematics much more of a challenge. However, the phrase "the problem with math is English" applies to *all* students, not just those whose native language is not English. Language struggles are embedded in mathematics, which in many ways is its own language. These problems often occur at the critical juncture of math instruction and content. Two major issues in mathematics education that result from this merger are often overlooked: (1) the language and symbolism of mathematics, which in turn greatly influence (2) the mathematics itself—the content that we teach—and by association, how we communicate that content. The following scenarios introduce some key concepts related to these issues, which this book will explore in-depth.

WHY LANGUAGE AND SYMBOLISM?

Imagine you are a middle school student taking the state's required progress exam in mathematics. As you begin the test, you feel confident about your answers to the first few items. But then you read Item 5: "Find the arglif of a nopkam if the betdosyn is 12." Try as you will, the problem has you stumped. You finally give up, make a guess, and move on to the next problem. Unfortunately, you come across 14 other test items that confuse you in similar ways. Once again, the best you can do is guess at the answers. Later, you find out you did not pass the exam primarily because of those 15 items.

When most people see or hear the term *mathematics*, the initial thoughts that come to mind are numbers, computation, rules, and procedures. But the root cause of the student's inability to solve Item 5 is not because of a lack of knowledge of computation, rules, or procedures. If the strange terms *arglif*, *nopkam*, and *betdosyn* meant "area," "circle," and "diameter," respectively, Item 5 would become the following: "Find the area of a circle if the diameter is 12." However, if a student does not know the meanings of *area*, *circle*, and *diameter*, the terms might as well be *arglif*, *nopkam*, and *betdosyn* because they still hold no meaning.

This scenario is a rudimentary example of the key role that language plays in the understanding of mathematics. The student's difficulty is not in reading English, but in understanding the language of mathematics, and it makes no difference whether the student is fluent in English or not. A language problem still exists. Although perhaps not obvious, language is as critical in mathematics as in any other discipline. Moreover, the role of language in mathematics entails far more than vocabulary or definitions, encompassing a broad landscape of language-based issues, which are explored in this book.

Beyond Words: The Symbolism of Mathematics

Box 1.1

Solve the two tasks below:

a. $n = 1 + 3 + 5 + 7$

b. $\sum\limits_{n=1}^{4} 2n - 1$

For many people, the first problem in Box 1.1 is child's play, whereas the second poses a serious challenge. The interesting paradox about these two problems is that although the second seems far more difficult, they are, in fact, the same problem. They are just presented differently. The first problem seems simple because most people can easily interpret what the numerals and symbols are telling them to do. The second problem, however, will literally be Greek to many people because they have no idea what those symbols mean. The problem becomes much simpler once the symbols are explained. The symbol $\sum$ is a summation symbol. The $n = 1$ in the subscript means that 1 is the first value of n in the expression $2n - 1$, and the superscript 4 indicates the last value to be used in that expression. Thus, the task is to determine the value of $2n - 1$ when n is 1, 2, 3, and 4, and then to find the sum of those values. These steps result in the expression $1 + 3 + 5 + 7$. Simple!

These two problems illustrate the key role of symbolism and visual representation in mathematics. The interpretation and subsequent understanding of mathematics concepts are heavily dependent not only on language but also on the symbols that are an inherent component of the discipline. These two problems also illustrate a scenario seen in far too many classrooms when concepts or ideas in mathematics that are actually quite simple are presented in a way that is far more complex, much to the detriment of student learning. In other words, there are too many instances in mathematics instruction where a simple concept or idea is somehow prodded and molded, either by the math education system or teachers, and unveiled to students as something that appears to be far more complicated than it really is.

The Language of Mathematics Instruction

Box 1.2

You have been teaching the challenging concept and skill of division by a proper fraction. You write the problem $10 \div \frac{1}{2}$ on the board. You then state, "Class, how many times does $\frac{1}{2}$ go into 10?"

Refer to the question asked in Box 1.2. If teachers tend to teach the same way they were taught, it follows they will tend to teach *using the same language*. Over the years, numerous elementary and middle school teachers have presented the expression $10 \div \frac{1}{2}$ as the question, "How many times does $\frac{1}{2}$ go into 10?" As students themselves, these teachers accepted this interpretation of the symbols and moved on regardless of how much sense the interpretation made—or did not make—to them. Once they became teachers, they used the same language, thus passing on the torch to their students. Quite honestly, what can a student create to model a context where $\frac{1}{2}$ *goes into* 10? The question as posed really makes no sense. The language of instruction in mathematics often makes the conceptual meaning almost impossible to grasp, but students survive by blindly following procedures that enable them to get the correct answers that result in good grades. As educators, however, we must reflect and ask ourselves what level of mathematics are students actually learning, and is that depth of knowledge acceptable?

WHAT WE ARE TEACHING

Box 1.3

Next week's unit of instruction will focus on the multiplication of mixed numbers. You need to ensure that students have the prerequisite skills and knowledge to learn this new topic. What are these prerequisite skills and knowledge? Make a list.

Your generated list from Box 1.3 would likely include many prerequisite skills or concepts that focus on *how to* multiply mixed numbers. Think of your experiences as a math student and, if applicable, as a math teacher. Much of the instruction and learning in math classrooms is focused on how-tos. In the United States, we value good old American know-how. To learn mathematics at a deep conceptual level, however, know-how is not enough. Just as important, if not more so, is good old American know-what and know-why. In other words, students need to understand *what* a basic concept is and *why* that concept works as it does. In the scenario in Box 1.3, students need first to understand what multiplication is conceptually, then use that knowledge to understand why the process works as it does. Knowing only how to multiply, at best, results in basic memorization of rules and procedures.

Not surprisingly, many adults in the United States perceive mathematics simply as a conglomeration of facts, rules, computations, and procedures. After all, that is the type of mathematics they were taught. The K–12 math education system often focuses on arithmetic and efficiency (or algorithms), but mathematics is far more than that. If teachers only know, and subsequently teach, arithmetic and algorithms rather than a conceptual understanding of mathematics, then that limited knowledge will be the baton passed on to future generations.

What Is Missing: The Need for Definitions

An interesting paradox in mathematics is that one can know *how to* do something without understanding *what* the concept or process truly is. For example, students can know how to multiply without understanding what multiplication is conceptually. I successfully navigated numerous math courses knowing how to use π in formulas while having no clue as to what π meant as a concept. Quite literally, the *what* is missing from math instruction. Since a definition tells us what something is, it makes sense to emphasize definitions as a core element of instruction.

Defining key mathematical terms helps students build their understanding of important concepts. Students should be able to provide precise yet simple definitions of basic terms, such as those in Box 1.4. For teachers, these types of definitions paint a clear picture of students' depth of understanding. Incorrect student responses can reveal misunderstandings and gaps in knowledge. In addition, patterns that emerge from students' definitions of basic concepts can provide clues about the effectiveness of instruction, the curriculum, and even the larger mathematics education system.

Patterns of Misunderstanding

As a young high school math teacher, I often made assumptions regarding students' content knowledge, especially their mastery of fundamental concepts in earlier grades. I adopted the strategy of having students define basic math concepts not only to build understanding but also to expose the areas where students' knowledge was weak. The approach revealed some interesting patterns over the years. For example, high school students in higher-level math classes most commonly define an equation, one of the most basic concepts in mathematics, as "when you solve for *x*." This definition is a clear misconception of what an equation is, but the root cause was not so evident. After much reflection and analysis, I realized the origin lay in the state's mathematics content standards. In the state standards in effect at that time, the term *equation* did not appear until the sixth grade. Moreover, the context for this first appearance focused on learning to solve simple linear equations. This initial focus had likely contributed to students' misconception of an equation being "when you solve for *x*."

The concept of an equation is usually defined as a mathematical sentence that states that one quantity is the same as another quantity. In other words, the quantity expressed on the left side of the equal sign is the same as the quantity expressed on the right side, regardless of how those quantities are represented. For some reason, the U.S. educational system often waits to formally include the idea of equations in state mathematics standards until fifth or sixth grade. However, do students not begin their experiences with this concept early in elementary school? Is $2 + 1 = 3$ not an equation? There is no requirement that an equation must involve variables! Yet even many adults struggle with the correct definition and gravitate back to the notion that an equation must have "letters" and that a solution must be found.

Earlier in the chapter, I discussed how the mathematics education system sometimes takes something that is relatively simple and manages to make it inordinately complex. An equation is actually an extremely simple concept that can be ingrained very early in a child's education. Young children love to learn what they think are complex or sophisticated words. So why do we not simultaneously teach that $3 + 4 = 7$ is an equation when students learn basic arithmetic? This early introduction would help solidify students' fundamental understanding of an equation and simultaneously reduce the misconception that an equation must somehow involve a variable and be solved.

Similarly, when I asked high school students to define the term *graph* as a noun, their responses revealed another interesting pattern. What emerged was the common idea of a graph as the grid itself or the x and y axes. An investigation of the possible root causes of this off-target perspective of a graph pointed to both instruction and curriculum materials as the culprits. How many times have math teachers instructed students to plot the points or to draw the curve "on the graph"? How many textbooks ask students to illustrate their responses "on the graph"? With this phrase repeated ad nauseam, is it any wonder that students begin to define a graph as the grid itself? These patterns reinforce the importance and impact of language, both written and oral, on students' perceptions and understanding of fundamental mathematical concepts.

TURNING THE TIDE: A SAMPLING OF APPROACHES

Mathematics instruction is an extremely complex enterprise with multiple interrelated factors. However, logically, the foundation for instruction should be the mathematics itself—the concepts and big ideas—not skills and algorithms, although they do play an important role. This conceptual foundation, in turn, necessitates a paradigm shift from the how-to of mathematics to the what and the why. The result is language-focused instruction based on conceptual understanding. The following examples provide a sampling of approaches used in this type of instruction and an overview of the chapters to come.

Multiple Perspectives

Box 1.5

You have taught your students the multiplication of mixed numbers using the standard algorithm: Convert to improper fractions, multiply, then simplify and convert back to a mixed number if applicable. You are tutoring Michael because he still does not get it. Using $3\frac{1}{2} \bullet 2\frac{1}{2}$ as an example, think about how you would go about helping Michael gain a conceptual understanding of mixed-number multiplication using other perspectives or approaches. Write down an explanation of how you would help Michael.

Review the example in Box 1.5. If you had difficulty thinking of different approaches to help Michael understand how to multiply mixed numbers, you are definitely not alone. As mentioned, we tend to teach not only how we were taught but also *what* we were taught, with multiple implications. Teachers can teach only what they know and only to the depth of their own understanding. If teachers' only experience with the multiplication of mixed numbers is the standard algorithm and their college training, or subsequent professional development has not taken them beyond that, then that one approach is what they will teach.

Out of training and habit, teachers can easily begin to view a concept or approach a problem from just one perspective. We know students learn in different ways; thus, we should teach mathematical concepts and skills using multiple approaches and perspectives that relate to how individual students learn. So what can we do for Michael in the above scenario? We might try teaching multiplication of mixed numbers from a numeracy perspective using the definition of multiplication. Or we might try a geometry-measurement perspective using an area model. We could also try an algebraic perspective through the use of the distributive property. All these approaches and the power of the connections among them can help students develop conceptual understanding. This instructional scenario will be revisited in Chapter Eight to illustrate how to use multiple perspectives to help students understand the concept of multiplying mixed numbers.

So What Was the Question?

Box 1.6

You have been teaching the challenging concept and skill of division by a proper fraction. You write the problem $10 \div \frac{1}{2}$ on the board. You then state, "Class, how many times does $\frac{1}{2}$ go into 10?" The question is followed by silence. Finally, one student volunteers and states, "I sort of understood back when we had stuff like how many times does 3 go into 12, but no matter how hard I try, I can't picture in my head how many times $\frac{1}{2}$ can go into 10. What does that mean?" How do you respond?

The scenario in Box 1.6 is an extension of the one in Box 1.2. Again, the focus is on the tendency for teachers to use the *same language* used to teach them. Suppose the students are older, and a high school teacher poses this same problem to review basic computation. A few students give the incorrect solution of 5, while others give the correct solution of 20 but with trepidation and uncertainty. The teacher then challenges the students to state the expression $10 \div \frac{1}{2}$ as a question without using phrases such as "goes into" or "divided by." It should come as no surprise that the high school students are stumped despite their maturity and experience.

The scenarios in Boxes 1.2 and 1.6 reveal how teachers' language choices, often unconsciously influenced by how they were taught, can confuse students and even erode the understanding of the mathematics involved. Most teachers would be at a loss to explain what it means for $\frac{1}{2}$ to "go into" 10 or to describe division without using this phrase. And without a deeper understanding of division, the high school teacher above would not be able to pose that challenge to students as an instructional strategy.

This dilemma illustrates two additional problems in K–12 mathematics instruction. First, instruction tends to focus on finding answers without any focus on students' *understanding of the question*. When students truly understand the question being asked, they can answer it correctly with full confidence. But often, students will present a correct answer hesitantly, revealing a lack of real understanding of the task. Second, despite being in high school, many students, even high-achievers in advanced math classes such as Algebra II, still do not truly understand basic concepts such as division. True, students can easily recite facts such as 42 divided by 6 is 7, but they do not understand division *conceptually*. There is a huge difference between using procedures or memorizing facts and truly understanding concepts and why procedures work. And the language used can contribute to this lack of understanding.

MATHEMATICS IS ABOUT RELATIONSHIPS

Box 1.7

Solve the following:

The state champion in football is determined by a single-elimination playoff system: If you lose, you are out. How many games would the state need to hold if 37 teams were involved in the playoffs?

Refer to the task in Box 1.7. One could solve this problem by laboriously drawing playoff brackets to determine the number of necessary games. There is, however, a much simpler approach to the solution. The key is to look for the *relationships* in the problem. In this scenario, each game produces one winner and one loser. The loser is out, and the winner continues. The state champion must go through the playoffs undefeated. Since the playoffs involve 37 teams and only one is crowned the state champion, then 36 of the 37 teams must lose. Each game produces one loser. As a result, you need 36 games to produce the necessary 36 losers.

The simplicity of this process may be surprising. However, it is not actually a simple process. The key is to search for the relationships among the variables in the context of the problem. Clearly, not all mathematics problems will have an alternative approach or method of solution. However, finding and understanding relationships should be an integral part of the problem-solving process in any mathematical context. An unknown author once wrote, "Arithmetic is about computation; mathematics is about relationships." Using this perspective and approach can make a huge difference in the level of mathematical understanding students attain. Both teachers and students should focus on mathematics as relationships; otherwise, they are simply doing arithmetic.

CONNECTING THE PIECES AND LOOKING AHEAD

To understand mathematics at a deeper conceptual level, students need to develop a strong foundation by learning to define basic concepts, make connections, and unearth relationships; an understanding of the language, symbolism, and visual representation of mathematics is integral to this process. The chapters that follow explore these concepts in greater detail. Although attention is paid to instruction and instructional strategies, the focus is on mathematics content and all it entails. This overview illustrated that mathematics is not simply about numbers. Language and symbolism play a pivotal role, one often neglected in classrooms. More often than not, this neglect occurs because the educational system has not recognized the importance of language and symbolism in mathematics. My goal is to help you identify and address language-based problems in mathematics instruction and learn how to present mathematics content in a way that simplifies it, yet transforms it from shallow and procedural to deep and conceptual. With a deeper conceptual understanding of mathematics, teachers, and in turn their students, gain the power to make connections, identify relationships, and view mathematical concepts from multiple perspectives. The approach in this publication is not a silver bullet, nor will it revolutionize mathematics instruction. But it does provide a new vision of mathematics through a neglected perspective that provides a conduit for a much deeper understanding of fundamental mathematics—advanced fundamentals, if you will.

Why a Language Focus in Mathematics?

chapter
TWO

Mathematics and language are inextricably intertwined. You do not need a degree in education to realize that language is the primary vehicle used to convey mathematics knowledge. Students' understanding is dependent on their comprehension of both the academic language of mathematics as well as the instructional language used to teach it. Every lesson, regardless of content, presents students with terms, symbols, and context they must grasp to learn the new material. Yet, hidden within the language are numerous landmines that can sabotage student learning, arising from the complexities of English itself to poor practices entrenched in traditional instruction (discussed in Chapter Three).

THE CONVERGENCE OF MATHEMATICS AND ENGLISH: MORE THAN JUST VOCABULARY

The U.S. educational system has long viewed mathematics and English as separate: Math class is for math; English class is for English. Fortunately, this bias is fading with the growing movement to integrate literacy instruction into all content areas. But what does the intersection of mathematics and literacy instruction look like in a K–12 math class? For math teachers, it would be easy to fall for the illusion that merely increasing their focus on vocabulary would satisfy the issue. In truth, a closer investigation reveals that integrating literacy requires teachers to address an intricate web of factors related to language and symbolism that can affect the instruction and learning of mathematics—and vocabulary is just the start.

11

It Starts with Vocabulary

Admittedly, a strong mathematics vocabulary is essential. This vocabulary constitutes the foundation for understanding key concepts, which in turn enables students to solve real-life mathematical problems. Without an understanding of the language used routinely in instruction, textbooks, and word problems, students are handicapped in their efforts to learn mathematics. To maximize math achievement, a program of vocabulary development should be an integral part of instruction. However, several systemic issues can limit the effectiveness of mathematics vocabulary instruction.

Vocabulary Instruction—Not a Simple Enterprise. One major issue is the traditional lack of emphasis on teaching the specialized vocabulary of mathematics in most K–12 math classes. Reflect back on your elementary and secondary mathematics education. Likely, few of your teachers strongly emphasized the vocabulary and language of mathematics, even though research indicates that formal instruction in vocabulary is far more effective than relying on the informal acquisition of words.

Because of this historically limited focus on vocabulary, many math teachers lack experience in how best to teach it. When teachers do cover vocabulary, their efforts are often insufficient to make a significant impression on students. Frequently, vocabulary instruction is incidental to, or separate from, the solution process for contextual problems. But mere exposure to definitions is not enough. Students need to think about and discuss vocabulary terms and the concepts they represent in context to internalize them. Providing vocabulary instruction and practice in isolation through test-like exercises does not necessarily transfer to conceptual understanding or problem-solving ability. Transfer is more likely to occur if teachers have students practice in the actual situations in which the transfer is desired. In other words, vocabulary instruction should occur as an intrinsic part of math lessons in the classroom.

Limited Use of Mathematics Vocabulary. Another issue restricting the meaningful acquisition of mathematics vocabulary is the fact that some terms are rarely used outside of a math classroom. The old adage, "If you don't use it, you lose it," definitely applies. How often do you think two middle school students walk down the hall at school chatting about negative integers? Words such as *perpendicular, divisor,* and *quotient* are not commonly used outside of math contexts. Although numerous parallels exist between math instruction and reading instruction in the way language is taught, unique differences exist as well. Key among these differences is the amount of reinforcement needed for mathematics language compared with everyday language. Whereas everyday language is used constantly in the classroom, at home, and in social interactions, mathematical language is not. This lack of reinforcement in daily use is exacerbated by a lack of any type of formal structure or system to enable or support the reinforcement of mathematics vocabulary outside of the math classroom.

PROBLEMS BASED ON THE ENGLISH LANGUAGE

On top of these vocabulary issues are a number of even more serious issues inherent in the English language itself. English is a complex language. It has scores of rules that often have multiple exceptions, numerous homonyms and words with multiple meanings, words that are often pronounced differently from how they are spelled, and a slew of idiomatic expressions. This complexity can ratchet up the difficulty level of mathematics and leave students, particularly those who are younger or are learning English, dazed and confused.

Abstract Terms

One problem with English is that many mathematical terms are abstract, representing concepts rather than objects. Words such as *quotient*, *sum*, and *factor* describe concepts that have no unique, unambiguous representations in the real world to help students get the meaning or definition. For example, the term *blue* in everyday language can be construed as somewhat abstract, but one can easily resort to real-life representations of that color to enable students to understand the meaning. However, teaching a student what a term such as *multiple* means is exponentially more difficult because there is no tangible or solid representation to help students visualize and understand the term. This inherent problem of defining abstract mathematical concepts reinforces the need to define mathematical terms in context.

Polysemous Terms

Another difficulty of the English language resides with polysemous terms, words that have more than one meaning or definition. Numerous words, such as *difference*, *product*, *scale*, and *factor*, have specific mathematical meanings as well as commonly used everyday meanings. For example, the cost of materials, labor, and transportation are *factors* in the manufacturing of a *product*, whereas 7 and 4 are *factors* that when multiplied result in the *product* 28. Another example is the word *volume*. Should we be surprised that a student in math class might define *volume* as "how loud the music is," particularly if the child does not fully comprehend the mathematical concept the word represents?

Some polysemous terms further cloud the issue because they not only have different meanings in standard English but different definitions within different areas of mathematics. For example, within mathematics, *degree* can refer to statistics (*degree* of freedom), geometry (*degree* of an angle), algebra (third *degree* equation), or measurement (*degree* as a unit of temperature). Further complicating matters, outside of mathematics, *degree* can refer to education (a *degree* of learning), geography (a *degree* of latitude or longitude), medicine (the *degree* of a burn), or law (the *degree* of a crime). That is one hard-working word and, for students, a potentially very confusing one.

The examples are many. Within mathematics, the term *second* can mean an ordinal number, a unit of time, or a more exact measure of an angle. Meanwhile, the term *translation,* in geometry class, can refer to the geometric connotation (slide) that involves a change of location while preserving size and orientation; while in algebra class, it can refer to converting a word problem into an appropriate algebraic expression or equation.

Homonyms and Similar Spellings

Adding yet another layer of confusion are the many English words with similar pronunciations or spellings. We are all familiar with the difficulty of homonyms, words that sound alike but have different meanings. Homonyms can be especially tricky if students do not have a context to assist them or if the information is oral rather than written. For instance, a teacher might give students the problem $3 + 12 + 7 + 8$ and explain that the *sum* of the numbers might be easier to obtain if students rearrange *some* of them. Students still trying to master the concept of *sum* have enough to think about without the added noise created by the homonym *some*.

Likewise, students may be confused by words with similar spellings but different pronunciations. For example, students learn how to pronounce *algorithm* and *logarithm*, but must stop and think twice when they learn the word *paradigm*. Although the third word ends with a similar spelling, its pronunciation is entirely different.

Ambiguous and Idiomatic Expressions

Part of the complexity of English is due to the lexical ambiguity and idiom that most adults take for granted, but which can result in serious misunderstanding for students. For example, the use of ambiguous, idiomatic spatial terms in mathematics instruction can complicate understanding for students. Suppose that a teacher gives students the problem in Box 2.1 and instructs them to "add the numbers up."

Box 2.1

$$24$$
$$+\ 35$$

Should it surprise the teacher when some students place the solution *above* the 24? That placement is literally what the student was told to do: Add them *up*. Yet the convention is to place the answer at the bottom, which makes one wonder why the instruction was not to "add them *down*." Adults have learned to associate the term *up* with addition and the idea of "more," and to disregard the spatial connotation when not applicable. However, students, particularly those learning English, may struggle with these nonliteral associations.

Another example of ambiguity is the fundamental idea of a pair. If a parent takes a little boy shopping and buys him a pair of socks and a pair of pants, what is the child to think about the meaning of *pair*? In one instance, there are two items; in the other, one item. What do we tell the boy when he asks, "Where are the other pants?" Then, when the parent and child arrive home, the little boy is given a pear as a snack!

Compounded Ambiguity

The potential for confusion mounts when one or more language-related issues, such as polysemous terms and ambiguity, intersect. Examine the problem and answer in Box 2.2. The directions have two possible interpretations that on the surface may appear humorous, but can be problematic for students. The definition of *reduce* in standard English is "to make smaller." Given the directions in the problem, a student could make a valid argument that the literal response shown is correct.

Box 2.2

Reduce: $\dfrac{6}{8}$

Student Answer: $\frac{6}{8}$

Similarly, given the directions in Box 2.3, students could make a valid argument that the answer shown is correct because of the definition of *expand* in standard English.

In Box 2.4, ambiguous directions once again provide students with a valid argument that the answer shown is correct. Students were instructed to "find *x*" rather than to "find the value of *x*." The answer, thus, reflects a literal interpretation of the directions.

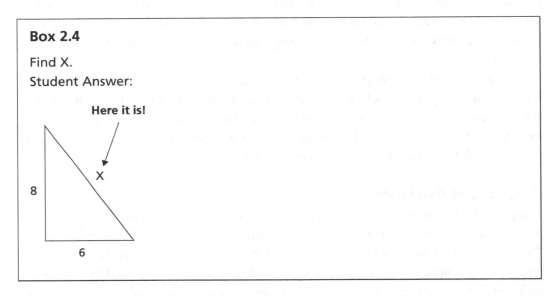

Box 2.4

Find X.
Student Answer:

These issues illustrate why math teachers must be mindful of the language, both in instruction and within mathematics, and whether students understand it. With the complexity of English, the opportunities for confusion are numerous. Moreover, familiarity with meanings and habitual repetition make most adults oblivious to the language's nuances, which can be especially problematic when those adults are teachers.

A NUMBER OF PROBLEMS WITH *NUMBER*

As a case study for examining language-based issues in mathematics, consider the fundamental mathematics concept of *number*. On the surface, the concept seems relatively simple. Yet, it serves as an important example of the confusion that can be caused by the merger of the complexity of English with mathematics. Examine Box 2.5, which is disaggregated into three parts.

Box 2.5

a. Which is larger?

37   **5**

b. Which number is larger?

37   **5**

c. Which numeral is larger?

37   **5**

What is the language issue in each problem? In the first, Problem 2.5a, there is definitely a high degree of ambiguity. The exact intent of the question is unclear: Does it refer to the physical size of the symbols or to the quantities represented by each? A teacher might pose this question with the expectation that students would recognize this ambiguity and explain the rationale for the two possible responses. In contrast, the language issue in problems 2.5b and 2.5c is not ambiguity, but easily confused mathematics terms. The key lies in knowing the difference between the definitions of *number* and *numeral*. The term *number* refers to the actual quantity represented by one or more symbols. Thus, the *only* correct response to Problem 2.5b is 37. On the other hand, *numeral* refers to the symbol itself. Based on that definition, the *only* correct response to Problem 2.5c is 5. These examples highlight the importance of precise academic language in mathematics and foreshadow the importance of teachers' content expertise. Obviously, if teachers are not aware of the differences between *number* and *numeral*, they cannot teach those differences to their students.

Other issues inherent in the concept of *number* in mathematics may cause confusion as well. For example, a number can still be mathematical in nature, but not refer to a quantity. Rather, a number may refer to a code, such as a phone number or a social security number. A number can be used in conjunction with letters to designate a location, such as 30218 Main Street. These representations do not denote quantities, and it is important that students recognize this distinction and the difference in the meaning of the numerals in these cases. For this reason, teachers need to give students experience with these types of contexts and guidance in recognizing the distinct interpretations of the symbolism.

Taking Ambiguity to Another Level

The idea of *number* can become even more problematic via spoken English. An investigation of the pronunciation of numbers unearths these additional issues. Consider the questions in Box 2.6.

Box 2.6

a. What are some ways to say 2,632?

b. How can these two addresses be confused?

   3218 Main Street

   30218 Main Street

c. How are these numbers often pronounced, and what is problematic about those pronunciations?

   2,560

   $25.60

d. How is this number often pronounced, and what is problematic about that pronunciation?

   25.6

Problem 2.6a illustrates the confusion that can result from pronouncing the same numerical quantity in multiple ways. Some interpretations, such as "two thousand six hundred thirty-two" or "twenty-six hundred thirty-two," retain the integrity of the numeric value; while more careless pronunciations, such as "twenty-six thirty-two," erode what the symbols represent. The street addresses in Question 2.6b also demonstrate the need for precise pronunciation of values. In these cases, orally stating the symbol 30218 as "thirty-two eighteen" would not suffice because that pronunciation fits 3218 instead. Consider the pronunciation of 2,632 in Problem 2.6a as "twenty-six thirty-two" and the pronunciation of 3218 in the street address in Problem 2.6b as "thirty-two eighteen." We can see that the cross-pollination of the two contexts may have slowly evolved to the acceptance of the abbreviated and numerically incorrect pronunciation of 2,632 as "twenty-six thirty-two."

Problem 2.6c brings to light additional problems and confusion that can result from inappropriate pronunciation in monetary contexts. We are often guilty of pronouncing both 2,632 and $26.32 as "twenty-six thirty-two," both of which are mathematically incorrect pronunciations in those contexts. The two numbers represent different quantities, and we confuse students by pronouncing them the same way. These examples are analogous to parents naming one daughter Margaret and another daughter Magdalena, and then calling them both Maggie. A connection can also be made among the three contexts of the first three questions above: a street address, a numeric value, and a monetary value. Given a street address of 4578 Sunset Drive, the pronunciation of "forty-five seventy-eight" gradually spilled over to become a socially acceptable pronunciation for 4,578 and $45.78, much to the detriment of students struggling to learn mathematics and to develop number sense.

Problem 2.6d introduces the further pollution of numeric understanding through the pronunciation of decimals. A number such as 25.6 should be pronounced as "twenty-five and six tenths" to preserve the numeric value and enhance student understanding of place value. Yet, we add additional complexity by pronouncing 25.6 as "twenty-five point six," further eroding the idea of place value rather than enhancing it; the word *point* does nothing to reinforce the place value of the 6 or of any of the other digits.

Number: Associated Terms

Fundamental concepts in mathematics, such as *number*, often have several terms associated with them that students must learn to understand the central concept fully. Thus, these terms can add complexity and confusion if not understood as well. When students learn about number, they also need to learn related terms such as *numeral, amount, place value, digit,* and *quantity*. Another associated term that is especially problematic is *figure*. This confusing term can refer to both a symbol itself (a numeral) or its quantity (a number). *Figure* also has a different meaning in geometry (a geometric *figure*, such as a circle) and a similar connotation in the context of skating (such as a *figure* eight). It has other meanings in standard English as well, such as in reference to the human body (a slender *figure*) or to a person (a historic *figure*).

Number: Nonmathematical Meanings

Although used primarily in mathematical contexts, the term *number* is another polysemous word with multiple meanings outside of mathematics. Students (and teachers) must be able to distinguish the meanings of *number* in mathematics from its many other meanings in standard English, such as those shown in Box 2.7.

Teachers must be cognizant of both the overt, glaring problems created by the merging of mathematics and language as well as the more covert and subtle problems created by the nuances of the two areas. It is important to reiterate that the phrase "the trouble with math is English" by no means has only to do with students whose native language is other than English. Rather, the statement is meant to express the overarching idea that language in the context of mathematics encompasses a wide continuum of components and issues. From a content perspective, this broad idea emphasizes the crucial role of language in both the teaching and learning of mathematics.

Teachers face an array of challenges in addressing language-based problems in mathematics. However, the first step is an awareness and acknowledgment of the issue. The second step is the realization that there are no easy solutions, especially when faced with teaching both math content and English to English Learners (ELs). For example, the use of cognates is recognized as an effective EL strategy. To assist Spanish speakers in the classroom, a math teacher could use the term *numero* in teaching the concept of number. However, based on the issues and examples presented in this chapter, it should be fairly obvious that the cognate strategy falls far short of addressing all the number-related problems that English learners will face.

Keep in mind that language-based issues in mathematics are problematic for *all* students. This chapter offered only a small sampling of the language-related obstacles students will encounter in understanding mathematics. Focused reflection on the contents of the chapter should yield a realization of both the complexity and inconspicuous nature of the role of language in the learning of mathematics. In a way, a lack of attention to language in math instruction is analogous to a lack of attention to diabetes. Because of no obvious symptoms or pain, the problem often goes undetected for years. But silently, the disease is damaging the body (of knowledge) and can eventually lead to serious consequences if not diagnosed and treated.

Language and Symbolism in Traditional Instruction

An old adage states that to enjoy life fully, we need to take time to stop and smell the roses. Likewise, mathematics instruction needs to take time to examine symbolism and language to help students appreciate fully the concepts and relationships being represented. Yet, traditional math instruction often breezes past symbolism and language with only a cursory sniff. Little attention is paid to the critical role they play or to the many language-based problems that can hinder student learning. As a result, traditional instruction not only perpetuates but often adds to the language-based problems in math.

A common understanding of what is meant by traditional instruction is necessary before continuing. Within the context of this book, traditional instruction encompasses the following characteristics:

- Lecture-based instruction

- Passive students

- Repeated drill and practice

- Memorization of facts and procedures

- Emphasis on answers rather than explanations

Note that none of these characteristics deals with any type of emphasis on the language and symbolism of mathematics. True, teachers in traditional math classrooms do stop and define words such as *factor* and have students memorize symbols, such as the difference between the less than (<) and greater than (>) symbols. But traditionally, few attempts are made to focus on language and symbolism to the depth and breadth that is illustrated and recommended in this book.

One major reason for this neglect is that many educators experienced traditional instruction as students. As touched upon in Chapter One, research (such as Conference Board of the Mathematical Sciences, 2001) indicates that teachers tend to teach in the same way as they were taught. Fortunately, over the years, much attention has been given to examining and improving how teachers teach. The bulk of education research and reform efforts has focused on this area, and most teachers would agree that the majority of their training and professional development has as well. However, we must not forget the related corollary: not only do teachers tend to teach *how* they were taught, they also tend to teach *what* they were taught. This assertion includes not only mathematical content but also the language and symbols used in instruction. Yet, little attention is given to this critical area. Consequently, without intervention or professional development, teachers will continue to teach *their understanding of mathematics* (the "what") using the same language used to teach them.

SHORTCOMINGS OF TRADITIONAL INSTRUCTION

Traditional math instruction has a number of shortcomings related to language and symbolism. Beyond the major problem of not sufficiently emphasizing or addressing these topics, traditional instruction often glosses over the critical role of terms and symbols and what they represent. In addition, many traditional practices, such as the reliance on shortcuts, minimize or cloud symbolic connections and relationships in math. These language-based shortcomings can be broken down into four categories, which we examine in turn:

1. Careless vocabulary
2. Shortcuts
3. Confusing logic and mismatched symbolism
4. Naked numbers

Careless Vocabulary

Just like their teachers before them, many math teachers tend to use a traditional set of terms in their daily instruction. The problem is that some of these terms can be extremely confusing or misleading, and others are flat-out inaccurate. This careless vocabulary often involves terms that have other meanings outside of mathematics. Box 3.1 lists six commonly used math terms that can prove problematic for all students, not just those learning English.

Box 3.1: Six Examples of Careless Mathematics Vocabulary

1. The bigger half
2. Carry the 1
3. Borrow a 10
4. Cancel the 2s
5. Reduce a fraction
6. 2 goes into 8

The Bigger Half.   Although a seemingly innocent phrase, one can easily determine that the notion of *the bigger half* is mathematically erroneous. By definition, two halves must each be the same quantity, so there is no such thing as *the bigger half*. This error is more likely to occur at home, rather than at school, in a scenario such as when a parent instructs an older child to give a younger child *the bigger half* of a cookie. Regardless of the location, the term is an example of how easily the mathematical meaning of a concept can be inadvertently eroded. Students already have enough difficulty with topics such as fractions without further confusing the issue with careless statements such as this one.

Carry.   The term *carry* has long been repeated in numerous elementary and middle school classrooms and is firmly entrenched in the vocabulary of traditional math instruction. The confusion for students lies in the standard definition of *carry* as an action of holding and transporting an object, as in "carrying a bag of groceries to the car." Thus, the term not only can confuse students but also fails to explain what is actually happening mathematically. It's a missed opportunity, really. Fortunately, new curricula and texts are changing the terminology of addition and replacing *carry* with terms such as *regrouping*. Contextual examples, such as converting 16 pennies to 1 dime and 6 pennies, would add clarity in those scenarios.

Borrow.   The use of the term *borrow* in subtraction is analogous to the use of *carry* in addition, with both terms being equally entrenched in traditional instruction. The confusion for students again lies in the standard definition of the term. In standard use, *to borrow* suggests that one receives something with the implied or expressed intention of returning that same item to the lender. So if we borrow a 10 in a subtraction problem, are we supposed to pay it back at some point? Changes are slowly being made in new curricula and texts to replace the use of *borrow* and incorporate the idea of converting and regrouping in the basic operations of addition and subtraction.

Cancel. The term *cancel*, especially as it pertains to simplifying a fraction or rational expression, is especially problematic because it implies that something is deleted, eliminated, or otherwise brought to nothing. In science, one of the laws of conservation states that energy is neither created nor destroyed within a system, but rather changes form. This basic idea has a parallel in mathematics: Quantities and expressions can be changed to equivalent forms that may appear different and give the illusion that something was eliminated. The reality is that most mathematical contexts where something appears to have been *canceled* are in fact instances where an expression was simplified to either 1 or 0. The insidious idea of cancellation is connected to the overuse of shortcuts, which we address in the next section.

Reduce. It is probably a safe assumption that, with rare exceptions, almost all adults who went through the U.S. school system were taught to reduce fractions. The careless use of the term *reduce* in mathematics is in direct contradiction to the standard English definition, "to make smaller." Is it any wonder that some students get confused and think that $\frac{1}{2}$ is smaller than $\frac{3}{6}$? After all, they get $\frac{1}{2}$ by reducing $\frac{3}{6}$, and since 1 and 2 are smaller than 3 and 6, $\frac{1}{2}$ must be smaller than $\frac{3}{6}$. What's more, traditional instruction further reinforces this type of misconception because, in the process of reducing a fraction, we eliminate some stuff by canceling! Sure, many students eventually manage to overcome this careless use of the language and figure out fractions (although there are plenty of adults who still are mystified by them). However, teachers are not doing students any favors by continuing to use this term when discussing fractions and rational expressions. Here again, progress is being made by new curricula and texts referring to this process as *simplifying* a fraction rather than *reducing* it.

Goes into. The notion of *goes into* is probably the most senseless use of language in mathematics instruction. In English class, elementary students learn that a person *goes into* a room or that a bear *goes into* a cave. Then in math class, these same students are told that 2 *goes into* 8 and that 3 does not *go into* 10. Somehow students adapt and accept the terminology even though it is unclear how in the world 4 *goes into* 12. Things go fairly smoothly until students confront division by fractions and teachers continue to use the same terminology. Think back to the problem $10 \div \frac{1}{2}$ from Chapter One. Many students are taught to interpret this expression as, "How many times does $\frac{1}{2}$ *go into* 10?" How can students visualize a context where such a phenomenon could occur? They cannot because the expression makes no sense. Literally, what does $\frac{1}{2}$ going into 10 look like? So the question is why does traditional mathematics instruction insist on the continued use of such confusing and nonsensical terminology?

Clearly, some expressions in the English language have an implied and traditionally accepted meaning even if they make no sense grammatically. For example, the driver of a vehicle is told to "make a left," but a literal translation leaves one wondering how the driver can *manufacture* a left. However, we are expected to know that the implied meaning is to "make a left *turn*." In that context, would it not be better to just say "turn left?" This statement is shorter, simpler, and clearer. For whatever reason, careless and confusing expressions such as the six cited here have become deeply entrenched in mathematics and, like revered traditions, been passed along from one generation to the next. As a result of such language, teachers often *mystify* rather than *simplify* mathematics, which unfortunately reinforces the myth that only a select few can master this discipline. To improve math instruction, we should be telling students to turn left rather than to make a left.

Shortcuts

Another tradition deeply instilled in mathematics instruction is the use of shortcuts. Math teachers love shortcuts. They imply efficiency, and what teacher does not want students to do math efficiently? However, if applied incorrectly, this efficiency comes at a cost. If procedures and algorithms are taught using shortcuts too soon or too often, then efficiency comes at the huge cost of conceptual understanding. An overreliance on shortcuts often prevents students from truly understanding the mathematics involved. In other words, a deep understanding of the "what" and the "why" of a mathematical process is sacrificed in favor of the "how to." A direct correlation exists between shortcuts and learning: The less students do with paper and pencil (or keyboard and screen), the less they do with their brains. Conversely, the more students write and see visually, the more that thinking occurs.

Simplifying Fractions.   The process of simplifying a fraction provides an excellent example of the shortcomings of shortcuts. Box 3.2 illustrates the typical shortcuts used in simplifying a fraction.

Box 3.2: Simplifying a Fraction: Short Method

$$\frac{6}{8} = \frac{3 \bullet 2}{4 \bullet 2} = \frac{3 \bullet \cancel{2}}{4 \bullet \cancel{2}} = \frac{3}{4}$$

Although efficient, this short method leaves students with a fuzzy notion of what really happened. All students really learn is that this process is the way the teacher showed them to do it, so this is the way they need to keep doing it. This lack of understanding is only exacerbated when students are told erroneously to "*cancel* the 2s" as part of the process.

Contrast the above approach with the same problem done without shortcuts, as shown in Box 3.3.

Box 3.3: Simplifying a Fraction: Long Method

$$\frac{6}{8} = \frac{3 \cdot 2}{4 \cdot 2} = \frac{3 \cdot 2}{4 \cdot 2} = \frac{3}{4} \cdot 1 = \frac{3}{4}$$

This longer method, showing all the critical steps, guides students through the process, leading to a more thorough understanding of what simplifying a fraction involves and why it works. Meanwhile, students using the short method are taken down the blind path of cancellation, where we can only hope they stumble across some understanding.

By including each step, the complete process instills a conceptual understanding of the multiplicative identity: the basic idea that any number multiplied by 1 remains the same. That critical fundamental property is the linchpin for a deep understanding of what truly happens when simplifying a fraction. More important, the multiplicative identity is one of the primary algebraic tools in solving equations. By insisting that students use the full process above, teachers help them establish a key algebraic foundation through arithmetic. Nothing is eliminated or canceled. Instead, the expression is manipulated in such a way as to create an equivalent expression involving some quantity multiplied by 1. Because an amount multiplied by 1 remains the same, the " • 1" portion of the expression in the fourth step can be dropped. Thus, working through the complete process builds students' understanding of not only the process of simplifying fractions but also the process of solving algebraic equations.

Adding Fractions.   As with simplifying fractions, many math processes taught in the lower grades establish an important foundation for higher-level concepts taught later. For example, examine the expression in Box 3.4. This expression represents a basic property in mathematics often found in Algebra I textbooks. In my experience, this property initially confuses many students, who feel it makes no sense. Moreover, they often claim to have never seen it before. Sometimes we cannot see the forest because of the trees!

Box 3.4: Property for Adding Fractions

$$\frac{A+B}{C} = \frac{A}{C} + \frac{B}{C}$$

Box 3.5 shows the arithmetic processes for fractions, which students usually learn in elementary school. Do you see the property from Box 3.4? And more important, where do you see it?

Box 3.5: Adding Fractions: Short and Long Methods

Typical shortcut:

$$\frac{2}{5} + \frac{1}{5} = \frac{3}{5}$$

Expanded method:

$$\frac{2}{5} + \frac{1}{5} = \frac{2+1}{5} = \frac{3}{5}$$

Notice, the preferred expanded method for adding fractions is exactly what the algebraic property states. So, in essence, students have been using that property for years prior to their formal Algebra I course. True, when variables are involved in mathematics, for some inexplicable reason students' comprehension ability seems to plummet to unimaginable depths. Still, why is the algebraic expression so foreign to them? The answer is fairly obvious. The constant use of the shortcut has masked what is really happening, even though students have been using the property. Although the shortcut helped speed through problems, it prevented students from reaching full understanding; once in algebra, they found themselves right back at square one.

Multiplication and Division.   The use of shortcuts is also an inherent part of the basic multiplication and division algorithms, shown in Box 3.6.

Traditional math instruction focuses on the efficient application of the procedures for multiplication and division. The ultimate goal is the prompt attainment of the correct product or quotient. Students, more often than not, memorize the process with little

Box 3.6: Multiplication and Division Algorithms

Multiplication Algorithm

```
        28
   ×    34
       112
        84
       952
```

Division Algorithm

```
      35
 7 ) 245
     21
     35
     35
```

understanding of the steps or the reasons for them. When using the multiplication algorithm above with multidigit numbers, students in many cases are taught that after obtaining the first partial product, they must move the second partial product one place to the left, with no explanation as to why. That's just the rule. In a similar fashion, in the division example, students are instructed to "bring down" the 5, with no notion as to why they are doing it. In both algorithms, the fundamental concept of place value is crucial to an understanding of the process, but gets totally lost in the shuffle.

Shortcuts in and of themselves are not necessarily bad. The key lies in the sequence of events that occur in the learning. Mathematics instruction must first ensure that students' conceptual understanding is deeply embedded. If students are truly learning mathematics, they should be able to show all the detailed steps in a process, explain why those steps occur, and connect the process to related concepts. Once this level of understanding is gained, students can be exposed to more efficient shortcuts. A reliance only on algorithms and procedures with a focus on shortcuts transforms instruction to teaching efficiency, not mathematics. Shortcuts can become a race to get to the answer, bypassing conceptual understanding. This loss in understanding is not worth the lessened paperwork and gain in speed.

Confusing Logic and Mismatched Symbolism

Another critical problem in traditional mathematics instruction is that some of the language and symbols used just do not make logical sense. Many adults who came up through the U.S. school system have accepted these mismatches and, as a result, do not really see them as problematic. Furthermore, teachers may not see this incongruence as an issue. However, instruction should never make mathematics more difficult or confusing for students. The following are some illogical obstacles that students must overcome to understand mathematics.

Number Values Go Both Ways.   The representation of the value of numbers provides an interesting example. Consider the value of numbers as represented on a number line. As one moves *right*, the values of the numbers increase. Now, consider the numeric notation we use to represent quantities. If we consider the number 65,374, what happens to the digits with respect to place value? For whatever reason, the value of each digit increases with each step to the *left*, the opposite of what happens to values on a number line! Again, as adults we do not give this disparity a second thought, but students often grapple with such contradictions alone unless teachers deliberately address them.

Which Is Simpler?   One of the interesting phenomena in mathematics is the idea of having students convert an expression or number *into its simplest form*. Another objective is for students to develop number sense and determine the reasonableness of a solution. Examine the two problems in Box 3.7.

Box 3.7: Two Radicals

a. Estimate the value:
$$2\sqrt{13}$$

b. Estimate the value:
$$\sqrt{52}$$

The first radical is actually the simplified form of the second, as shown in Box 3.8. Which form of the two values was easier to estimate? Most people would likely say that 3.7b was easier because it lies between 49 (7^2) and 64 (8^2). Since 52 is much closer to 49, then a reasonable estimate would be about 7.1 or 7.2. Even if one had the square root of 13 memorized, estimating 3.7a would probably be more difficult. So from a number sense perspective, 3.7b is *in a simpler form* for estimating its value. However, algebraically, the first expression, and not the second, is *in simplest form*. Thus, the two objectives (simplifying an expression and number sense) are contradictory in this context. Numerically, 3.7b is in a form that makes it *simpler to estimate*; algebraically, 3.7a is *in simplest form* because its radicand has no square factors.

> **Box 3.8: Simplifying a Radical**
>
> $\sqrt{52} = \sqrt{4 \bullet 13} = \sqrt{4} \bullet \sqrt{13} = 2\sqrt{13}$

Multiplication Mysteries: X Marks the Spot. Multiplication, one of the most prevalent operations in mathematics, also has some of the most confusing and contradictory uses of language and symbolism. For example, why do we use the letter x as the most common algebraic variable as well as the symbol for multiplication ($\times$)? It is as if we want to confuse students. And this mystery is only the start.

In arithmetic, we use expressions such as $2 \cdot 3$ to represent basic multiplication contexts involving a certain number of sets, all of which are the same size. But in the expression $2 \cdot 3$, what do the *2* and the *3* each represent? Is the *2* the number of sets, or is it the size of each set? The same question applies to the meaning of the *3*. Surprisingly, research has not found any definitive answer to this query. Although most people consider $2 \cdot 3$ to represent 2 groups of 3 ($3 + 3$), some educators and mathematicians consider $2 \cdot 3$ to mean 3 sets of 2 ($2 + 2 + 2$). For the purpose of this book, we will assume that $2 \cdot 3$ represents 2 groups of 3, where the first numeral represents the number of groups and the second numeral represents the size of each group.

Already, you can see how easily students might become confused. But the problems only continue. Consider how a multiplication expression, such as $3 \cdot 5$, is usually pronounced. Is that pronunciation problematic, and if so, why? Under traditional instruction, most people pronounce $3 \cdot 5$ as "three times five." If we assume that $3 \cdot 5$ means 3 sets of 5, then what we have is $5 + 5 + 5$. Should that be "five three times" instead? Yet, we pronounce $3 \cdot 5$ as "three times five." Would it not be simpler and more sensible to say "three fives"? The word *times* seems only to add confusion in the context of multiplication.

From an algebraic perspective, it makes sense for $3 \cdot 5$ to mean 3 sets of 5. Consider the expression $3y$. Would it make more sense for students to see $3y$ as "three y's" instead of "three times y"? Imagine yourself as a young student learning multiplication. Which would be easier to visualize? Students can take that interpretation ($3y$ as three y's) and make a simple transition to a more complex algebraic expression, such as $3(y + 5)$. If students have the solid understanding of $3 \cdot 5$ being 3 sets of 5, rather than 3 times 5, the expression $3(y + 5)$ can readily be interpreted as 3 sets of $(y + 5)$, or $(y + 5) + (y + 5) + (y + 5)$. Having this interpretation firmly entrenched in students eliminates the common mistake of $3(y + 5) = 3y + 5$, where students fail to completely distribute the multiplication by 3. The term *times* as it is used in describing multiplication is problematic and confuses rather than clarifies the operation, especially in the early grades.

Naked Numbers

Naked numbers refer to the prevalent use of numerals in isolation, without any descriptors, units, or context. Traditional instruction continually uses naked numbers, especially in the form of drill and practice geared to student memorization of facts or procedures. As a result, students can easily lose sight of the meaning of numbers and numerals, resulting in a diminished view of mathematics.

In large part, mathematics is our way of quantifying the world around us. Picture a group of primitive hunters. Even then, people needed to quantify their environment. On a hunting trip, a scout who had been sent ahead might return to report seeing 5 deer in a valley and 3 deer on a hillside for a total of 8 deer. The numbers had meaning attached to them. How confusing would it be if the scout only reported seeing 5 in the valley and 3 on the hillside? The other hunters would have no idea what he was talking about because the numbers would lack meaning. That confusion and lack of meaning is exactly what has happened in mathematics. Over time, our method of representation transformed this scouting report into $5 + 3 = 8$. Without any context, teachers and students alike forget the meaning of the numerals and the key idea that they represent *something*. Exercises such as finding $17 - 6$ or $23 \cdot 8$ result in solutions that are void of meaning and slowly erode the idea that each of those numerals and symbols represents something. At this juncture, it is not readily apparent why this fundamental idea is so critical to the learning and understanding of mathematics, but the idea will be made more evident, particularly in Chapters Four, Five, and Six.

In looking at student performance on state-mandated exams, measurement is one of the areas where students historically perform poorly. Why is this? Based on my professional experience, naked numbers are one of the prime offenders lurking behind this poor performance. Measurement is not just about inches and pounds and liters. It must be perceived from a much broader lens. We must zoom out and look at the bigger picture of mathematical representation and symbolism and at where measurement falls within that picture. (Chapter Nine provides a look at this bigger picture.) Unfortunately, educators and the public in general consider the measurement strand of mathematics strictly from the perspective of units of measure. But numerals and symbols in mathematics do not occur in isolation—each represents or means *something*. Thus, we need to connect the idea of measurement to the larger idea of representation in mathematics. As noted previously, students consistently work with naked numbers and tend to forget what they really represent. For this reason, students' poor performance in the measurement strand could be a symptom of the system's lack of emphasis on the language and representation of mathematics, and not just an indication that students have trouble with standard units of measure.

Compounding the Problem

Unfortunately, the problems that have been discussed do not occur in isolation. Often these shortcomings occur simultaneously and reinforce each other, thus compounding the confusion and misconceptions of students. Revisit the problem $10 \div \frac{1}{2}$. The use of careless vocabulary occurs when students are taught to interpret this expression as "how many times does $\frac{1}{2}$ *go into* 10?" Add to this confusing language the lack of instructional emphasis on what those naked numbers mean. Just what do the *10* and the $\frac{1}{2}$ actually represent? Even if students manage to block out the confusion, do they really understand the procedure? If students do attain the correct solution, do they have any idea what the correct answer of 20 represents? And because they divided, can they make sense of why the resulting quotient was "larger" rather than "smaller?" (Chapter Eleven will further address the notion of "answers.")

Addressing this combination of issues with the problem $10 \div \frac{1}{2}$ is not a simple task. This quandary is analogous to a forest fire. It begins as a simple spark, sometimes the result of a human mistake. Initially, the spark is a small problem, but under the right conditions of fuel, low humidity, high winds, and so on, the combination of factors results in a raging inferno that is difficult to extinguish or get under control. The combination of instructional mistakes, shortcomings in mathematics content, and inattention to language issues can similarly work in concert to incinerate learning.

MORE LANGUAGE AND SYMBOLISM ISSUES: ADDING FUEL TO THE FIRE

There is more to the mathematics and language story. On top of its shortcomings, traditional instruction includes some habitual practices that make learning more difficult. Traditional math instruction can actually perpetuate language-based problems and impede students' ability to learn mathematics as well as obscure the meaning of terms and symbols that limit students' mental flexibility to see other interpretations and solutions. Some of this is actually inadvertent because instruction often involves habits and practices that were part of teachers' own learning in K–12 mathematics and are thus perpetuated, often-times unconsciously. Examples include treating the reading of math as analogous to the reading of English and the unintended consequences of using simple examples without addressing the necessary transitions when examples become more complex. Assuming that students understand basic symbolism can also be a problem.

The language of mathematics is not static. Similar to a living creature, it changes and evolves. Although some language-related problems in math are systemic, due to the nature of the English language, others are manufactured creations that evolve through the education system and, in time, become standard practice. These changes add fuel to the fire and can make the language and symbolism of mathematics even more complex and confusing for students than it already is. For this reason, teachers need to stay alert, questioning changes and knowing when to resist adopting them.

Reading Mathematics

Examine the problem in Box 3.9. This problem illustrates the clash in the U.S. school system between what students are taught in language arts versus mathematics. Because students are taught to read from left to right, there is a natural tendency to read mathematics in the same way. And math teachers often perpetuate this tendency. But interpreting the expression $3 < x < 8$ as "3 is less than x is less than 8" can leave students bewildered. What can they even visualize as a reference and framework to understand such an odd phrase? Yet, year after year, students must struggle to untangle such phrases because mathematics instruction generally offers no objection or alternative to using the rules of English to read mathematics.

Box 3.9

Write out the following in words: $3 < x < 8$

What if the teacher instead tells the class, "I have a number between 3 and 8"? With this interpretation, students can easily visualize the mathematical relationship. However, breaking the habits of English does not come easy, particularly for native speakers. Teachers must provide direct instruction and practice to help students learn the specialized skill of reading and interpreting mathematics in new ways. And teachers must learn the skill as well, which later chapters address. This approach to interpreting math may be unorthodox and deviate from what is taught in language arts, but using it will help students gain a strong understanding of the concepts, relationships, and nuances of mathematics.

Simple to Complex: Unintended Consequences

It is unfortunate that there are scenarios in which we do a good job of teaching a math concept or process, yet we may still inadvertently be handicapping students in their learning of related topics in the future. Box 3.10 gives examples of problems that confuse students because of the unintended negative consequences of math instruction. When students first learn to solve simple linear equations, either formally or informally, teachers have a natural tendency to limit the examples to those that yield nice whole number solutions. Problems such as $3y = 12$ and $7x = 35$ are the norm. Students become accustomed to this pattern, so it should come as no surprise when they insist that there is no solution to $2h = 13$. Math educators need to recognize this unintended but false belief and intervene accordingly to help students transition beyond the notion that only whole numbers are viable solutions to equations.

Box 3.10

You assign the following problems to your class. Students assert that neither problem has a solution. What is causing the confusion?

a. Solve $2h = 13$

b. If y and some other number add up to 9, find the other number.

The confusion caused in 3.10b is even more pronounced. As another unintended consequence of traditional instruction, students become indoctrinated that the answer to a problem must be a specific number, such as 12, or even a mixed number, such as $4\frac{1}{2}$. To students, a problem like 3.10b does not contain enough information and, therefore, cannot be solved. One remedy is for teachers to enrich students' idea of what constitutes a "solution" by exposing them to more contexts like 3.10b. By doing so, teachers can emphasize the thought process in interpreting such expressions and help students realize this type of context can produce alternative expressions of numbers rather than just numeric answers.

In the specific case of problem 3.10b, teachers need to guide students through a series of steps where students propose possible values and look for patterns in the arithmetic. For example, if two numbers add up to 9 and one of the numbers is 3, what is the other number? Students may easily determine the answer is 6, but the key for teachers is to help students discover the steps they used to arrive at that answer. Repeating the process several times helps students see the pattern for both the solutions and the thought process.

Students will realize they attained the solution by subtracting the known number from 9 (for example, $9 - 3 = 6$). By building on this process, students will see that if the "known" number is y, the correct response must be $9 - y$. This deeper understanding of representations of quantities can be instilled at earlier elementary grades, perhaps through the use of empty boxes, question marks, or blank lines, rather than waiting until Algebra I to spring variables on students.

Do Not Forget Symbols

Mathematics can seem like a Cold War cipher, full of strange symbols and arcane formulas that students must decode to solve various puzzles. Traditional instruction, however, often forgets to provide students with one essential tool: the complete code book. Box 3.11 exemplifies the confusion this oversight can cause.

Box 3.11

If $y = 2$, then $5y =$ _____.

    You assign the problem above and notice that several students fill in the blank with 52. What are these students' misconceptions?

As Box 3.11 shows, traditional instruction often does a poor job of helping students decode the meaning of symbols, including the related concepts needed to interpret them. To solve the problem in 3.11, students need to understand several concepts related to the symbolism. First, students must understand place value along with the value of numerals. This understanding includes knowing that 52 is actually 5 tens and 2 ones, which can also be expressed as $50 + 2$. Second, students must understand mixed numbers and that a number such as $5 \frac{1}{2}$ can also be shown as $5 + \frac{1}{2}$. At this point, the general rule seems to be that addition of the value of the digits is the norm.

In time, students will be exposed to an expression such as $5y$ and in this new context, the rules change on them. Teachers must stop and ensure that students understand the differences and ramifications of the symbolism. For example, students need to understand the difference between 52 and $5y$: that $5y$ is actually an expression of multiplication versus one of place value, as is the case with 52 or a mixed number such as $5 \frac{1}{2}$. For each context, teachers must take time to ensure that students understand all the nuances of the symbolism, something that most likely was not done during the teachers' own K–12 experience as students.

"Fluid" Math Terms and Taking Liberties

For whatever reason, the mathematics educational system sometimes invents new terms or changes the meanings of terms already in standard use. The term *fluid* as an adjective suggests that something is variable or subject to change, and "fluid" mathematical terms are those with invented or changed definitions. Such fluidity in terminology can be problematic, resulting in the same name for different concepts or contradictory definitions.

Which Definition?   As an example, many of you may be surprised to learn that a new definition of the term *average* has come into use. For most Americans, *average* is synonymous with the *mean*. However, a new definition has emerged where *average* is defined as the umbrella term for all three measures of central tendency: mean, median, and mode. That's quite a promotion. According to this new definition, median, mean, and mode are all types of averages. This change raises two critical questions: Who or what authorized this new definition, and which definition is correct? The answers to these questions have definite instructional implications. As a teacher, I would want to know which definition to teach my students and which definition would apply to the state accountability exam. As a parent, how would I learn about this new definition and in turn, decide which one to use when helping my child with homework?

The term *trapezoid* has developed a split personality as well. Two distinct definitions of the term are now in use: One definition claims a trapezoid is a quadrilateral with *only one* pair of parallel sides; the other asserts a trapezoid is a quadrilateral with *at least* one pair of parallel sides. The definition chosen most definitely affects the dynamics of a trapezoid and its relationship to other quadrilaterals. Again, as a teacher, I would want to know which definition is the correct one to teach my students.

Although the focus has been on definitions, an analogous situation exists regarding the interpretation of symbolism in mathematics. Just as with terminology, a need exists for a consistent and uniform interpretation of symbolism. For example, as previously discussed, the interpretation of multiplication expressions, such as of $3 \cdot 2$, is not consistent. Does this expression represent 3 sets of 2 each or 2 sets of 3 each? The confusion and ambiguity regarding the interpretation affects the meaning of the symbols. Someone should really make a decision! Otherwise, how do educators know what to teach their students?

New Terminology.   In addition to changing definitions, teachers and publishers sometimes take it upon themselves to rename math terms. For example, the commutative property is one of the most common properties in mathematics. It is applicable to both addition and multiplication, and can be found in elementary arithmetic. However, some elementary teachers and publishers have renamed the commutative property as the *order* property. The logic for this change is that elementary students need an easier word (*order*) to replace the more difficult term (*commutative*). Several arguments can be made against this change. Some educators argue that elementary students enjoy a challenge and like to show off their knowledge of big words, thus making the learning of *commutative* logical and developmentally appropriate. Other educators argue that replacing academic language with easier terms poses potential confusion for students down the road. At some point, students will have to spend time and energy to unlearn the order property and learn it anew as the commutative property. Would it not make more sense to simply learn the property by its proper name once and avoid the whole unlearning and relearning process?

Taking Liberties. The field of mathematics does not have a definitive authority or governing body to oversee and make decisions regarding mathematics content. Subsequently, organizations, publishers, and even individuals seem to think they can take poetic license with mathematical language. This tendency is seen in cases where a definite name has never been established for a basic property or rule in mathematics. The result is often a confusion of ever new and competing names. For example, the expression $-(-x) = x$ is often referred to as the Property of -1; but some texts cannot resist coining more creative names, such as the Op-Op Property. Fun to say, but did we really need another name?

Another tendency is to change or invent terminology for the explicit purpose of making mathematics "fun." Take, for example, the basic idea of the multiplicative identity, which states that any number multiplied by 1 produces a product that is unchanged. In the name of making math fun, some textbooks have given the multiplicative identity cute names, such as The Magic One or The Onester. Such practices can erode a term's mathematical meaning and hinder students' understanding of the concept. In addition, down the road students once again will have to unlearn the cute names and relearn the concept under its proper academic name.

This phenomenon is not limited to elementary or middle school, either. For example, over the years, many high schoolers in the United States, myself included, have learned the FOIL method. Guess what? There is no such method! Someone at some point invented this name, which is actually an acronym for the distributive property, as a mnemonic to guide students in the order (**F**irst, **O**utside, **I**nside, **L**ast) to use when multiplying two binomials, such as $(x + 3) (x - 2)$. The FOIL method not only creates extra work for students, who have to learn the term, but also creates an additional layer of complexity that obscures the fundamental understanding of the distributive property.

It Comes with the Territory

Other obstacles related to mathematics language are an inherent part of the educational system. These unavoidable issues are either embedded in the system or in the language itself. As a result, not much can be done to change them; they come with the territory. Teachers can only be cognizant of the issues and impart the knowledge to their students.

Inadequate Definitions. Some mathematics terms span the entire spectrum of K–12 instruction. Thus, these terms require elementary or middle school definitions that are often insufficient in higher-level mathematics. One example is an exponent. The elementary-level definition of *exponent* is a numeral that indicates how many times the base appears as a factor. This perspective works well for expressions such as $7 \cdot 7 \cdot 7$, which can be expressed as 7^3. But what happens later in advanced algebra when students come across an expression such as $7^{\frac{1}{2}}$? Imagine the confusion of students who legitimately ask how the base (7) can appear as a factor $\frac{1}{2}$ of one time. The initial definition was well intended and worked in middle school and elementary algebra, but it no longer suffices in an expression with a rational (fractional) exponent. There is little teachers can do in such situations other than change the perspective and definitions of the terms in question so that they fit the higher-level mathematics applications.

Multiple Meanings and Redundant Terms. Another inherent obstacle that comes with the territory of mathematics is academic language that, for one reason or another, is naturally problematic. For example, as mentioned previously, some math terms have more than one definition or meaning within mathematics. One example is the term *ounce*. It honestly makes no sense to have a unit of measure with two distinct meanings, yet *ounce* can refer to both weight and volume. At this point, we cannot rename those units of measure, so we just need to find ways to help students navigate this confusing terminology.

Similarly, some mathematics terms seem to have an unending number of applications. One such term is *inverse*. This term is associated with numerous mathematical contexts, including inverse function, inverse operation, multiplicative inverse, additive inverse, inverse matrix, inverse variation, and so on. Unfortunately, terms with multiple meanings are part of the language of mathematics, so teachers and students alike must find ways to deal with the difficulties these terms create.

TELL ME AGAIN WHY THE LANGUAGE FOCUS IN MATH?

The schematic in Box 3.12 illustrates the simple logic behind a deliberate, focused emphasis on the language and symbolism of mathematics. What do mathematics content and instruction have in common? Where do they intersect? The common intersection is language, both academic and informal. Language provides the integral connection between the content of mathematics (what is taught) and the instruction (how that content is taught). As the age-old saying goes, language enables us to kill two birds with one stone. A language-focused strategy ensures that the content is correct while simultaneously preventing misconceptions or misunderstanding that can result because of the language of instruction. Through a deliberate and insightful focus on the language of mathematics and what it entails, teachers can simultaneously improve both content and instruction, ensuring that students gain a deep understanding of mathematics.

Box 3.12: Logic Schematic for Emphasis of Language and Symbolism in Math

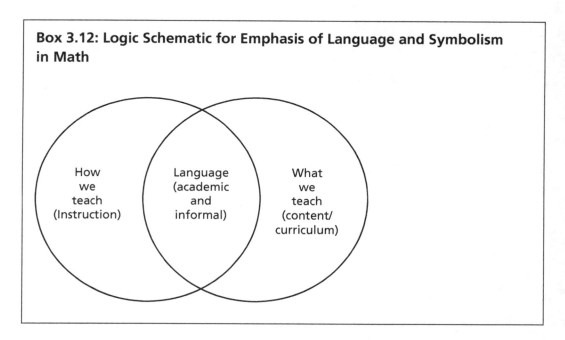

So What Does Conceptual Understanding Look Like?

In *Adding It Up: Helping Children Learn Mathematics* (Kilpatrick et al., 2001), the National Research Council identifies five competencies required for students to attain "mathematical proficiency." These interwoven competencies, based on studies of students in pre-kindergarten through eighth grade, are noted below:

1. Conceptual understanding—comprehension of concepts, operations, and relations

2. Procedural fluency—carrying out procedures flexibly, accurately, efficiently, and appropriately

3. Strategic competence—ability to formulate, represent, and solve problems

4. Adaptive reasoning—capacity for logical thought, reflection, explanation, and justification

5. Productive disposition—habitual inclination to see mathematics as sensible, useful, and worthwhile, coupled with a belief in diligence and one's own capacity

It may not be an accident that conceptual understanding tops the list of competencies of mathematical proficiency. Conceptual understanding is the bedrock on which the other four components are grounded. So given its vital importance, what exactly does conceptual understanding in mathematics look like? To answer this question, we must examine this multifaceted and complex idea from multiple perspectives. From a content perspective, conceptual understanding goes far beyond "how to." Students should know not only what a concept is, but also why it works as it does, how it connects to other concepts, and what it looks like symbolically and graphically. Such understanding enables students to view a concept from different angles. From a language perspective, conceptual understanding includes a thorough mastery of the academic language and symbolism that are critical components of mathematics. Thus, students should be able not only to recognize and understand nuances in the language and symbolism but also to decipher the meanings of words and symbols in different mathematical contexts and to distinguish the mathematical meanings of words from other meanings those words may have.

An examination of traditional instruction, state content standards, and textbooks reveals that mathematics instruction tends to focus primarily on procedural fluency. True, knowing algorithms and procedures is important and should be emphasized, but not to the point of minimizing conceptual understanding. Rather, procedural fluency should be a complement to and a byproduct of conceptual understanding. To gain the first without the latter is analogous to an automobile with a smooth and powerful engine but no steering wheel. The car can run and accelerate, but it has no way to direct this power and will undoubtedly veer off the road or crash, never reaching its final destination.

The power and value of conceptual understanding cannot be overstated. Yet even with the use of descriptions, envisioning what this level of understanding looks like can still be difficult. To help, this chapter examines three major attributes that are indicative of conceptual understanding in mathematics: (1) deep and thorough definitions of key terms and concepts, (2) connections among key topics that deepen understanding, and (3) insightful interpretation and translation of the language and symbolism of mathematics.

IT STARTS WITH DEFINITIONS

The basis for building a conceptual understanding of mathematics is providing deep and thorough definitions of key concepts. True understanding is not possible without a solid grasp of what a concept is, yet even the most adept students often possess rather shallow and incomplete definitions of key ideas. Because procedural fluency is frequently the sole focus of instruction, students can successfully progress through mathematics without ever moving beyond superficial definitions and understanding. For instance, students can get by without a conceptual definition of multiplication if they know their multiplication facts. Likewise, students can find the area of a circle with only a shallow knowledge of π being 3.14; for computation, a conceptual understanding of π is not needed. Unfortunately, being adept at performing algorithms and procedures might serve students well on standardized tests, but it does not necessarily build the fundamental understanding students need. Later, this lack of understanding will prove problematic if students want to take higher-level math classes or hope to pursue a math-related career.

Simple Yet Deep

The paradox is that the shallow definitions often taught in K–12 math classes are, at the same time, often rather complex. Students are usually not exposed to deep yet simple and concise definitions of fundamental mathematical concepts. Although the idea seems contradictory, it is possible to simultaneously simplify and deepen math content. But we as educators rarely use this "simple yet deep" strategy for building conceptual understanding. When done correctly, however, a simple yet deep definition of a basic mathematical concept can be powerful, applying to many contexts and revealing relationships and connections to other concepts. Obviously, since such a definition must include words, the issue of language is again at the forefront. And this language plays dual roles: both in the actual definition of a concept and in how that definition is taught.

An unknown sage once said, "It's a simple task to make things complex, but a complex task to make things simple." Developing a mathematics definition that is simple yet deep can be daunting. The task requires experience and a solid foundation in multiple areas of math. However, just like a locomotive that is building up speed, once momentum is attained, speed is much easier to maintain. Simple yet deep definitions connect to and build on each other, as this and subsequent chapters will show. Thus, once you have some deep definitions of fundamental concepts in hand, they leverage the learning of related terms. As a note for the pure mathematicians out there, the definitions proposed may seem a bit unorthodox. However, they remain true to the mathematical ideas being defined while enabling students to build conceptual understanding. So what does a simple yet deep definition look like?

A Look at Five Examples

With the explosive growth of the Internet, it's a snap to look up definitions for every mathematical term and concept that exists. Popular resources include online dictionaries and encyclopedias as well as websites geared to K–12 math teachers and students. But do these online definitions pass the "simple yet deep" test? Not all of them do. However, evaluating the strengths and weaknesses of definitions online and in other resources provides an excellent method for developing simple yet deep definitions. Through this process, teachers can identify elements to include in definitions and, even more important, fallacies and shortcomings to avoid. The following examples illustrate this process by assessing definitions found in popular resources to develop simple yet deep definitions for five key math terms.

Defining Graph. As mentioned in Chapter One, many students incorrectly define a graph as a grid or the x and y axes because directions so often say to show results "on the graph." Teachers need to provide students with a strong definition of the term *graph* to counter such misconceptions. In addition, since the two most common areas for the use of a graph are in data representation and algebra, this definition would be even more beneficial if it included and connected these two areas.

Examining definitions of the term *graph* in popular K–12 resources reveals a number of limitations. Some definitions focus on a graph as a drawing used to represent data, but this meaning is too simplistic and limited in context to data. Other definitions of a graph tend to use an algebraic perspective. These definitions focus on a graph as a set of points and use such terms as *discrete*, *continuous*, and *functions*. However, the focus on algebra is also restrictive, implying that a graph exists primarily in the context of a coordinate plane with x and y axes. Keeping students in mind, we do not want definitions that are too shallow or complex with limited applicable contexts. We need a definition that enables students to gain a solid holistic understanding of a graph as a concept.

Now, consider the following simple yet deep definition: "In mathematics, a graph is a picture of a relationship (or relationships)." This definition should suffice for elementary and middle school, with a transition over time to a slightly more sophisticated vernacular, where a graph is defined as "a visual representation of a relationship or relationships."

One of the tests of a good definition is whether it is applicable in the majority of possible contexts or uses. From a data perspective, pie charts, bar graphs, and so on show the relationships among the quantities in data. For example, a vertical bar graph could illustrate the relationship of the average monthly temperature in a city for the past year. From an algebraic perspective, a graph (typically two-dimensional on a coordinate plane) is a visual representation of the relationship between whatever is represented on the two axes. As an example, if the vertical axis represents a person's weight and the horizontal axis represents time in days, the graph would show patterns of the person's weight over time. Even on a number line, which is a one-dimensional graph, the focus is on the relationship of the numbers represented. For example, a number line could show the relationship between two numbers, such as 15.3 and 18. Of course, there is a lot more to understanding graphs, notably how to interpret them, but that is another focus to be investigated separately. However, the conceptual understanding of a graph must be based on a simple yet deep definition.

Defining Logarithm.   What is meant by the term *logarithm*? Because the focus of this book is primarily on fundamental mathematics, you may wonder why we are addressing such a high-level concept. There are three reasons. First, did you experience a twinge of fear when you realized this section covered logarithms? That fear is based primarily on the fact that for most adults, the idea of a logarithm is a concept reserved only for the mathematically gifted. Many of us consider logarithm and similar concepts to be firmly nestled high up in a mathematical aerie, far beyond our reach. But this idea is inaccurate. Second, even with modern technology and the wealth of information available online, a student would be hard-pressed to truly understand the concept of a logarithm based on the definitions in many resources. Third, in mathematics, a logarithm is but one of many concepts inexorably connected to other concepts. As a result, students' full understanding of a new concept is often dependent on a knowledge of related concepts, making it essential that we expose students to simple yet deep definitions of fundamental ideas in mathematics—including logarithm.

Take a few minutes and find a definition of *logarithm*. The one you found may define the term via an example: if $y = b^x$, then $\log_b y = x$. Or the definition may explain the term to some extent, but in a roundabout way, such as stating that a logarithm is the power to which a base must be raised to equal a given quantity. Whatever definition you found, in all likelihood, it left you still wondering what a logarithm is.

The following is a simple yet deep definition of a logarithm that even younger students can grasp: "A logarithm is an exponent." That basic idea is all students need as a start. Building on this definition, teachers can then add the idea that we use logarithmic equations when we do not know the exponent. True, students must know a lot more, such as the conversion of exponential equations to logarithmic equations, but this basic definition is a solid yet simple foundation for this mathematical topic. So if students are confronted with an equation such as $2^x = 30$, they automatically see that there is an exponent involved and that the exponent (logarithm) is unknown. This basic understanding then helps students realize an equation in logarithmic form is used to find a solution. With this sound start, students will be ready, when it is time, to soar high and learn the properties and procedures involved in working with logarithms.

Defining Exponent.   Clearly, since the term *logarithm* is synonymous with the term *exponent*, one cannot fully comprehend the first without a conceptual understanding of the latter. Several representative definitions of *exponent* can be found, with some being good and others being incomplete or even misleading. A definition that focuses on an exponent being the number of times that a base is used as a factor is an excellent example and should be the one taught to students. Such a definition provides a correct, concise explanation of an exponent that lacks only the idea of the symbol appearing as a superscript to the right of the digit (known as the base) in this context.

There are others that as stand-alone definitions are incomplete. A definition that refers to an exponent as a number that indicates repeated multiplication establishes only the involvement of multiplication, but nothing else. You might find definitions that are only examples of an exponent by citing an expression such as y^x and then explaining that y is called the base and x is called the exponent. Such definitions refer only to the symbolism used to represent an exponent, but do not explain the actual concept. These shortcomings represent one of the most prevalent and devastating problems in K–12 mathematics: Many of the definitions presented are either incomplete or woefully inadequate. Rather than define a term conceptually, many definitions provide only a scant description or describe only what a term looks like. How can we expect students to apply mathematical concepts if they do not know what those concepts are?

The words we use in definitions are obviously critical. One danger is that the language used can actually result in incorrect definitions. As a result, we inadvertently pass along misconceptions that mislead students. A search for the definition of an exponent will surely uncover some that define an exponent as the number of times the base is multiplied. At first, that seems correct, but is it? Consider 7^2 as a test. Based on such a definition, the 2 is the number of times the 7 is to be multiplied. In expanded form, 7^2 is expressed as 7 · 7. Isn't that just *one* multiplication, not *two*? But based on the definition, we are supposed to do two multiplications for 7^2, which would actually look like this: 7 · 7 · 7. Take 5^1 as an additional test. The interpretation of that last definition suggests one multiplication involving 5. However, in expanded form, 5^1 is simply 5; there are no multiplications of 5 involved at all! Thus, a closer examination of a definition that states that an exponent tells you how many times the base is multiplied is mathematically incorrect. Even as an informal definition, it is still confusing and not a viable option. Unfortunately, that is the definition being learned by many students.

Just as the term *logarithm* requires a knowledge of *exponent*, so the term *exponent* requires a knowledge of related terms, such as *power* and *base*. Such connections can be both a blessing and a curse. On the positive side, teachers can leverage students' understanding of one concept to support their learning of related or connected ideas. On the negative side, students' misconception of just one fundamental concept can lead to a domino effect of misunderstanding related terms. When math terms are incorrectly defined or used, and this problem is coupled with the poor use of language in instruction, the devastation can be exponential. One example that illustrates this potential for creating devastating problems is the concept of rounding a number in mathematics.

Defining Round.   Rounding is an integral part of estimation and will be found in most, if not all, fundamental math curricula. It is hard to imagine anyone not having at least some experience with the process. It is not a complex process, yet one that is difficult to define.

This section finds us looking for several representative definitions of the mathematical term *round*, used as a verb. These definitions illustrate the importance of having a simple yet deep definition for a concept.

Some definitions explain rounding as reducing or increasing the digits in a number while trying to keep the value similar to the original. Such definitions are problematic in that the idea of reducing is not necessarily applicable, and the idea of trying to keep a value similar is not the actual intent of rounding. We should never use the word being defined as part of the definition, yet one can find definitions that say *rounding* means to express as a *round* number. Using the word being defined in the definition itself renders the definition vague, confusing, and of little utility.

There exist informal definitions that assert that rounding a number refers to taking a number and *bumping it up* or *bumping it down* to a nearby number. Such a definition is no better than the previous because it is too generic, using standard English words such as *bump* and *nearby* that really have no mathematical meaning and which do not define the term at all. Other definitions of rounding explain it as a process of approximating a number to a nearby one. That type of definition is an improvement as it connects rounding to the central idea of approximation. However, such phrases as *to a nearby number* do not have any mathematical precision and cloud the meaning.

Any of the cited definitions would leave students without a conceptual grasp of rounding. It is apparent that the definition should include the idea of approximation. One can find definitions that refer to rounding as a process of approximating a number with additional details on how to do it. However, such definitions exemplify our tendency in math to include the "how to." Describing how to round a number in the definition is not necessary and only adds complexity. Save the "how to" for exactly that—the additional instruction to show students how to round a number. With this in mind, the definition of rounding should avoid how to do it and have embedded within it a connection to the idea of approximation as well as the critical component of accuracy, which is the covert link to the role of place value in the process of rounding. Adjusting the last definition produces the following simple yet deep definition of *round (noun)*: "A method of approximating a number to a specified degree of accuracy." With that established, *round* as a verb would mean the application or use of such a method.

Conceptual understanding in mathematics includes the ability to recognize the line between *what a concept is* and any how-to procedures involved with that concept. Making this distinction is one of the keys to a simple yet deep definition. A definition that includes a lot of how-to information can actually hide the meaning of a concept. And isn't the purpose of a definition to describe what something *means*? The true litmus test for a definition is whether it describes what the term being defined is. If not, it is not a definition. For that reason, this text often uses the phrase *conceptual definition,* as opposed to just *definition,* as a reminder of what a definition should do.

The focus of this point has been on the definitions themselves. However, the language used in establishing fundamental concepts in classroom instruction is also influential. The teaching of rounding is a good example of some of the superfluous and haphazard language that finds its way into teaching scenarios. Any given lesson on rounding can reveal a multitude of language pitfalls. For example, a common strategy in the process is to underline the digit that is being rounded. But in some cases *digits* are mistakenly referred to as *numbers.* You'll recall from Chapter Two that, simply put, a *number* is the actual quantity, and a *numeral* is the symbolic representation of that quantity. Furthermore, a *digit* is a single numeral (in the U.S. system, the symbols 0, 1, 2, ... 8, 9). Note, the three terms are interdependent and connected, but they are not synonymous; they have different definitions. If one has a deep understanding of these ideas, then the inadvertent mistakes will not occur.

After the digit that is to be rounded is underlined, the next step is to determine if that digit should remain the same or be increased by one. It is at this point that the tendency to make a simple idea inordinately complex emerges. When looking at a multidigit numeral, there is the simple idea of the location of the digits in relation to each other, which connects to the meaning of place value. Quite simply, digits appear to the right or left of each other. However, there are scenarios where the location of the adjacent *numbers* (incorrect) is described as being behind or in front of it, which means to the right or to the left, respectively. When I grew up, there was a big difference between being behind something as opposed to being to the right of it. And being in front of something did not mean I was to the left of it. Why not stick to the basic ideas of left and right, which are better descriptors of the location of a digit in place value and number line contexts? Without previous experience, it takes some thought to figure out what is meant by one digit being behind another. When teaching place value, do we say the ones place is *behind* the tens place? No, so this misplaced terminology adds a layer of unnecessary confusion for students.

As if that were not enough, an inspection of some resources revealed that more confusion is added with the invention of the term *neighbor number,* which, incidentally, should technically be *neighbor digit.* This would be a digit adjacent to the digit to be rounded. Why introduce yet another irrelevant layer with this phrase? Why not reinforce students' previous knowledge and refer to a digit with respect to its place value? If students are rounding a number such as 376 to the nearest ten, it makes more sense to keep it simple and reinforce previous academic language (place value) by referring to the 6 as the ones place; no need to cloud the issue by bringing in *neighbor number*.

The result of all these inappropriate or new terms is to make rounding far more complex than it is. Such adaptations and invention add a layer of complexity and also create the need for students to relearn the proper terminology. High school math texts do not include the idea of a *neighbor number* in the process of rounding. And amid all this instruction, nowhere do students receive a simple yet deep definition of rounding—all they typically are shown is *how to* round. It is tempting to use or invent new terminology to make mathematics more fun or interesting. Teachers can accomplish that by making the activities creative and interesting rather than the terminology.

Defining Slope. Slope is a concept of paramount importance in mathematics. Needless to say, a thorough understanding of this fundamental concept is essential. Finding an appropriate definition in available resources is a difficult task with definitions ranging greatly in quality. Interestingly enough, one can find definitions in math based on the use of an example. There are definitions of slope that simply point out that in any equation in the form $y = mx + b$, *m* means slope. Clearly, this is not a definition at all. Literally translated, *m* means slope? No matter the perspective, this description gives students no idea whatsoever of what slope is.

There are definitions that are based on trigonometry that describe slope as the tangent of the positive angle formed between a given straight line and the x-axis. Such a definition, despite its impressive appearance, is actually a better description of a trig ratio than a slope. Other definitions focus on the coordinate plane and describe slope as the rate at which the y coordinate (ordinate) of a point on a line changes with respect to a change in the x coordinate (abscissa). This definition hits on the fundamental idea of a slope, but still falls short of a clear description. Although both of the last two definitions are mathematically correct, they are inordinately complex and better suited for mathematicians, not students. Such complex yet paradoxically shallow definitions offer students no real understanding and reinforce the false belief that mathematics can be understood only by a privileged few.

An informal variation of the last definition above is that slope is the difference of the y coordinates over the difference of the x coordinates, otherwise known as the infamous *rise over run* definition of slope. This approach is inadequate because it attempts to define slope by describing *how to* find or compute it. For the term *slope*, the following is a simple yet deep definition: "Slope is the rate of change." That's it. It's that simple. Everything else is window dressing that connects to the application and representation of slope. This basic understanding of slope as a rate of change serves as the foundation for a multitude of processes and applications in mathematics.

Drifting Away. Knowing simple yet powerful definitions is the foundation for mathematical proficiency. Even when armed with a deep repertoire of these definitions, there is a language-based danger that can erode them. This problem must be acknowledged so that educators can recognize the issue and take action to minimize the impact. Refer to Box 4.1 and perform the task to see if you exhibit the symptoms.

Box 4.1: Real-Life Example

Give a real-life example of slope.

This task is an example of what we will refer to as "drifting." Experience has shown that with rare exceptions, the responses usually deal with some type of incline. Common responses include examples such as a hill, roof, boat ramp, mountain, or stairway. True, these are examples of slope, but they are all representative of the standard-English definition of slope which revolves around the notion of an incline or slant. In this particular case, for whatever reason, the thinking drifts toward the standard-English version of slope and away from the mathematical perspective. This idea of drifting occurs in many other instances and for different reasons, although it seems to occur primarily because of some type of habitual practice or repetition. Drifting will be mentioned at various points in the text with an additional emphasis presented in Chapter Ten.

Armed with the definition of slope as a rate of change, people who are asked for real-life examples of a slope could offer many that have nothing to do with an incline. Such examples could include $3.49 per gallon of gas, a loss of 3 pounds of weight per month, a study that shows 7 ounces of plant food yields 2 inches of plant growth, and a worker who earns $15 per hour. The drifting toward thinking of slope as only an incline would be eliminated, or at least minimized, if participants possessed a conceptual definition.

Definition Summary

Concepts such as graph, logarithm, exponent, and round are integral components of mathematics. By providing simple yet deep definitions, teachers can help students—even in elementary and middle school—build an understanding of fundamental concepts in mathematics. Some overarching concepts such as slope are especially critical. Its importance is immeasurable and cannot be overemphasized. There must be no compromise because the alternative would be for the majority of our citizenry to only think of slope as the incline of a mountain. The educational system must insure that without exception every student is well grounded in this concept. To do otherwise leads to misunderstanding and confusion, or shallow knowledge at best, which almost assures poor performance in any measure of mathematical knowledge.

Definitions are just the start to mathematical proficiency, but they are critical. We have all heard the expression *connect the dots*. In essence, simple yet deep definitions constitute those dots. The more powerful the definition, the stronger the possible connections because the definitions provide the spark, the energy, and the synapses for making connections in math.

MAKING CONNECTIONS IN MATH: BEYOND CONNECTING DOTS

Math teachers know well that mathematical concepts are highly interrelated and build on each other. For this reason, the second key component of conceptual understanding is making connections among concepts and ideas. In many ways, these connections make learning mathematics easier because students' knowledge of one topic often constitutes part of what they need to learn about another topic.

Imagine that the two circles in each figure in Box 4.2 represent two math topics or concepts. The intersection represents what content is common to both. The first is an example of a poor connection. The small intersection can result because of multiple reasons. If the topics are not well related, there is obviously not much that can be done to improve the connection. However, closely related concepts can look like Figure A in Box 4.2 if those concepts are poorly defined. If the concepts are well defined in a simple yet deep way, then the relationship can look like Figure B. Since the intersection of the two is large, what was taught in the first concept has resulted in students already subconsciously understanding the second topic, which of course saves teachers time and energy!

As an example, if students have a firm and deep grasp of the definition of multiplication, then they automatically have a partial understanding of division because of its close connection. Students' deep understanding of division can then be used to help them link to the connected concept of an average. (See Chapter Six for a discussion of multiplication and division.) Some of these connections are fairly obvious to students, but others can be seen only through a conceptual lens. For instance, a conceptual understanding of ratio, slope, and rate enables students to see that the concepts overlap and are variations of the same overarching theme—relationships.

Box 4.2: Poor Connection Versus Strong Connection

A. Poor Connection

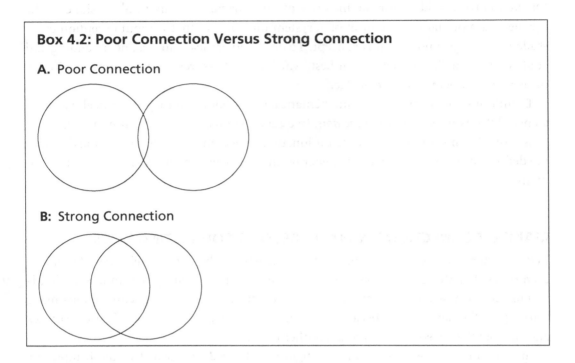

B: Strong Connection

By clearly making and explaining such connections, elementary and middle school teachers can help students understand the degree of interdependence that exists among mathematical concepts. Thus, as students learn simple yet deep definitions of key terms, teachers should point out related terms and explain how they connect to and build on the initial terms. For example, we saw with the definition of *round* that knowledge of the term *approximation* is needed as well. Likewise, to understand the term *digit*, students need to understand both its connection to *numeral* and how both terms differ from the term *number*.

An excellent example for how to make connections to build and extend students' conceptual understanding is the distributive property. This property is usually associated with multiplication. However, a conceptual understanding of the distributive property coupled with a simple yet deep definition of multiplication enables students to connect and extend the distributive property to division. Consider the problem in Box 4.3 and the solution presented by one fifth-grade student:

Box 4.3: Covert Distributive Property

Problem: $156 \div 4$

Solution:

$$156 \div 4$$

$$
\begin{aligned}
&= 25 \\
&\quad\ 12 \quad \tfrac{1}{2} \\
&+ \ 1 \quad \tfrac{1}{2} \\
\hline
&\quad 38 + 1 = 39
\end{aligned}
$$

Although the thought process is evident, the student's work is missing the key element in the solution process: the breaking up of the dividend into place-value pieces prior to the division by 4. Box 4.4 symbolically illustrates the student's complete thought process:

Box 4.4: Distributive Property Applied to Division

$$
\begin{aligned}
156 \div 4 \\
&= (100 + 50 + 6) \div 4 \\
&= 100 \div 4 + 50 \div 4 + 6 \div 4 \\
&= \quad\ 25 \quad + \quad 12\tfrac{1}{2} + 1\tfrac{1}{2} \\
&= \ 39
\end{aligned}
$$

This solution involves a confluence of different understandings. In addition to the conceptual knowledge of multiplication and the distributive property, the solution shows an understanding of the connected meanings embedded in the symbolism. One of the many shortcomings of the traditional instruction of division is the illusion that we have no options with the dividend, which in this example is 156. Traditional instruction embeds the idea that a dividend is like a solid block of cement that we must use as is. However, much of arithmetic, which includes multiplication and division, is focused on either taking things apart or putting things together. An in-depth investigation of the student's work reveals an understanding of those basic ideas.

A teacher focused on making conceptual connections could improve on the solution process even further by connecting to the idea of factors. Rather than breaking up the dividend (156) based on place value, as the student did, a better option is to break it up into chunks that are divisible by 4. For example, 156 can be broken up into 120 + 36. Box 4.5 illustrates this approach.

Box 4.5: Distributive Property with Division Using Factorable Chunks

$$156 \div 4$$
$$= (120 + 36) \div 4$$
$$= 120 \div 4 + 36 \div 4$$
$$= 30 + 9$$
$$= 39$$

Yet another option is available, as shown in Box 4.6. In this method, students split the dividend into chunks divisible by 4, but from a subtraction perspective. Thus, 156 is transformed into 160 − 4 to produce the solution process shown.

Box 4.6: Distributive Property with Division: A Subtraction Perspective

$$156 \div 4$$
$$= (160 - 4) \div 4$$
$$= 160 \div 4 - 4 \div 4$$
$$= 40 - 1$$
$$= 39$$

The distributive property is one of the more powerful properties in mathematics. Yet its power is greatly limited if applied only to multiplication contexts. By clearly making the connections between multiplication and division, teachers can help students extend the distributive property to contexts involving division and subtraction. Many students in the United States graduate from high school with the mistaken notion that division has only one solution process—the algorithm restricted to working with the dividend in full. However, several alternative and often superior approaches exist if students have a conceptual understanding of how key mathematical principles connect.

THE INTERPRETATION AND TRANSLATION OF MATH

The third major component of conceptual understanding is the interpretation and translation of mathematical language and symbolism. This final piece of the puzzle is integral to and interwoven with the other two components. Thus, to understand conceptual definitions and make connections among concepts, students must be able to interpret the meanings, nuances, and contexts of the language and symbolism used. At the same time, students need a level of conceptual understanding to be able to translate terminology and symbolism into plain English. For example, students need to be able to understand formal definitions provided in math textbooks. And as this chapter has shown, these formal definitions often need to be distilled into simpler language.

Meaning, Nuance, and Context

Take the commutative property of addition as an interpretation example. This property has a formal definition replete with symbols and abstract mathematical terms. Most mathematical resources define the commutative property of addition as follows: "For any distinct real numbers b and c, b + c = c + b." Such a statement might seem incomprehensible to young students with no previous knowledge of the concept. They could recite the given definition hundreds of times, yet still have no idea what it means. For students to make sense of it, they must be able to translate the definition into a simpler form. For example, the teacher may help students develop an interpretation such as, "When adding two numbers, if I change the order, I will still get the same answer." A more precise yet still informal translation would be that the commutative property of addition states that changing the order of the addends does not change the sum. Note that this definition requires an understanding of the terms *addends* and *sum*. Another way to help is to provide a real-life example: One person puts the right shoe on first, then the left shoe. Another person puts the left shoe on first, then the right shoe. But the end result for both people is that they have each put on two shoes.

As the previous example shows, mathematics often requires interpreting and translating formal language intermixed with symbols—not only for students but also for teachers. The Common Core State Standards for Mathematics provide many symbol-heavy statements. In the domain *Number and Operations—Fractions*, the third-grade objectives include the following example:

Understand a fraction $\frac{a}{b}$ as the quantity formed by a parts of size $\frac{1}{b}$.

At first glance, this statement might be intimidating to some elementary teachers. By developing a conceptual understanding of the symbols, however, a teacher can translate such a statement into something that makes more sense, and be ready to help students do the same. Often, a first step in interpreting symbol-heavy statements is to replace any variables with numbers. For example, the statement above could be rewritten as follows:

Understand a fraction $\frac{3}{5}$ as the quantity formed by *3* parts of size $\frac{1}{5}$.

Next, creating a visual representation, such as the one shown in Box 4.7, can enhance understanding.

Box 4.7

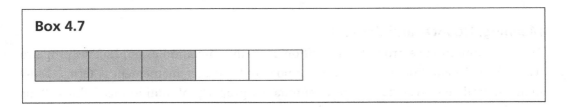

In the illustration, each of the parts is $\frac{1}{5}$ of the whole, and three of the parts are shaded. The statement is now beginning to make sense. In essence, the fraction $\frac{3}{5}$ says that you have three one-fifths. Similarly, the fraction $\frac{2}{7}$ is the quantity formed by 2 parts of size $\frac{1}{7}$ (or two one-sevenths), and the fraction $\frac{4}{9}$ is the quantity formed by 4 parts of size $\frac{1}{9}$ (or four one-ninths). Using the numeric examples, a pattern develops, and the statement is much clearer than on the initial reading. Understanding instills confidence. Once a teacher successfully translates statements that involve variables or other symbolism, that type of interpretation becomes easier. However, it is an acquired skill that takes practice.

Another component of translation that requires practice is learning to interpret the nuances and contexts associated with mathematical symbols and language. This skill is also key for conceptual understanding. Consider the problem in Box 4.8. What nuances associated with the symbols in this problem must students understand to solve it correctly?

Box 4.8

Solve: 63 − 32 + 1

The correct answer to the problem is 32. Some students may be tempted to take a shortcut and add the 32 and 1 to get 33, then subtract from 63 to get 30. However, that process and solution actually fit the expression $63 - (32 + 1)$, which is not the same as the expression in Box 4.8. The key is an understanding of the negative ($-$) symbol. Note that in the original expression, the negative sign applies only to the 32; thus, the 32 is the only amount subtracted. This scenario is not the same as the one in $63 - (32 + 1)$. In that context, the negative sign applies to all the numbers inside the parentheses, which in essence changes the positive 1 to a negative 1 if the parentheses were dropped. This example emphasizes the importance of conceptual understanding and having a trained eye to correctly interpret the nuances of mathematical symbolism. With this type of understanding, students faced with the problem in Box 4.8 would have the flexibility to interpret $63 - 32 + 1$ as $63 + (-32) + 1$.

As mentioned in Chapter Three, interpreting mathematical symbols correctly also frequently requires breaking away from traditional reading practices based on the rules of English. Consider the expression in Box 4.9. What issues might students face in reading and interpreting this expression?

Box 4.9

Interpret the following in words: $b - c = b + (-c)$

If students read the expression as "b minus c is equal to b plus negative c," it may have no meaning for them. Honestly, what depth of understanding can we expect students to get from such a statement? In actuality, the expression above can clarify for students why expressions such as $3 - (-2)$ are the same as $3 + 2$. But to reap this benefit, students must have the conceptual understanding to translate the expression correctly into concise and clear English. A loose translation of the above might state that "subtracting a number is the same as adding its opposite." Thus, subtracting a negative 2 is the same thing as adding a positive 2. Of course, teaching students the subtraction of integers is an involved process that should include manipulatives of some type. But understanding begins with the proper interpretation of the general expression in Box 4.9, preferably as a conclusion reached by students in a series of discovery activities with manipulatives. Once students understand the pattern that subtracting a number is the same as adding its opposite, the next task would be for them to determine how to express that idea mathematically using symbols.

Some Minuses of the Negative Sign

You may have noticed that the two previous examples both involve the use of the negative sign. This is not surprising given that it is one of the more problematic symbols in mathematics. The negative sign has three primary interpretations, underscoring the need to be hyperaware of the nuances of mathematical symbols and the context in which they are used. In some contexts, the negative sign indicates the operation of subtraction, usually interpreted as "minus," "subtract," or "take away." In other contexts, it indicates a value less than zero, such as -5, usually pronounced as either "minus 5" or "negative 5." Note that the interpretation "minus 5" for a negative number may prove to be problematic because it can also indicate the operation of subtraction. Adding further potential for confusion, the negative sign is sometimes shown as a superscript to indicate a negative number, as in $^-5$, but that placement is not always consistent. Students must be flexible and interpret the negative sign based on context and meaning regardless of how it appears in print.

The third interpretation of the negative sign is the least used but arguably the most important. This interpretation is "the opposite of." The most common context for this meaning occurs when a negative sign applies to more than one number or to a variable. For example, the sign in front of the parentheses in the expression $-(b - 3)$ should be interpreted as *the opposite of* $(b - 3)$, which is the same as $-b + 3$. Consider the expression $-c$. A common mistake is to pronounce this expression as "negative c" rather than "the opposite of c." This problematic pronunciation leads students to the false conclusion that the expression represents a negative number. What if $c = -3$? In this case, the value of $-c$ is $-(-3)$, or a positive 3. The difficulty in an expression such as $-(-3)$ is that each negative sign must be translated differently. The negative sign outside the parentheses should be translated as "the opposite of," while the sign inside the parentheses should be translated as "negative," for the full interpretation, "the opposite of negative 3." This interpretation enables students to understand better why the end result is a positive 3. By using "the opposite of," students will be able to make more sense of the negative sign when it is used with variables or with grouping symbols, such as parentheses.

Obviously, both teachers and students need to be precise in how they interpret the negative sign. The interpretation must match the context. Since old habits can be hard to break, teachers must exercise due diligence to make certain they and students pronounce the sign correctly. Doing so may be the difference between a correct and incorrect solution. But more important, using the proper interpretation can add to students' depth of understanding and eliminate confusion or the creation of cumbersome and often incorrect terminology. For example, $-(-8)$ is equivalent to 8, not because *a double negative is a positive*, but rather because the opposite of a negative 8 is a positive 8. By distinguishing these three interpretations of the negative sign, teachers not only simplify and deepen content understanding but also simplify instruction by eliminating inaccurate rules such as "two negatives make a positive." This rule is yet another example of how the U.S. education system often makes mathematics far more complex than necessary.

When students reach high school, they will encounter even more meanings of the negative sign. One of these is as part of an exponent. Refer to Box 4.10. In that context, the negative sign indicates a reciprocal. Those students who have a strong conceptual understanding of the above three interpretations of the negative sign will be better prepared to add these new meanings to their symbolic library—definitely a plus.

Box 4.10: Not Your Typical Negative

$$6^{-2} = \frac{1}{6^2}$$

Some Habitual Offenders

We all know how troublesome bad habits can be, and how difficult they are to break. In the math classroom, several habitual practices of traditional instruction hamper students' ability to interpret and translate symbols and terminology. We touched on some of these offenders in Chapter Three. In this section, we examine them again with a focus on their effect on conceptual understanding.

As noted above, the rules and practices of reading English do not always align with the best way to read and translate mathematics. Take the inequality $y < 0$ as an example. The literal translation is "y is less than zero." If a number is less than 0, then it must be a negative number. Thus, the expression $y < 0$ really says "y is a negative number." True, there is nothing wrong with reading the expression as "y is less than 0," but the context at hand and the potential numbers involved will be much clearer to students with the interpretation "y is a negative number." By the same token, students who interpret $m > 0$ as "m is a positive number" have a more direct and immediate clarity as to what numbers are involved. To break the bad habit of reading math like English, teachers need to explore the best way to read mathematics expressions and instruct students in using and practicing this skill. Although difficult at first and perhaps unorthodox, learning to read math in a new way will build conceptual understanding and give students a clear advantage.

Another habitual practice that is actually a sin of omission is the failure to provide sufficient instruction devoted to learning and reviewing key symbols and what they represent. Box 4.11 illustrates the dangers of this neglect.

Box 4.11

$$8 + 4 = \boxed{} + 5$$

The problem illustrated in Box 4.11 was given to elementary students as part of an elementary-level research study (Falkner, Levi, & Carpenter, 1999). The results showed that the vast majority of students in grades 1–6 filled in the square with the incorrect response of 12. The fact that most fifth and sixth graders missed the problem as did younger students indicates the cause was more than carelessness or a lack of proficiency in addition. The study concluded, rather, that the equal sign had lost its conceptual meaning for students. Instead of representing two equal relationships, the equal sign had become a prompt that signaled to students that they needed to do something, typically a computation. It was no coincidence that 12 was the most common incorrect answer. Students who gave this answer added $8 + 4$ and then filled in the square with the sum of 12, with no regard for the additional task of adding 5. Some students even got creative and after filling in the square with 12, inserted another equal sign to the right of the 5 and wrote the new sum of 17!

Without any corrective guidance or review of the symbolism, repeated tasks such as $3 + 4 = $ _____, $8 - 5 = $ _____, $4 \cdot 8 = $ _____, start a process where students slowly drift away from the real meaning of the equal sign and begin to see it as a prompt to perform some type of operation and then write down "the answer." To investigate this phenomenon further, I did informal research at the middle school level. I gave a small sample of students a strip of paper with a similar problem to the one in Box 4.11 and asked them to quickly write in the solution and hand back the completed strip. Interestingly, the informal results at the middle school paralleled those in the elementary school study. The most common answer was the sum of the two numbers on the left side of the equation. This informal trial, although unscientific, showed that even with older seventh and eighth graders, a serious problem with the concept of equality existed, one that students had not outgrown with age and experience. To break the bad habit of students' drifting away from symbols' true meanings, teachers need to emphasize and review symbolism, assess students' understanding, and provide appropriate intervention as needed to prevent students from veering off course.

A third habitual practice that affects conceptual understanding is the repeated use of naked numbers, or numbers provided without any context. Although not obvious, naked numbers often lead students to make assumptions. This tendency compounds the fact that mathematical representation is already plagued with assumptions, another issue frequently slighted in classrooms. For example, in a simple problem such as $3 + 4$, unless otherwise noted, the assumption exists that both the 3 and the 4 represent the ones place value. Examine the problem in Box 4.12. What assumptions might be involved?

Box 4.12

How can this statement be made true?

$2 + 8 = 28$

The fact that no context is provided for the problem does not imply that the 2, 8, and 28 are inert or void of meaning. By definition, a symbol represents *something*. Thus, the symbol 8, for example, represents something in the problem above. In mathematics, 8 is more precisely defined as a numeral, and without any context, we assume it represents a quantity of 8 *ones*. Since convention assumes that each of the numerals above represents *ones*, the equation as stated is false. However, it could be true if the equation identified specific representations for each numeral: 2 *tens* + 8 *ones* = 28 *ones*. Another true interpretation could be the following: 2 *dozen* + 8 *halves* = 28 *ones*. To break the bad habit of overexposing students to naked numbers, provide examples like the above to illustrate that numbers represent something and these representations affect how we interpret math. Providing contexts such as these is thought-provoking for students; but more important, it serves as a reminder of the conventions and assumptions that need to be an integral part of the knowledge base in mathematics.

CONCLUSION

As these examples illustrate, conceptual understanding requires a simple yet deep knowledge of key terms and concepts, the ability to make connections among concepts, and the ability to interpret and translate the meanings and subtleties of mathematical symbolism and representation. This depth of understanding includes the ability to identify and understand where and why assumptions are being made, particularly in symbolism, and the ability to translate mathematical expressions into English, and vice versa.

Mark Twain once said that the difference between the right word and the almost-right word is like the difference between lightning and a lightning bug. This adage applies to mathematics as much as it does to the English language. A firm grasp of the language of math, whether in the form of words, symbols, or visual representations, is critical for understanding. With such a grasp, students and teachers can see through the confusion to gain clarity.

Back when I taught high school mathematics, a sign above my classroom door read *Se Habla Algebra*. This motto communicates an overarching focus of this book: Mathematics is a foreign language and, as such, requires learning how to interpret and translate its words, symbols, and visual representations. There are multiple aspects of conceptual understanding in mathematics, but the foundation is a deep understanding of the terminology and symbolism.

The Order of Operations: A Convention or a Symptom of What Ails Us?

chapter
FIVE

Please excuse my dear aunt Sally. Praise every mom, dad, and sister. Pandas enjoy merrily dancing and singing, but pranksters earn math detention after school. Figured out the pattern yet? These sentences are mnemonics for PEMDAS, the acronym that stands for "parentheses, exponents, multiplication, division, addition, and subtraction." Over the years, many math students have used such memory aids as a way to remember the order of operations.

The standard method for teaching the order of operations highlights the preoccupation of the U.S. mathematics education system with procedural fluency and instruction over conceptual understanding and content. This traditional focus emphasizes the memorization of facts, skills, and procedures, demonstrated in isolation through repeated practice and with the sole goal of getting the correct answer. Think back on your experience as a student learning the order of operations. If you attended school in the United States, you likely were instructed to memorize an acronym such as PEMDAS to remember the list of rules. Your teachers may have explained that these rules ensure that everyone reaches the same answer for a given computation. In all likelihood, you and your classmates accepted the order of operations as gospel, with no idea as to where it came from or why it worked. Unfortunately, the same assertion can be made for most procedures and algorithms in mathematics. The rules are accepted with little fanfare and with little thought as to their origin or conceptual basis.

63

THE ROOTS OF THE RULES

My experience as a student was no different. I learned the order of operations in the typical way, accepting the rules as some magical incantation of age-old origin. I continued to hold this view throughout my career as a high school math teacher and later as a professional development provider for the Southwest Educational Development Laboratory (SEDL). As part of the SEDL experience, I participated in a project that ended up changing my entire perspective of the order of operations. This project involved creating and providing professional development for middle school mathematics teachers. In order to match the professional development activities with their needs, we began the project by polling math faculties at selected middle schools in Arkansas, Louisiana, New Mexico, Oklahoma, and Texas to learn which math topics teachers thought were the most difficult for students. High on the list was the order of operations.

To address this problem area, I was assigned the task of developing a two-hour training module on the topic. In no time, however, I came up against a dilemma. The traditional methods and rules for teaching the order of operations did not come close to filling the allotted time for the module. The task of stretching "Please Excuse My Dear Aunt Sally" into two hours was daunting. I needed more information. As a focus for my research, I considered the purpose and origin of the order of operations. If the purpose was to ensure consistent solutions, then some astute mathematician or group of experts from years past should have received recognition for this great contribution to the body of mathematical knowledge. So I began looking to answer the question, Who established and formalized the order of operations? Surprisingly, my research yielded no answers. No one was credited with having developed the rules. There was not even any record of a mathematical council or body having approved the order of operations as correct. However, my research did uncover one thing: No training modules or manuals were currently available that focused on the order of operations. In fact, I could not even find any conference presentations or sessions on the topic. Perhaps educators considered the topic too simple to warrant special attention or focus even though it is problematic for students. After all, in the typical lesson on the order of operations, students are supposed to memorize a list of rules and learn that as long as they follow those rules, they will get the correct answer.

Traditionally, the set of rules known as the order of operations has been viewed as a convention. In this case, a convention is defined as a principle or procedure that experts in the field of mathematics have agreed is correct. What is interesting is that educators have begun to refer to this specific convention as the "order of operations agreement." An

Internet search of this phrase yields thousands of sites using this expanded expression. If the rules of the order of operations truly are the result of an agreement, then who made it and where's the record of it? We don't know. In effect, the order of operations is a prime example of the U.S. education system's tendency not to question mathematical procedures and rules but rather to focus on how to use them to solve problems. And I was among the guilty. I was, after all, a product of the system and, as a result, had always taken this same narrow view of the order of operations.

The demands on a classroom teacher did not give me the luxury of time to thoroughly investigate the math we are teaching, especially on a topic that appears fairly simplistic. Until this research I was guilty of blind acceptance of the rules that constitute the order of operations. My research for the person or group that decided that these were the governing rules for performing multiple operations came up empty. This was both an aggravation and a motivation. This dead end, however, totally changed the direction and focus of my efforts. If there was no answer as to the originators of these rules, then logic dictates that the answer must lie *in the mathematics itself*. This hypothesis was the driving force behind the search for an understanding of a mathematical justification of the rules and provided the reflective thinking needed to develop an effective model for teaching the order of operations. Through this process of discovery and focus on the mathematical foundation of the rules, I gained a much deeper understanding of their conceptual basis and completely shifted how I thought about them. With this insight, I developed a model for teaching the order of operations from a new perspective.

THE NATURAL ORDER: A MATHEMATICAL PERSPECTIVE

To help students truly understand the order of operations, the teaching model I developed explores the fundamental concepts behind the rules from a mathematical perspective. Instead of presenting students with PEMDAS and a list of rules and mnemonics, this method takes students on a process of discovery similar to the one I took myself. Using a constructivist learning approach, teachers use relevant examples and questions to help guide students to a conceptual understanding of the basis of the order of operations. Armed with this knowledge, students have much more powerful mathematical tools at their disposal than a simple list of rules. This model has been used in intensive site work as part of math-focused SEDL projects with positive evaluations and results. This section borrows from that training module to present the approach in much the same way, taking the reader on a process of discovery.

Understanding Relevance: Order Matters

This process begins with the relevance of the order of operations. Students need to understand how order affects both real life and mathematics. If one considers everyday activities or actions, many of them involve a series of steps in which order matters. For example, when getting dressed in the morning, you must put on some articles of clothing before others. To drive to work, you must unlock the car, get inside, place the key in the ignition, and turn the key to start the engine. In contrast, many everyday activities involve steps where the order does not matter. For example, some drivers may prefer to put on their seat belts before starting their cars' engines; other drivers may prefer to do the opposite. But both sequences of events produce the same result. Such real-life examples help students understand the natural role of order.

In mathematics, real-life examples also illustrate how the order in which operations are performed makes a difference. For example, if a car purchase involves a rebate as well as a sales tax, the order in which the two are calculated makes a difference in the car's total cost. Let's say the price of the car is $21,000, and the deal includes a $1,000 rebate and a 6% sales tax. The salesperson tells you that the rebate check will be mailed six weeks after the sale, so the upfront sales price is $21,000. You must pay the 6% sales tax on $21,000, which is $1,260. You will later get the $1,000 rebate check, making the total cost $21,260. When you complain, the sales manager intervenes and agrees to apply the $1,000 rebate now. This changes the selling price to $20,000, with a 6% sales tax of $1,200. The new total cost is $21,200. So the second sequence saved $60. Such examples help students discover the importance of the order in which operations are performed in mathematics.

Prerequisite Knowledge

An integral component of planning a lesson is the identification of the prerequisite knowledge needed to understand the new mathematics topic to be taught. The identification of the important prerequisite mathematics knowledge necessary for a student to learn and understand a new math topic is critical. With that in mind, what are the prerequisite skills and understandings that students need to learn the order of operations? A typical list usually consists of facts and procedural skills, such as knowing basic addition and multiplication facts; knowing the symbols for the four basic operations; knowing the basic rules for operations regarding integers; and knowing the use of other symbols, such as parentheses and the fraction bar. Keep this typical list in mind for comparison purposes later in this chapter.

Discovering the Underlying Principles

Examine the following questions about the rules that make up the order of operations. These questions provide a framework for exploring those rules and the concepts behind them. On another sheet of paper, try to answer each of these questions.

1. Why are multiplication and division done before addition and subtraction?
2. Why are addition and subtraction done last?
3. What is the connection between the distributive property and the order of operations?
4. What is the role or purpose of grouping symbols?
5. What can you conclude about the rationale for the establishment of rules in the order of operations?

The answers to the above are the key to a very different, mathematically founded perspective of the order of operations. Don't worry if you did not know all the answers. These are difficult questions: those that ask *why* typically are. Continuing our constructivist approach, we examine the questions in turn to discover the conceptual basis of the order of operations.

Why Multiplication and Division Before Addition and Subtraction?

Consider a class of middle school students who have not received any formal instruction in the order of operations. In your opinion, would the students be able to correctly simplify the expression in Box 5.1a? In the training sessions I've led, the overwhelming majority of teachers say no. The main reason they give is that students tend to perform mathematics operations from left to right, just as they read English. As a result, the typical student would add $3 + 7$ to get 10, then multiply by 5 to get the incorrect sum of 50.

Box 5.1

a. $3 + 7 \bullet 5$

b. How much money would Jane have if she had 3 pennies and 7 nickels?

Now, consider the problem in 5.1b. Do you think the same group of middle school students would be able to answer this problem correctly? In this case, in the training sessions I have led, the majority of teachers say yes. Unlike the first problem, the second provides contextual clues, such as the words *pennies* and *nickels*. These clues help students intuitively know they cannot immediately add the 3 and the 7. Based on those clues, students convert the nickels and get the correct response of 38 cents.

As you probably realize by now, problems 5.1a and 5.1b are the same, just expressed differently. An investigation as to why students can do one but not the other is necessary in order to discover why the multiplication and division must be done before the addition and subtraction. True, the context in the penny and nickel scenario is key in giving students the clues they need to correctly determine the total amount. However, an answer of "because of the context" is not sufficient to get to the bedrock of the order of operations. To get at this root understanding, consider what it is *about* the context of the pennies and the nickels that leads students to the proper order of the operations. How did students know to convert the nickels into cents? And how did they know to take this step before adding? Of course, knowing the answer enables the facilitator or teacher to know what probing questions to ask based on the audience responses.

Slowly but surely, the truth hidden in the context of the pennies and nickels begins to surface. Obviously, adding 3 pennies to the 7 nickels will not give the total amount. The intuition that makes middle school students realize that the nickels must be converted to cents is actually a subconscious ingrained notion that was embedded in elementary school. Deep in long-term memory is the knowledge that when they added and subtracted in those early years, the items being added or subtracted were always *the same things*. The roots can be traced to concepts learned in elementary school. Elementary students first learn the process of addition with concrete objects. Problems provide contexts, such as 3 apples plus 4 apples is 7 apples, or 5 cows plus 1 cow is 6 cows. In essence, these types of problems teach students the fundamental numeric and algebraic property that you can only add or subtract *like items*! By middle school, most students have an ingrained, but dormant understanding that when they add and subtract, the items must be the same things.

Somewhere along the way, though, teachers drop the context and use only the numeric symbols, such as $3 + 4 = 7$ or $5 + 1 = 6$. Students are bombarded with these naked numbers, without any context to explain what each symbolic notation represents. Is it any wonder that students soon lose sight of the simple fact that one can only add apples with apples and oranges with oranges? Even adults can forget that in the expression $2 + 3$, there is a huge assumption that the 2 and the 3 both represent the same thing and can therefore be combined.

The critical understanding that only like items can be added or subtracted is the mathematical basis for the order of operations. Reviewing the problem $3 + 7 \cdot 5$, one begins to realize the key role of the property of like items. In the context of pennies and nickels, students unconsciously apply this idea when they convert the two types of coins into cents, because the amounts to be combined must be the same things. When context is not provided, those students who understand the meaning of multiplication and how to interpret its symbolic representation will realize that 7 • 5 represents "seven sets of five." As a result, the 3 and the 7 • 5 do not represent the same things and cannot be combined until converted to like items. This understanding clarifies the order in which the operations must be done: first multiplication to convert, then addition to combine. Unfortunately, without a context, most students will answer the problem incorrectly, not only because they are accustomed to reading from left to right, but also because they have forgotten the principle of like items and the symbolic representation of multiplication.

By this point, the logic behind doing multiplication and division before addition and subtraction is clear. From a mathematical perspective, multiplication or division must be done first to determine how many like items there are. In some contexts, the multiplication or division literally converts whatever is involved to like items. For example, the 7 • 5 converted nickels to pennies. Once the quantity of like items is known, we can add or subtract those items. Thus, in an expression such as 3 • 4 + 6 • 7, we have to assume that we have 3 sets of 4 *somethings* added to 6 sets of 7 *somethings*. We multiply to convert each of the groups to two subtotals (12 + 42) of the same *somethings*. Now, we can add these two sets of like items to get a sum of 54 *somethings*.

Order of Operations Incognito.   The rule to multiply and divide before adding and subtracting produces a "chicken or the egg" scenario. Which came first, the standard multiplication algorithm or the order of operations? Examine the multiplication procedure shown in Box 5. 2.

Box 5.2

```
        46
  ×     35
       230
       138
      1610
```

Notice that in the standard algorithm for multiplication, all the multiplications are done first, and then the addition is performed last. Does this sound familiar? In the absence of grouping symbols, this sequence is the one called for in the order of operations. Is this mere coincidence? No, the order of operations is built into the standard multiplication algorithm! Also, notice that the procedure instructs us to move the 138 one place to the left. For people who experienced traditional instruction in the United States, this rule may have been provided with no explanation or understanding as to why it is necessary. In actuality, the second partial product is 1,380, not 138. Knowing this enables us to line up the partial products correctly. But why must they be aligned?

Consider the task of adding 2,417 and 752. The traditional method calls for the numbers to be written vertically, as shown in Box 5.3.

Box 5.3

```
  2,417
+  752
```

The numbers must be aligned on the right to ensure that we are adding properly. In other words, we must ensure that we are adding ones with ones, tens with tens, hundreds with hundreds, and so on. Does this sound familiar? We have been emphasizing the property that we can only combine like items—and the above alignment ensures exactly that! Thus, we align the place values in vertical addition and subtraction to adhere to the basic property of like items. The reality in the example is that even though there is no real-life context, "things" are being added, as shown in Box 5.4.

Box 5.4

```
2 thousands + 4 hundreds + 1 ten  + 7 ones
+                7 hundreds + 5 tens + 2 ones
```

Unfortunately, like items do not always appear in such overt forms as shown above. Rather, they are often hidden in symbols, as in the number 2,417, where each digit actually represents its appropriate place value. As mentioned in Chapter Four, a deep conceptual understanding of mathematics includes the ability to make connections and to see how one concept supports or reinforces another. Such is the case here. The cornerstone for the order of operations is the fundamental property that addition and subtraction require like items; and that property, in turn, is closely linked to place value. If students understand all these concepts and how they connect, then like items become visible where before they weren't. For example, given the problem 12.47 + 5.3, students can connect these concepts and understand why the decimal points must be lined up when adding. Students will see that each digit is not a naked number at all. For example, 5.3 is really 5 *ones* and 3 *tenths*, and the decimal points are lined up to ensure the addition of like items—ones with ones, tenths with tenths, and so on. It is exciting to see students' eyes light up when they begin to see these types of connections.

The Distributive Property Connection

You can begin to see just how embedded the property of like items is in fundamental mathematics. It drives the order of operations, requiring that we multiply and divide to convert sets of items into like items before we add and subtract. The property is an integral component of the standard multiplication algorithm, placing addition last to ensure that like items are being combined. So, building on this logic, what do you think is the connection between the distributive property and the order of operations? You may recall that this was the third of the five questions you answered at the start of this section. How would you answer the question now?

Although not overtly, this section has already discussed the answer. Refer back to the multiplication procedure for 46 • 35 in Box 5.2. The procedure presents the standard multiplication algorithm in a vertical format. Now, consider the similar expression 23 • 65, but with a horizontal layout instead of the typical vertical format. Box 5.5 shows this multiplication process.

Box 5.5

23 • 65
  = (20 + 3) • (60 + 5)
  = 20•60 + 20•5 + 3•60 + 3•5
  = 1200 + 100 + 180 + 15
  = 1,495

The horizontal approach above illustrates that the standard multiplication algorithm is a direct example of the distributive property. Although not readily apparent, the distributive property was also utilized with the expression 46 • 35, but each of the four distinct partial products was not detailed as they are in Box 5.5. In the standard algorithm, only two partial products are traditionally written down when multiplying two 2-digit numbers.

However, the distributive property can be overtly illustrated in a vertical format, as shown in Box 5.6.

Box 5.6

```
        46
×       35
        30
       200
       180
      1200
      1610
```

Regardless of vertical or horizontal format, the distributive property is used in the multiplication algorithm. And in both cases, the multiplication is done first, and then the addition. Educators tend to forget that the proper name is not the "distributive property," but rather the "distributive property of multiplication *over* addition." However, there is a language problem embedded in the proper name of this property because multiplication does not have power *over* addition. So perhaps a more appropriate name would be the "distributive property of multiplication *before* addition." The distributive property and the order of operations can lead some educators to think of multiplication and division as more "powerful" operations than addition and subtraction, and to see this power as the justification for multiplying and dividing before adding and subtracting. This misconception clouds the true reason for this order: multiplication and division are done prior to addition and subtraction to convert groups of items into subtotals of like items that can then be combined into one total.

The Role of Grouping Symbols

Building on this knowledge, you can probably now see the logic for the placement of the *E*, the exponents, in PEMDAS. Exponents are simply a short way of showing multiplication; thus, their order falls in line with the mathematical foundation already presented for multiplication. That leaves us with the *P* in PEMDAS, which refers to parentheses. So what about grouping symbols? What is their role in the order of operations? This was the fourth of the five questions.

Consider the expression $20 - 5 \cdot 1.08$. Without context or additional direction, we would multiply before subtracting to solve this expression. But suppose this expression represented a scenario where a cashier needed to take a $5 discount from a $20 item prior to assessing an 8% sales tax. In this context, the expression 20 − 5 • 1.08 would not suffice because we need to subtract before multiplying. As a result, we use parentheses to regroup the elements so that they accurately reflect the computation that is needed in that context. In one of the training sessions I led, an astute participant commented that we could refer to the order of operations as the *natural* order of operations because the order of computation is how it would be done naturally due to inherent rules in the mathematics. However, a little artificial help is sometimes needed to get the appropriate computation—in this case, to force the subtraction of the discount before we multiply to get the cost with tax. Grouping symbols, such as parentheses, serve as this artificial intervention. They enable us to perform mathematical operations in a different order than how they are done naturally.

As another example, remember the expression 3 + 7 • 5, used to represent the context of having 3 pennies and 7 nickels? Suppose we wanted to express a situation where one person has 3 nickels and another person has 7 nickels, and we want to know the total amount of money the two people have together. The expression 3 + 7 • 5 would not suffice because the solution would be 38 cents, which is not accurate. We need to use grouping symbols to indicate that the operations should be done in a different order than what occurs naturally in mathematics. By inserting parentheses so the expression reads (3 + 7) • 5, we know to do the addition first, then the multiplication by 5 to get the correct total of 50 cents.

Grouping symbols give us control over the natural order of computation. However, this intervention cannot be justified mathematically from a theoretical standpoint. This aspect of the rules of the order of operations is more a convention dealing with mathematical representation and symbolism than with pure mathematics. However, this convention can be eroded based on the interpretation of the symbolism. Consider the scenario in Box 5.7.

Box 5.7

24 ÷ 4A

Let A = 2.

Solve mentally.

This problem illustrates a difficulty associated with mathematics language and symbolism, as opposed to the order of operations itself. This difficulty has led to the creation of two camps: those who argue that the answer should be 12 and those who insist it should be 3. When the value of A is placed into the expression $24 \div 4A$, the first camp says the result is $24 \div 4 \cdot 2$. Following the order of operations, the solution is 12. Then why does the other camp insist that the solution is 3? This second camp considers the 4A to be an inseparable expression. As a result, filling in the value of A results in the expression $24 \div (4 \cdot 2)$. Now, following the order of operations produces a solution of 3.

Each camp's stance depends on whether the $4A$ is inseparable. This issue underscores the need in mathematics to clarify assumptions and ambiguity in symbolism. Of all the disciplines, mathematics in particular should not be having such arguments in the first place. One way for a teacher to avoid such assumptions and ambiguity is to present an expression such as the one above as $24 \div (4A)$ if the desired interpretation is to see the $4A$ as inseparable. This added clarification clearly changes the substituted expression to $24 \div (4 \cdot 2)$, resulting in the solution of 3. Reaching consensus on the interpretation of an expression such as $24 \div 4A$ is beyond the scope of this text. Refer to Box 5.8. It is interesting that most algebra texts evade this problem by expressing division with a fraction bar rather than the division sign. The fraction bar can actually be used as a grouping symbol in the same manner as parentheses.

Box 5.8

$$\frac{24}{4A}$$

Earlier in the chapter introduction, it was noted that the justification we often give for the order of operations is to ensure that we all get the *same* answer rather than stating the *correct* answer. How do we define *correct*? You just experienced a scenario where two camps reached different solutions because of a different interpretation of the symbolism. This notion of *correct* in mathematics is sometimes founded on adherence to some rule or property. Without guidance, an expression with several operations could be simplified in a variety of ways, resulting in different answers. I would imagine that the primary objective of the order of operations was to prevent that from happening. Adherence to the rules would assure that the same result was obtained by all, and since the rules were followed, the answer would also be considered correct.

Going Nature's Way: The Rationale for the Order of Operations

You may have noticed that one question remains from the original five presented at the start of this discovery process. What can you conclude about the rationale for the establishment of the rules in the order of operations? Did some long-forgotten person or group sit down and deliberately establish these rules? Or are they rather the *natural* order of operations, based on the property of like items and related concepts? The research and the evidence soundly support the latter. In essence, the order of operations may be analogous to the FOIL method for the multiplication of two binomials. Is there really a FOIL *method*, or is it simply an acronym and memory trick for the distributive property? If students truly understand the mathematical concepts discussed in this chapter, they will be able to compute an expression such as $4 + 6 \cdot 5$ without formal training in the order of operations. Rather than have students memorize and blindly follow a list of rules to ensure they get the correct and, perhaps more appropriately, the *same* answer, educators should have students dig deeply into the fundamental mathematics that serves as the rules' basis instead.

Communicating the Order of Operations

In keeping with the focus on language and symbolism, another issue related to the order of operations is the language used to communicate it. As mentioned, the language we use in instruction can sometimes create unintended confusion or misconceptions. At the same time, when used correctly, language can help part the clouds and reveal understanding.

Think back over the chapter's discussion about the order of operations. Might the terminology involved give students the impression they have no choices or alternatives and must follow PEMDAS in every case? Consider the two examples in Box 5.9. How would you best simplify each one to get the solution?

Box 5.9

a. $25 \cdot 13 \cdot 4$

b. $4\frac{2}{3} + 3\frac{1}{7} + 6\frac{1}{3}$

In the multiplication problem, the computation is easier if one first multiplies $25 \cdot 4$ to get 100, then multiplies $100 \cdot 13$ to get 1,300. Likewise, in the addition problem, it is much simpler to first add $4\frac{2}{3}$ and $6\frac{1}{3}$ to get 11, and then add that subtotal to $3\frac{1}{7}$ to get the final sum of $14\frac{1}{7}$. For these computations, the order of operations is clearly not the best approach. However, the rules state that in the absence of grouping symbols, the above computations should be done in order from left to right, *period*! Because of the way in which the rules are often stated, students—especially those who rigidly follow instructions to the letter—may think they have no options and must multiply and divide, or add and subtract, strictly from left to right.

The reality is that there is a missing piece to this aspect of the order of operations. The rules should state that, in the absence of grouping symbols, we are to multiply and divide (or add and subtract) from left to right *unless* some valid mathematical property enables us to perform the computations in a more efficient manner while still adhering to the spirit of the rules. By making connections to related ideas such as the commutative and associative properties, teachers can help students see that such properties can supersede and complement the order of operations and thus make computation much easier.

Teaching the Order of Operations

An effective instructional strategy that teachers can utilize is to actively engage students in discovering or constructing new knowledge as recommended by the National Council of Teachers of Mathematics (NCTM) and other organizations. Rather than just telling students the order of operations, teachers can present relevant scenarios and ask probing questions to guide students to discover and understand the mathematical justification for those rules. Box 5.10 provides two sample scenarios teachers might use in this approach.

Box 5.10: Sample Scenarios to Foster Student Discovery

Scenario 1: The football team scored 4 touchdowns, worth 6 points each; kicked 3 extra points, worth 1 point each; and kicked 1 field goal, worth 3 points. What was the team's final score? Express the relationship using an informal sentence; then use that sentence as the framework for writing a mathematical equation of the problem. Explain and justify the computation step by step.

   Scenario 2: You have three $20 bills, two $5 bills, eight $1 bills, and seven quarters. How much money do you have? Express the relationship using an informal sentence; then use that sentence as the framework for writing a mathematical equation of the problem. Explain and justify the computation step by step.

With Scenario 1, students will likely be tempted to solve the problem in their head. However, teachers should insist on no shortcuts. Students need to write the relationship out in words and then translate those words to an equivalent statement using numerals and symbols. This process will help students not only build knowledge and understanding but also master this essential skill in mathematics. Box 5.11 shows possible answers for Scenario 1.

Box 5.11

Translate into an informal sentence:

The total score is made up of four touchdowns worth six points each, plus three extra points worth one point each, plus one field goal worth three points.

Translate into a mathematical expression or equation:

Total Score	is	4 touchdowns	+	3 extra points	+	1 field goal
T	=	$4 \cdot 6$	+	$3 \cdot 1$	+	$1 \cdot 3$

Intuitively, the students probably have already solved the problem and know the total score is 30. However, teachers must ensure that students work through the next step and show that the initial equation then becomes $T = 24 + 3 + 3$. The key is to ask probing questions so that students ultimately understand why they did the multiplications first and then the additions. In this scenario, the touchdowns, extra points, and field goal all had to be converted to points (like items) before the three subtotals could be combined for the total score.

The solution to Scenario 2 would parallel the process illustrated for Scenario 1. The only difference would be the context and the numbers and computation involved. The process and the desired discovery of why the multiplication is done prior to the addition are the same as before. One distinction is that there might be a slight variation on the like item that students utilize. Some may distill the amounts down to dollars and use decimals while others may convert all the monetary amounts to cents or pennies.

While still in the realm of teaching, refer back to the earlier list of prerequisite knowledge for teaching the order of operations. Note that most of the items deal with *how to* do things, especially in computation. This is a reflection of and a connection to the tendency to focus on procedural fluency rather than conceptual understanding. Note that the topic of like items was nowhere on the radar, which is no surprise because this is a different approach to the order of operations. A key learning from this list that can be generalized to other areas is an awareness of content. Review lists of prerequisite knowledge and make note of how many deal with how to do math versus more conceptual items that focus on the what and the why of math topics.

CONCLUSION: A CONCEPTUAL UNDERSTANDING OF THE ORDER OF OPERATIONS

From a mathematical perspective, can you now see how the order of operations is far more than a list of rules needed for consistency in computation? This perspective reveals that the topic is rooted in basic mathematics principles and can serve as a powerful model for illustrating the connectivity of mathematics concepts. This view also illustrates the key role of language and symbolism in the order of operations. The idea of like items deals with the things that numerals represent. As noted, in the early grades, there is an emphasis, albeit an informal and unconscious one, that only like items can be combined. However, because language and symbolism usually are not the focus of attention, this critical idea of like items fades away with the loss of context in upper elementary and middle school math classes, until it finally reemerges in a formal Algebra course. Even then, the connection back to arithmetic is fragmented at best because the focus is on the new idea of variables. Once forgotten, the property of like items is virtually ignored in everyday computation. Even when it reemerges, this basic principle seems to somehow be isolated and encapsulated in formal Algebra only in the form of expressions such as $7y - 2y$, and in teacher statements such as "No, you can't add 4b and 8y."

Is the order of operations really a convention in terms of the mathematics involved? I contend that it has mathematical foundations and is a convention only with respect to mathematical representation and symbolism. The mathematics community may not accept the arguments in this chapter as sufficient mathematical proof for the order of operations. Perhaps the basic ideas presented comprise too simplistic a justification for the origin of the order of operations. However, that discussion is not the real issue. The primary focus is the way in which we view and teach the order of operations, and how that approach directly parallels the way in which U.S. educators have traditionally viewed and taught mathematics. And I contend that this approach is a symptom of what ails us.

Traditionally, the order of operations has been viewed and presented as a set of rules or procedures to follow blindly. In K–12 math classes, these rules are rarely questioned or examined from a mathematical perspective. This chapter has presented an alternative inquiry-based approach, one more in tune with recent research in mathematics education. This approach looks at the order of operations conceptually, with attention to the language and symbolism. There is a deliberate focus on the mathematical roots of the order of operations, and uses the topic as a vehicle to make rich connections among fundamental ideas. You are challenged as fellow mathematics educators to change PEMDAS to *promoting enriched mathematics discovery advances students*.

Using Multiplication as a Critical Knowledge Base

Besides basic ideas such as cardinality, addition, subtraction, and place value, perhaps no other fundamental concept in mathematics is more critical than multiplication. Unfortunately, the emphasis in traditional K–12 instruction is on performing multiplication, rather than defining and examining it from a conceptual perspective. This narrow approach leads to many missed opportunities and teaching moments because of a focus on superficial definitions and methods. In actuality, multiplication is far more than a simple operation. This chapter shows that with a deep understanding of multiplication, students can build a strong conceptual framework and make connections to other fundamental concepts. The result is a powerful mathematical knowledge base.

UNDERSTANDING KEY DEFINITIONS AND CONNECTIONS

The importance of how we define and connect fundamental concepts in mathematics cannot be overemphasized. Because such concepts provide the foundation of all that follows, the cost of a shallow or incomplete understanding is immeasurable. Teachers and students alike lose critical opportunities to leverage a conceptual understanding of these topics to learn new ones, make connections to related concepts, and view concepts from different perspectives. Multiplication is a special example of this because of the shallow definition and computational approach on one hand, and the surprising depth—as a mathematics topic—and breadth in connectivity on the other. The foundation is a simple yet deep definition, which in turn serves as the synapse for multiple connections. Examine Box 6.1 to begin the investigation of this rich topic.

Defining Multiplication

As a fundamental operation in mathematics, multiplication appears in a variety of contexts. This makes the task of defining it more difficult because, for example, multiplication in a quadratic function does not yield the same type of result as multiplication in an area context. The focus is on fundamentals, so we will concentrate on the multiplication most applicable to real-life contexts. These would be scenarios where a total is sought based on knowing the number and size of groups or sets. Based on this application, many teachers define multiplication as "repeated addition." Although true, this definition is woefully incomplete. Moreover, it substantially handicaps students' ability to connect to and understand critical related ideas, such as division and average.

A better way to define multiplication is as "a faster process of finding a total by using equal-sized groups or sets." The crucial idea to emphasize here is *equal-sized groups*. Instead of understanding $2 + 2 + 2$ as the repeated addition of 2, students should view the expression as three *equal-sized sets* of two, which we express mathematically as $3 \cdot 2$.

As noted in an earlier chapter, a national consensus does not exist as to which factor in multiplication represents the number of groups and which represents the size of each group. For the purpose of this text, the interpretation is that the first numeral represents the number of sets and the second represents the size of each set. Critical reasons exist for the use of this interpretation, which are detailed later in the chapter.

Division and Multiplication: Two Peas in a Pod

More often than not, teachers parallel their definition of multiplication with a definition of division as "repeated subtraction." Although true, this definition is also drastically incomplete. What's more, it creates a chasm between the concepts of multiplication and division because of the focus on repeated addition and subtraction. This focus reinforces the false notion that multiplication and division are completely different, whereas in actuality, the two are not only similar but inextricably connected.

So how are the two operations similar or connected? The key is that multiplication and division are conjoined by the idea of *equal-sized groups*. In most contexts, especially at the elementary and middle school levels, both multiplication and division involve three components: (1) a total, (2) a certain number of equal-sized groups, and (3) a constant and specific size for each group. These three common components are what make multiplication and division similar and enable students to easily connect the two concepts.

The only difference between multiplication and division is in which one of the three components is unknown. If we know the number and size of the groups and we want to find the total, we multiply. If we know the total and the size of the groups and we want to find the number of groups, we divide. Likewise, if we know the total and the number of the groups and we want to find the size of the groups, we divide. This critical connection provides a deeper level of understanding that students will likely miss if they only learn multiplication as repeated addition and division as repeated subtraction.

Defining Division

Without the focus on equal-sized groups, there is no bridge to link multiplication and division. And without this link, students lack a key part of their conceptual framework of understanding. From a colloquial perspective, multiplication and division are flip sides of the same coin. If students internalize the contents of the previous paragraph, they will already have an intuitive basis of the concept of division, which is not the same as the algorithm used to find a quotient. The focus of multiplication on equal-sized groups almost eliminates the need for a formal definition of division. Some will insist on a definition, so what should it be? Saying that division is the inverse operation of multiplication clarifies little, and seeing division as how many times one number *goes into* another is, well, ludicrous. A reasonable, simple, yet deep definition of division would be that it is a mathematical operation closely associated with multiplication and focused on equal distribution. The phrase equal distribution is almost synonymous to equal-sized groups and serves the same purpose. Equal distribution should be an integral component of the definition because students can easily envision breaking something apart into equal-sized pieces.

Defining Average

A related concept to multiplication and division is that of an average. (The term *average* as defined in this text is synonymous with the definition of the mean.) It is rare to find teachers or students who can define an average as a noun, much less conceptually. The vast majority of Americans define an average as a verb by explaining the process of how to compute it. Consequently, they never define *what* an average is. So how can an average be defined in a simple yet deeply conceptual way that fits most contexts? The key lies in the definition of multiplication, and in turn, the connection to division.

To help understand this connection, consider the following classroom scenario: Students are asked to determine how many individual beans are in a large two-pound bag. The main objective of the lesson is to observe how students count the beans to determine the total. At the end of the lesson, the teacher pours the beans into a bowl and instructs students to each take between one and five beans. Some students take more beans than others. The teacher then asks students how they could make the distribution fair by ensuring that everyone gets the same amount. The teacher instructs students to return their beans to the bowl and divide them up equally.

By retracing these steps, a teacher can model the exact computational process of an average. Students have different amounts of beans (between 1 and 5), but then pool them together. These actions represent the addition of the different amounts to obtain a total, which is the first major step in computing an average. Students then divide the beans equally, which parallels the next major step—division of the total by the number of groups, which in this scenario is the number of students. The resulting quotient gives how many beans each student gets—the size of each set of beans.

As with the definitions of multiplication and division, the key to making the leap to a conceptual definition of an average is the notion of equal-sized groups. This idea, in turn, connects to division via the idea of equal distribution. The only difference between the processes of division and averaging is the starting point. There is a need for clarification at this point. Some may argue that in a context where an average needs to be determined, only the number of sets is known. That is not true. Just as with division, the total is in the information, but is provided indirectly through the sets of unequal size. The total must be computed, which in some ways serves as a disconnect and clouds the connections among these concepts.

Based on that observation, the only difference between division and averaging lies in how the total number is provided: directly in division and indirectly with an average. A closer inspection reveals that for both division and averaging, the total is divided by the number of groups to determine the size of each group. By connecting the dots, one can then reason that if division is about equal distribution, then an average is simply an equal *redistribution*! Isn't that what really happened with the distribution of the beans? There was an unequal distribution, so the students had to pool the beans and do an equal *redistribution*. Thus, a simple yet deep definition of an average is "an equal redistribution."

Above-Average Clarity. This definition also addresses a common misconception about an average. The term *average* is often referred to as a measure of central tendency. However, this idea of an average converging toward the center steers students to an erroneous definition that the average will be somewhere "near the middle." Consider the task of finding the average salary of the members of the Lakeside School graduating class that included Bill Gates, the multibillionaire chairman of the software company Microsoft. Because Gates creates an outlier of such magnitude, the average salary would probably be in the hundreds of millions, which of course is misleading. The problem with an average as a measure of central tendency is that the presence of an extreme outlier causes the resulting quotient to be far from the location of the median. A set of data does not always conform to the notion of a normal distribution. The definition of an average as "an equal redistribution" is not affected by the presence of outliers, nor does it suggest that the result must be somewhere near the middle.

The Power of a Conceptual Foundation. Imagine how many times teachers have been asked this question by students: "What grade do I have to make on this last test to pass?" If students ask this question, they clearly do not have a conceptual understanding of the definition of an average. These students face a quandary because they only understand how to compute an average when all the grades are known. But a conceptual definition provides a way past this impasse. For the above question, let's assume that a passing grade is 70 and that the final grade is based on an average of four test grades. Students who are armed with a conceptual definition of an average would understand that they need a total of 280 points (four test grades at 70 points each) to pass the class. This connects to two of the three components—the size of the set and the total. The passing grade, 70, constitutes the size of each group. Students must have a total that they can redistribute equally, and this comes from having four sets of 70 each. The next logical step would be to add the three known test grades and subtract that sum from 280 to obtain the necessary fourth test grade to reach the 280-point plateau. The fact that so many students ask this question should raise a jumbo-sized red flag. This averaging question is an indictment of the focus of traditional K–12 instruction on superficial procedural definitions that do not enable students to gain a full understanding of basic mathematical concepts.

Leap of Faith. Teachers often use excellent activities to model what an average is. For example, a teacher may use vertical stacks of blocks that are of different heights. Students then take some blocks off the higher stacks and place them on the shorter stacks until all the stacks are of equal height. The students have, essentially, averaged the stacks. However, teachers might then assume that students have made the leap from the concrete model or representation to a conceptual understanding of the abstract. Unfortunately, this leap often fails to occur. Students can easily walk away from such an activity with only the memory that they "evened out the stacks." If so, the students remain at the concrete level and do not cross the conceptual bridge.

Remember, a deep understanding of a concept must include a definition of what that concept is and looks like symbolically as well as the ways in which that concept connects to related concepts. When teaching averaging, some type of concrete model or activity is essential, but teachers still need to ensure that they lead students to the conceptual understanding of an average as "an equal redistribution." This definition, in turn, requires an understanding of multiplication that is based on equal-sized groups and of the connection and similarity between multiplication, division, and average. These key definitions and connections combine to create a solid framework of knowledge.

One of the messages of this book is that the U.S. mathematics education system sometimes manages to take something that is relatively simple and to make it inordinately complex. The exact opposite is required to improve student learning. Content can be made accessible and still express deeper understandings and connections; simple does not have to mean watered down. The definition of an average presented above is an example of how math content can simultaneously be simplified yet deepened. The key strategy employed here was to revamp the definition from how to compute an average to a condensed yet insightful statement of what an average is. This simple-yet-deep strategy is one that teachers can use to enhance their own content knowledge as well as enable students to grasp and retain a deep understanding of mathematics concepts.

INTERPRETING MULTIPLICATION

How students interpret multiplication is as important as how they define it. As noted in Chapter Three, multiplication involves some of the more confusing and contradictory uses of language and symbolism. One of the most notable examples is the use of the word *times*. Long entrenched in the traditional instruction of multiplication, this word has almost no meaning. Consider the simple yet deep definition of multiplication provided above. This definition refers to equal-sized sets or groups. In addition, sets or groups are commonly used when teaching multiplication at the elementary level. So why not use that same language? Rather than interpret 2 • 6 as "2 times 6," would it not be more sensible to say "2 sets of 6 each." This language eliminates confusion, provides context, and further solidifies the actual quantities involved. And while on this topic, it seems more logical as well to refer to the times table as the *grouping* table, since students are memorizing the values of the possible groupings of totals up to 100. Although these changes may buck tradition, they can greatly deepen students' understanding of the concept of multiplication.

The use of *sets of* or *groups of* in reading multiplication raises the related issue of how we interpret the factors in an expression such as m • n. The previous section noted that this text interprets the first factor as the number of sets and the second factor as the size of each set. Mathematicians might argue that the commutative property makes this issue a moot point because the product of m • n is the same as the product of n • m. However, from an algebraic perspective, it makes sense for an expression such as 2 • 7 to mean "2 sets of 7" because students can then make the easy connection to an algebraic expression, such as 2(y − 3). The proposed interpretation and the solid understanding it provides bridges the arithmetic and algebra, so a student can readily interpret 2(y − 3) as "2 sets of (y − 3)," or (y − 3) + (y − 3).

However, an even more powerful argument exists for interpreting the first factor as the number of sets and the second factor as the size of each set. Refer to Box 6.2.

Box 6.2

How much more is the first product than the second? Explain your conclusion.
25 • 78 and 24 • 78

Experience has shown that the majority of students will multiply both expressions, then find the difference between the two products to obtain the result. Now, refer to the related problem in Box 6.3.

Box 6.3

Farmer Jones has 25 cows. Farmer Smith has 24 cows. How many more cows does Farmer Jones have than Farmer Smith?

Obviously, this is a simple word problem for students, most of whom can mentally determine the solution in a matter of seconds. But if we compare Box 6.2 and Box 6.3, aren't they basically the same problem? So why do students expend so much wasted effort on the first and not the second? The fault lies not with students but rather with the traditional U.S. system's neglect of the language and symbolism of mathematics. For example, the key to the problem in Box 6.2 lies in the interpretation of the symbolism.

Students will read 25 • 78 as "25 *times* 78," which unfortunately leads them astray. If they instead interpreted the expression as "25 sets of 78," students would immediately realize that the first expression contains one more set of 78 than the second. But the insistence on using the word *times* in contexts involving multiplication makes this simple understanding far more difficult to grasp than necessary.

Teachers and students need to be flexible in their interpretation of the symbols of multiplication. Limiting this interpretation to *times*, which merely indicates the operation of multiplication, handicaps students' ability to determine the context in a situation such as the one in Box 6.2. But by interpreting the first factor as a quantity, the multiplication symbol ($\times$ or •) as "sets or groups of," and the second factor as a noun, students have the flexibility to interpret an expression such as 25 • 78 as "25 sets or groups of seventy-eight each." Such a perspective has two powerful implications: (1) it gives students the flexibility to interpret an expression such as 5 • 7 as 5 iterations of the same item where they interpret the 7 as a noun and understand that you have 5 sevens, and (2) this interpretation aligns with and reinforces the standard English practice of placing adjectives in front of the noun. Given a context such as the problem in Box 6.2, students will understand that 25 seventy-eights is 1 more seventy-eight than 24 seventy-eights, in exactly the same way that 25 cows is 1 more cow than 24 cows. However, this interpretation and perspective does not come naturally. It must be taught and practiced!

This explanation is the primary argument for the need to interpret the expression m • n as *m* signifying the number of sets and *n* the size of each set—that is, *m* sets of *n* objects. Without such a consensus, we are left wondering if 3 • 2 means 3 sets of twins or 2 sets of triplets—and parents the world over can attest to the need to know the difference!

USING THE POWER OF THE DISTRIBUTIVE PROPERTY

The teaching and learning of multiplication invariably gravitates to the actual procedure or algorithm. As a result, no discussion of multiplication is complete without addressing the integral and powerful role of the distributive property. Much of fundamental arithmetic deals with taking quantities apart and putting them together. An important connection can be made to the distributive property because that property enables the taking apart and combining together to happen. Those decomposing and composing processes utilize the four basic operations. In addition, we are dealing with numbers and place value as integral parts of our number system. The power of the distributive property is that it can be viewed as the intersection of the four operations and place value, a topic that should be revisited and reinforced throughout K–8 mathematics. The distributive property is a powerful tool for providing this reinforcement and for integrating place value into the multiplication process. Unfortunately, the distributive property, and its power, remain on the shelf of many math classrooms.

The Multiplication Algorithm

Once students move beyond single-digit multiplication, the powerful use of the distributive property is manifested via the multiplication algorithm. For many students, the multiplication algorithm is a process void of meaning or understanding. This fact is especially true of the vertical format used in multidigit multiplication, where students blindly follow a memorized process with no clue as to why each partial product after the first is moved one place to the left. The U.S. education system focuses on algorithms because they provide efficiency, which we highly value. Algorithms also have universal applicability in most contexts because they work well regardless of the numbers used. Unfortunately, this focus has led our education system down the path of teaching efficiency, not mathematics. True, we need algorithms, but students also need the conceptual building blocks to understand why those algorithms work. In multiplication, the distributive property can serve as that foundation.

For simplicity, let us focus on two-digit multiplication. If the task is to multiply 36 and 45, the typical approach would be the standard algorithm, as shown in Box 6.4.

Box 6.4

$$
\begin{array}{r}
36 \\
\times 45 \\
\hline
180 \\
144 \\
\hline
1620 \\
\end{array}
$$

Teachers rarely use the distributive property when teaching the algorithm for multidigit multiplication. Why they fail to do so is a mystery because the distributive property, quite simply, is the foundation of the process. Without it, students have no grounding on which to build an understanding.

To incorporate the distributive property into the process, the initial steps involve the proper interpretation and manipulation of the symbolism. For example, the problem in Box 6.4 would begin with transforming 36 and 45 to $30 + 6$ and $40 + 5$, respectively. Following the steps in horizontal format, the process will look like the one in Box 6.5.

Box 6.5

$36 \cdot 45$

$= (30 + 6)(40 + 5)$

$= 30(40 + 5) + 6(40 + 5)$

$= 30 \cdot 40 + 30 \cdot 5 + 6 \cdot 40 + 6 \cdot 5$

$= 1,200 + 150 + 240 + 30$

$= 1,600$

Note that if we were to use the commutative property and rearrange the order of the partial products to $1,200 + 240 + 150 + 30$, we would get the two partial products of $1,440$ and 180, just as in the standard algorithm. However, by using the distributive property, place value is reinforced, and students can clearly see and understand what is happening throughout the process. In contrast, in the standard algorithm, students can easily lose track of place value. For example, students may forget that when the digits 4 and 6 are multiplied, the reality is that 40 and 6 are being multiplied. The standard algorithm also muddies the water with the "move to the left process." Unless students are taught to insert a zero as a placeholder, they may not see that the 144 is actually 1,440. In addition, the blind action of inserting zero as a placeholder may actually erode understanding of place value since students might not have a clue as to why that is done.

One can easily use the distributive property in a vertical format as well. The orientation is different, but the process is exactly the same, as shown in Box 6.6.

Box 6.6

$$
\begin{array}{r}
30 + 6 \\
\times\ 40 + 5 \\
\hline
30 \\
150 \\
240 \\
1,200 \\
\hline
1,620 \\
\end{array}
$$

True, the vertical process looks more cumbersome, but in reality, it has no more steps than the standard algorithm. What's more, the standard algorithm does, in fact, utilize the distributive property, but in a covert way. The key difference is the standard algorithm involves *shortcuts* because not every product is written down. Chapter Three illustrated the irreparable damage that can be done from the overuse of shortcuts in mathematics. Like algorithms, shortcuts are a form of efficiency, but this efficiency often comes at the expense of conceptual understanding—not an equal trade-off. With the distributive property, students can see all the partial products, making the big picture clearer and enhancing understanding of the process. Such applications of the distributive property bring place value to the forefront and constantly reinforce rather than disguise it. As an added bonus, using the distributive property enables students to recognize fraudulent methods and to more easily learn and understand multiplication of other types of numbers.

Building on Box 6.6, the next logical step in the progression is to combine the four partial products into two partial products, as shown in Box 6.7, which results in a connection to the standard algorithm.

Box 6.7

$$
\begin{array}{r}
30 + 6 \\
\times\ 40 + 5 \\
\hline
150 + 30\ =\ \ \ 180 \\
1200 + 240 = 1{,}440 \\
\hline
1{,}620
\end{array}
$$

By going through this progression, students can understand what really happens in the standard multiplication algorithm. For some students, the preference might be to retain all the partial products and not resort to any shortcuts in representation. Although perhaps not as efficient, this longer version helps students maintain the perspective of each step of the process. Algebra teachers will benefit greatly as well. Imagine that for years, students have been using the standard vertical algorithm to multiply multidigit numbers like $36 \cdot 45$. These students are at a complete loss when faced with an algebraic expression such as $(y + 6)(y + 5)$. But if students have avoided shortcuts and have been using the distributive property in both horizontal and vertical formats, then not much of a transition is needed to go from a problem such as $(30 + 6)$ $(40 + 5)$ to one such as $(y + 6)$ $(y + 5)$. Students will tell their algebra teachers they already know how to do that type of multiplication, except they have been using numerals, not variables.

The distributive property provides another advantage often overlooked. Although the standard algorithm is purported to be the most efficient, that is not always the case. Take the computation of $7 \cdot 45$ as an example. Following the script of the algorithm, we first multiply $7 \cdot 5$, write down the digit 5, and remember the digit 3 to add later to the number of tens. We then multiply $7 \cdot 4$ to get 28 and add 3, for a total of 31, which when written down gives us the product 315. But what if we utilize the distributive property and visualize $7(40 + 5)$? It seems easier to multiply $7 \cdot 40$ and $7 \cdot 5$ mentally, and then add 280 and 35 for the final product of 315. This process is not only easier to do mentally but also retains the integrity of place value.

As you can see, the distributive property provides a powerful flexibility, especially with regard to taking apart or combining numbers. To help students tap into that full flexibility, teachers need to ensure they understand how to incorporate different but equal representations when using the distributive property. In other words, a number such as 59 can be represented as $60 - 1$. For example, consider the problem $103 \cdot 97$. Not only can students break apart the two factors, they also can use addition and subtraction to create equivalent numbers to make computation easier. Thus, 103 can be presented as $100 + 3$ and 97 as $100 - 3$. Suddenly, the task is transformed into the much easier problem $(100 + 3)$ $(100 - 3)$. The use of the distributive property results in the partial products $10,000 - 300 + 300 - 9$, which simplifies to $10,000 - 9$, for a product of 9,991. By using the distributive property, students can start to see through the multiplication algorithm into the many ways that numbers can be manipulated to make computation easier and more efficient. Now that's power.

An Unlikely Marriage: The Distributive Property and Division

Another underutilized application of the distributive property is with division. As mentioned, the distributive property applies not only to multiplication but also to division. However, many people never take advantage of this use because of an instilled misconception that the dividend must remain intact and only one division can take place. This mistaken belief limits the property's power. Just as with factors in multiplication, a dividend can be broken into parts, and this decomposition need not be done strictly by place value. For example, examine the problem in Box 6.8 and follow the reasoning in each step.

If one used the standard long division algorithm, the steps would coincide exactly with the process above. Of course, the process is made easier by starting with a problem where the decomposition creates addends that are evenly divisible by 12. However, numerous combinations of addends can be extracted from the original amount, with each part being individually divided by 12. The point is that the distributive property gives students options that may make more sense to them than the standard division algorithm.

The FOIL Method: A Rose with a Different Name

Despite its power as a teaching tool, the distributive property is sometimes set aside in favor of alternate "methods" for teaching multiplication. Many of these "methods" do little to increase students' conceptual understanding, however, and some can even erode it. A popular example is the FOIL method. Generations of U.S. students, myself included, have graduated from high school and even college believing in the FOIL method. The truth is, no such method exists. Rather, it is yet another example of the extraneous junk that is piled on top of the already vast content students are asked to learn. FOIL is simply someone's invention, an acronym that describes an order for multiplying two binomials: First, Outside, Inside, Last. This order represents the positions of the factors in the two binomials. According to the FOIL method, to multiply $(y + 6)$ $(y + 5)$, one starts with the two "first" factors $(y \cdot y)$, followed by the two "outside" factors $(y \cdot 5)$, then the two "inside" factors $(6 \cdot y)$, and finally the two "last" factors $(6 \cdot 5)$.

The trouble for students (and the irony) is that the FOIL method is not a method at all, but rather an acronym that serves as a rather useless memory aid. Like shortcuts, memory aids can cause students to gain only a superficial understanding and can lead to misconceptions. For instance, the FOIL method may cause students to think they must multiply two binomials in that order. That's not true, however. Because of the commutative property, we can change the order of the multiplications and still get the same result. So a LOIF or an OFIL method would be just as valid! The FOIL method is a pretender, not a contender, because it deals only with order and is limited to one specific context of the distributive property: the multiplication of two binomials. With such limited applicability, why make students learn this extra method? With an understanding of the distributive property, students will know how to multiply two binomials plus far more. In fact, students will become multiplication masters! In the end, the FOIL method just adds an unnecessary layer of learning for students with little benefit and several downsides.

Other Methods of Multiplication: Distributive Property in Disguise

With the proliferation of information available on the Internet, a number of other methods for multiplication have also gained popularity. For the most part, these are *not* new methods, but rather variations of the representation of the partial products in the distributive property. The danger is that these methods could provide information that is misleading or incorrect. Below, we assess the strengths and weaknesses of two popular visual methods of multiplication: the lattice method and the intersecting-lines method.

The Lattice Method. The lattice method uses boxes and diagonal lines to visually depict the distributive property in multiplication. The approach utilizes partial products but presents them in a different layout. Consider the problem 17 • 48. Box 6.9 shows the computation for this problem using the distributive property and Box 6.10 through Box 6.13 show the progressive steps in the lattice method. Compare the two approaches.

Box 6.9: Distributive Property Process

$$
\begin{array}{r}
10 + 7 \\
\times 40 + 8 \\
\hline
56 \\
80 \\
280 \\
400 \\
\hline
816 \\
\end{array}
$$

Refer to Box 6.10. In this scenario involving 17 • 48, the lattice method begins by drawing a 2 by 2 square. The next step is to write the two digits of the first factor horizontally over the respective smaller squares, then repeat the process vertically with the two digits of the second factor. Complete this part of the process by drawing diagonals across the smaller squares, preferably past the boundaries of the large square.

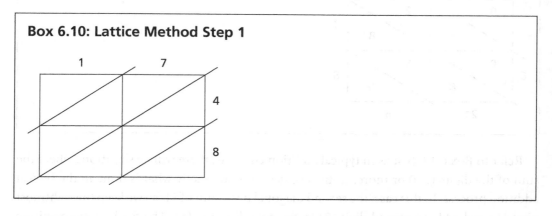

Box 6.10: Lattice Method Step 1

Refer to Box 6.11. The next step is to do the four separate multiplications. This is done by multiplying a horizontal digit and a vertical digit and placing the product in the corresponding sections of the appropriate square. For example, 7 • 8 is 56 and that product would be placed in the bottom right square. In a situation such as 1 • 4 where the product is only one digit, place a 0 in the appropriate section as illustrated in the top left square.

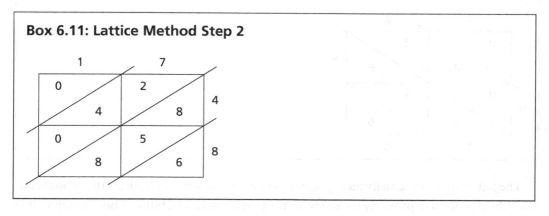

Box 6.11: Lattice Method Step 2

Refer to Box 6.12. After the partial products are computed, the next task is to add them. This is the purpose of the diagonals. It organizes the digits to be added. In this case, the sum of the first diagonal is only the 6, the sum of the second diagonal consists of 8 + 5 + 8, and the third sum would be from 2 + 4 + 0. Complete this step by placing each sum outside the large square but inside the boundary of the diagonal as shown.

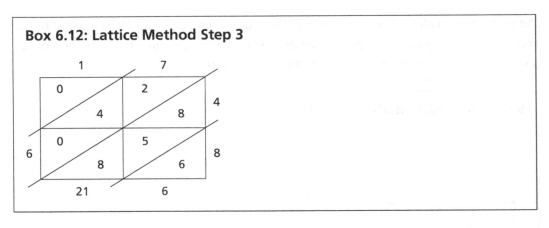

Box 6.12: Lattice Method Step 3

Refer to Box 6.13. Just as in typical addition contexts, there will be situations where the sum of the digits is 10 or more. In those cases, you do exactly what is done in the typical addition process. In this case, the second diagonal has a sum of 21, so we keep the rightmost digit (1) and add the second digit (2) to the next diagonal (6). The final digits constitute the product. Typically, the product is "built" by writing the digits from right to left. In this case, the final product is 816 as shown.

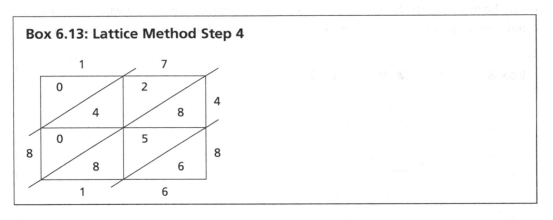

Box 6.13: Lattice Method Step 4

The lattice method actually incorporates solid knowledge of multiplication and incorporates the distributive property by listing all the partial products, but it is not readily visible because of the layout of the visual representation. As a result, the method's shortcoming is that it muddies the idea of place value in the process. Careful inspection shows that the bottom diagonal is in fact the ones place, the diagonal above that is the tens place, the third diagonal up is the hundreds place, and the top diagonal holds digits in the thousands place. What is uncertain is the extent to which teachers inform students of those facts regarding the diagonals and place value. A comparison of the digits in the columns of the vertical format of the distributive property (Box 6.9) with those of the lattice method (Box 6.11) shows that the digits in each of the place values coincide exactly. The lattice method is the application of the distributive property painted with a different brush. The danger is that without an astute teacher, this variation can easily erode the idea of place value.

The Intersecting-Lines Method. Another alternate method for multiplication found online employs the intersections of line segments and is touted under several names, including the Chinese, Japanese, and Mayan methods. Boxes 6.14 through 6.17 show the steps in this intersecting-lines method. You will quickly note a parallel to the lattice method which helps to understand the process. For simplicity, we will again use two-digit factors, in this case 31 • 24.

Refer to Box 6.14. This step involves drawing line segments with a positive slope (/) that match the quantity of each digit in 31, the first factor. In order, we first draw three segments, leave some room for clarity, then draw one more by itself.

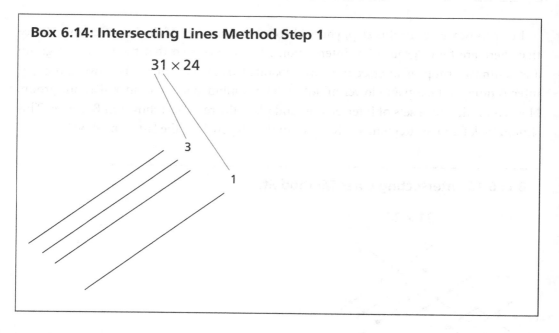

Box 6.14: Intersecting Lines Method Step 1

31 × 24

3

1

Refer to Box 6.15. This step repeats Step 1, with the difference being that the segments for the second factor, 24, are drawn with a negative slope (\) to correspond with the quantities of each digit. Draw them in such a way so that they intersect as they do in Figure 6.15. Highlight the points of intersection.

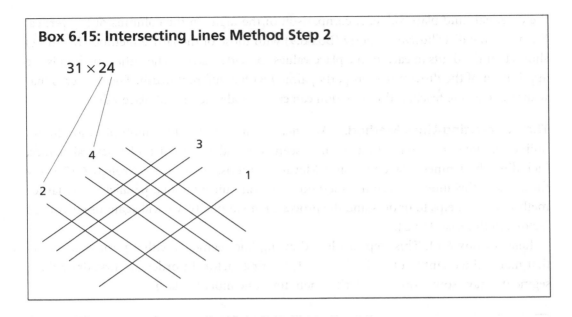

Box 6.15: Intersecting Lines Method Step 2

31×24

Refer to Box 6.16. In this step, you will count the number of the intersections. Notice that there are four "groups" of intersections. Draw curves so that the rightmost group and leftmost group of intersections are separated from the others. The two groups of intersections in the top and lower middle will be combined and considered as one group. Now count the three sets of intersections and place the results as shown in Box 6.16. This should look familiar. Remember the sums in the diagonals of the lattice method?

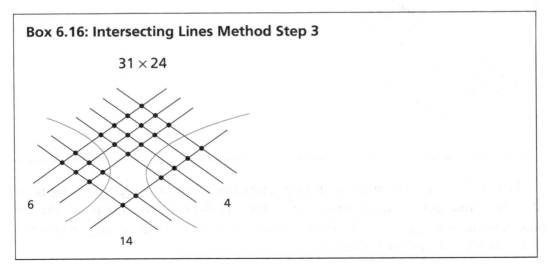

Box 6.16: Intersecting Lines Method Step 3

31×24

Refer to Box 6.17. The last action necessary is much the same as what happened in the lattice method example. Since there is carryover from the middle sum of intersections, follow the same procedure that occurs in normal addition to get the results below.

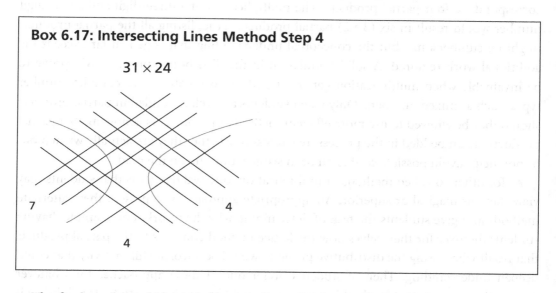

Box 6.17: Intersecting Lines Method Step 4

31 × 24

7

4

4

The final product of 31 • 24 is 744. You have noted the similarity between this method and the lattice method, which in turn connects back to the partial products in typical multiplication. The primary difference in the intersecting lines method is that the products are represented by the number of intersections at each of the different locations. The top right intersection is the product of 1 • 4. The upper left is the product of 3 • 4, which is combined with the bottom right intersection, which represents 1 • 2. The lower left intersection shows 3 • 2. The totals are then combined in a similar fashion to the lattice approach, although the diagonals needed to ensure the addition of the digits in the appropriate place values are not as obvious in this last method. This approach would certainly not be appropriate in contexts such as 89 • 78 because of the number of intersecting lines required. Also, the configuration would become difficult to decipher with larger numbers such as 347 • 3267. Again, this is not technically a different method of multiplication, but rather a different and more complicated representation of the partial products in the distributive property.

The Bottom Line

The key learning in all these examples is that students realize that multiplication involving numbers with multiple digits is actually the accumulation and combination of many multiplications. The total number of individual multiplications can be derived by multiplying the number of digits contained in the two factors. For example, the multiplication of two numbers that both have two digits results in four (2 • 2) multiplications, which corresponds to four partial products. The multiplication of a three-digit and a two-digit number would result in six (3 • 2) partial products. True, listing all the partial products might be cumbersome, but the conceptual understanding that is gained far exceeds the additional work required. A solid foundation in the distributive property will prove to be invaluable when multiplication gets ratcheted up to involve more complex number types, such as mixed numbers. Only when students are well grounded in partial products should they be allowed to use more efficient methods and shortcuts. Knowing that partial products are embedded in the process, regardless of whether they are actually written out or not, helps avoid possible confusion or misconceptions down the road.

As for other so-called methods of multiplication, one real danger is that students may view them as magical or superior. An appropriate approach is to present these alternate methods and give students the task of determining *why* they work. For example, having students discover for themselves how the lattice method connects to the partial products that result when using the distributive property would be a worthwhile activity that could deepen understanding. Then, if students prefer one of these approaches for whatever reason, they can use that method instead. The key difference is that students will know it is a viable alternative because they will understand why the method works.

FEELING NEGLECTED: THE UNITS IN MULTIPLICATION

Unfortunately, students will confront multiplication contexts more involved than determining a total based on knowing the number of groups and the size of each group. These contexts require more attention to the interpretation of the symbolism. For instance, one such context involves the multiplication of fractions. Starting with simple contexts such as $\frac{1}{2}$ • 6, students begin to interpret the multiplication symbol after a fraction as "of," so that they translate the previous equation as "one half *of* six." However, students need to realize this interpretation is limited and normally makes sense only if the first factor is a proper fraction. For instance, it makes no sense to read 6 • $\frac{2}{3}$ as "six *of* two thirds" or $2\frac{1}{4}$ • $4\frac{2}{5}$ as "two and one fourth *of* four and two fifths." Chapters Seven and Eight explore such issues related to fractions in detail.

Another key consideration in the operation of multiplication is the idea of units. Associated with the tendency to present naked numbers, or numbers without context, is the tendency to disregard the idea of units when performing the basic operations. Science texts actually address the units in operations to some extent. In mathematics, however, the unit in an operation is typically ignored. Examine the equations involving the four basic operations in Box 6.18.

Box 6.18

Fill in the blank with the appropriate unit.

a. 7 giraffes + 4 giraffes = 11 _____.

b. 23 oranges − 9 oranges = 14 _____.

c. 240 miles ÷ 4 hours = 60 _____.

d. 150 students ÷ classes of 25 each = 6 _____.

e. 5 feet • 6 feet = 30 _____.

f. 6 men • 4 hours = 24 _____.

Obviously, the involvement of units in the operations of addition and subtraction is fairly simplistic. As discussed in Chapter Five, only like items can be combined via addition and subtraction. So the process of adding or subtracting does nothing to the units involved. However, the issue becomes more complex with multiplication and, by association, division. In division, the resulting units for the quotient can typically be the number of groups or the size of each group, as in (d) where the result would be 6 classes (number of groups). In other division contexts, the resulting units often describe rates, such as miles per gallon, cost per ounce, or, as in (c), miles per hour.

Of the four basic operations, multiplication is probably the most problematic with respect to the resulting units. Even given the typical context involving a number of sets of a certain size, additional interpretation is involved when dealing with units. How do we get a unit of "total" when we multiply the number of sets and the size of each set? If you are buying 3 movies at $9.95 each, what does 3 • 9.95 really mean? Students must realize they are not multiplying movies and dollars! The key is to make the connection back to addition. What really happens in this movie context is the repeated addition of equal-sized sets. In the example, each movie is transformed to its price of $9.95. What you really have is $9.95 + $9.95 + $9.95, and the unit during the whole process remains dollars. The price of each movie, $9.95, is actually the size of the sets. Thus the thing (noun) that represents what constitutes each set remains as the constant unit. This holds true for any multiplication context involving a number of sets of a given size.

Another common context for multiplication involves area, as illustrated by example (e). Area is a difficult transition for students because it involves the transformation of one-dimensional units to two-dimensional units. Teachers need to model this situation with concrete manipulatives so that students experience how a linear unit (one-dimensional) changes to an area unit (two-dimensional). It is critical that students understand that a two-dimensional unit must literally be a *square* unit and that each of the linear dimensions must be described with the same unit of measure. For example, the length cannot be in feet and the width in inches. A different perspective for this context is that an actual transformation does not occur. If I have a piece of paper that is 7 inches by 5 inches, for example, I could argue that the 35 square inches that describe the area of the paper *already exist;* the square inches were not created from the linear inches. From this perspective, when describing the length or width of the piece of paper, inches would be the applicable units, because the length and width are linear components. When describing the area, square inches are the appropriate units. Therefore, we must choose the appropriate unit to describe one-dimensional and two-dimensional measures. The best alternative may be for students to understand both perspectives to better focus on the big picture.

Yet another scenario for multiplication involving units is provided in example (f), which results in a combined unit. A man-hour is a unit for measuring work in industry and is equal to the work done by one man (person) in one hour. Thus, the result of 24 man-hours is the amount of work done by 24 people in one hour. Of course, by considering the factors of 24, it is clear that the actual context may have been the amount of work done by 3 people working 8 hours each, which is a total of 24 man-hours of work. Other combined units include a foot-pound, which is a unit of work equal to a force of one pound moving a distance of one foot, and a watt-hour, which is a unit of energy equal to the power of one watt operating for one hour.

The merger of units and the operation of multiplication can be intimidating and frustrating for students. To provide the necessary support, teachers need to emphasize units as an integral component of mathematics instruction, particularly when covering multiplication. Operations in mathematics do not occur in a vacuum. Numerals typically represent a quantity of something, and students need to understand how each operation affects units. The focus on units puts clothing on naked numbers, and coupled with attention to how multiplication symbolism is interpreted, provides students with a whole new multiplication wardrobe.

CONCLUSION: SMALL DETAILS, HUGE IMPACT

We looked at two different worlds of multiplication: as a concept and as an operation. From a conceptual perspective, we saw why the correct definition is so important. The difference made by the inclusion and focus of the seemingly inconsequential idea of equal-sized groups opened up doors that would otherwise have been not just shut, but locked! Fundamental math includes computation, so we also focused on multiplication as an operation. And because multidigit numbers constitute the vast majority of multiplication contexts, the distributive property surged to the forefront. True, the distributive property is used constantly in the quest for products, but it is vastly underutilized in arithmetic as a means to continually resurrect and reinforce place value. This is manifested by means of partial products, another forgotten player relegated to sitting in obscurity on the bench, due primarily to that culprit we call shortcuts. Procedural fluency was given new meaning by the depth of understanding that can be attained by the proper application and representation of the distributive property. And speaking of representation, the neglected but crucial role of language, symbolism, and the interpretation of both was, again, an integral part of the conversation.

Fractions: The "F Word" in Mathematics

Fractions, more than any other topic in fundamental mathematics, can strike fear into students and teachers alike. Complex and demanding, the topic involves a new notation and long list of rules, posing challenges that can frustrate and confuse students and leave teachers struggling to help. It is no coincidence that fractions are also the area in fundamental mathematics most plagued with obstacles in the language and symbolism. This symbolism, which is fraught with assumptions and nuances, is used in many ways with different meanings, easily leading to misunderstanding and misconceptions. Issues related to *unit* and *whole* only add to this complexity. Truly, the confusion and anxiety are well justified, and it's no surprise if teachers curse when it's time to cover fractions!

DEFINING FRACTIONS: LIKE HERDING CATS

Faced with such daunting challenges, how can teachers best help students master fractions? Just as with any other topic in mathematics, a conceptual understanding begins with a simple yet deep definition of the term *fraction*. A perusal of different resources such as dictionaries and textbooks yields definitions with patterns of common characteristics.

The attempts to define a fraction fall into two general categories: those that focus on the representation of a fraction and those that approach it as a concept. Definitions centered on the symbolism of fractions refer to a representation such as $\frac{a}{b}$ where a and b are typically natural numbers that represent the numerator and denominator, respectively. This focus on the representation is misleading on two fronts. First, this focus is on what a fraction looks like but sheds no light on the meaning of a fraction. Second, the representation focus leads to a one-size-fits-all definition, which is misleading because the meaning of a fraction is dependent on the context.

For the definitions that fall into the category of concepts, a widespread theme is the idea of a fraction as a "part of a whole." This phrase is problematic because it describes only one of the many possible interpretations of a fraction. An issue of concern with some of the definitions in this category is their inconsistency with regard to related terms such as *rational number* and *ratio*. Both those terms refer to specific contexts that confer a specific meaning unlike the overarching perspective of the term fraction, yet they are sometimes treated as interchangeable with the term *fraction*. These examples highlight the three main issues with commonly used definitions of a fraction:

- The $\frac{a}{b}$ form used to represent fractions applies to a myriad of contexts and focuses on the representation rather than the meaning of a fraction.
- Traditional instruction presents "part of a whole" as the primary meaning of a fraction, resulting in a limited rather than universal interpretation of the term.
- Related terms, such as *ratio* and *rational number*, are treated as synonyms.

Because of the nature of the beast, developing a simple yet deep and universal definition of a fraction can be difficult. However, we can look to science, which excels at classifying things, as a guide for taming the fraction beast. In science, one of the broadest classifications is that of a kingdom, one example of which is the animal kingdom. Cardinals, frogs, and wasps are all part of the animal kingdom, but many people do not normally associate these examples with animals. Instead, we tend to associate them with their more specific classifications: cardinals are birds, frogs are amphibians, and wasps are insects. For whatever reason, the tendency for English speakers is to use a mammal, such as a dog or a cow, as an example of an animal.

In the same vein, students normally interpret a fraction, such as $\frac{7}{8}$, as 7 parts of a whole that has been subdivided into 8 parts. In fact, if asked to define a fraction, most adults who went through the U.S. school system would probably say a number that involves part of a whole. The everyday use of fraction in English also steers people to this part-whole interpretation. Phrases such as *fraction of a second, fraction of the workforce,* and *fraction of the cost* naturally result in this tendency. Moreover, math instruction at the elementary and middle school levels emphasizes the part-whole interpretation of a fraction. Unfortunately, this limited interpretation fails to address the many different contexts and meanings of a fraction and its symbolic representation.

Imagine that year after year as a child, you are told that dogs and cats are animals. After many years of dogs and cats, you are shown a spider and told that is an animal as well. Because your vision of an animal as a furry four-legged mammal has been so deeply embedded in your mind, you meet this new image of an animal as a scary eight-legged arachnid with confusion and resistance because it does not align with your default. This scenario is analogous to what happens with many students regarding fractions. Traditional instruction instills in students the definition of a fraction as indicating a part of a whole. After many years, it is difficult for students to adjust when confronted with an entirely new meaning.

Therein lies one of the major hurdles to understanding fractions. Many students develop tunnel vision, viewing fractions only as parts of a whole. They do not see the broader concept. Just as children learn to visualize the broader concept of a dog as well as to distinguish the different types of dogs, students need to learn the broader concept of a fraction as well as to distinguish the different uses of a fraction. Let's go back to people's tendency to suggest a mammal as an example of an animal. This tunnel vision would probably occur less if people were asked for an example from the *animal kingdom*. This phrase triggers the idea of that classification system and its various parts, and is more likely to lead to responses that include birds, amphibians, and insects as well as mammals. In the same way, visualizing a *fraction kingdom* can help students understand fractions in their broader sense as well as remember their different uses and meanings.

THE FRACTION KINGDOM

With an understanding of the fraction kingdom—the big picture of what a fraction is—students can develop a strong conceptual foundation on which to build. Box 7.1 shows one way to present this big picture. The Fraction Kingdom chart organizes fractions into major subdivisions, using $\frac{3}{4}$ as an example. Each subdivision is analogous to a phylum or class in a scientific kingdom, with each category exhibiting distinguishing characteristics. Using this overview as a guide, we can develop a simple yet deep and universal definition of a fraction.

A change in perspective from fraction to fraction kingdom accompanied by a visual representation such as this chart can trigger in students the realization that the generic term *fraction* can imply different possible meanings. For example, a fraction expressing a relationship is different from one expressing a quantity in much the same way a bird is different from an insect. This understanding is essential if students are to correctly interpret the symbolism and contexts of fractions.

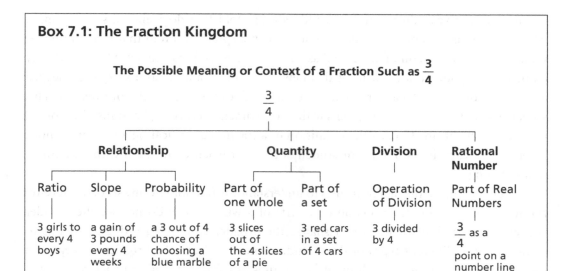

Box 7.1: The Fraction Kingdom

The Possible Meaning or Context of a Fraction Such as $\frac{3}{4}$

$\frac{3}{4}$

Relationship

Ratio — 3 girls to every 4 boys

Slope — a gain of 3 pounds every 4 weeks

Probability — a 3 out of 4 chance of choosing a blue marble

Quantity

Part of one whole — 3 slices out of the 4 slices of a pie

Part of a set — 3 red cars in a set of 4 cars

Division

Operation of Division — 3 divided by 4

Rational Number

Part of Real Numbers — $\frac{3}{4}$ as a point on a number line

Note: The chart presents only one possible visual representation of the Fraction Kingdom. The categories and terms shown were chosen for simplicity and to depict the main contexts for fractions. Other educators may want to use a different organization.

Definition of a Fraction: A Consolidation

The fraction kingdom chart makes it evident that the term *fraction* as currently used in mathematics is difficult to define because the symbol used to represent the concept encompasses a range of interpretations that are not synonymous. In addition, the definition must also be a universal one in the same manner that the symbol is an umbrella representation despite the multiple meanings. With that in mind, Box 7.2 contains a generic definition of the concept of fraction.

Box 7.2

Fraction *(n., mathematics)*. A generic expression in mathematics with multiple interpretations that is typically represented as $\frac{a}{b}$, where *a* and *b* are natural numbers. The possible meanings are dependent on the context and include an expression of a relationship, an expression of a quantity, the operation of division, and a subset of the real numbers.

Because of the tendency to gravitate to the "part of a whole" notion of a fraction, there is a focus on the universal nature of the term in order to clearly grasp the "big picture" of fractions. Although the U.S. mathematics education system does gradually cover other uses of fractions than parts of a whole, students rarely receive the big picture to serve as a foundation. As a result, when confronted with other uses, such as ratio and probability, students often struggle to wrap their minds around them. A solid definition and visual overview of fractions provide this needed foundation and make up for its lack in mathematics textbooks, standards, and traditional instruction.

A conceptual understanding of fractions requires more than a clear grasp of the big picture. Essential to a deep understanding of fractions is thorough knowledge of the constituent parts. Thus, the use of precise and consistent definitions for the terms associated with the components of the fraction kingdom, such as *ratio* and *slope*, are necessary so that students do not mistakenly assign the characteristics of one term to another. In science, students are expected not to make this type of mistake, such as confusing the characteristics of birds with those of insects. Mathematics should be no different. An examination of each part of the fraction kingdom is in order.

Fractions as Relationships

The first category in the fraction kingdom is the use of fractions to express relationships. This perspective is normally not introduced until well into middle school, so there is immediate dissonance because the accumulated experience of students consists of fractions as a quantity. This group contains three classes: ratio, slope, and probability. Once again, the first step is to define these related terms in a simple yet deep way.

Ratio. The initial journey is an exploration of the meaning of the term *ratio*. This investigation must begin with establishment of a simple yet deep definition so that it can serve as the standard of comparison for definitions commonly found in K–8 textbooks or online. This definition is expressed in Box 7.3.

Box 7.3

Ratio (*n*.). A comparison in mathematics, typically represented as $\frac{a}{b}$ where a and b are natural numbers, that establishes a relationship between the numerator and denominator. (A ratio can also be represented as $a{:}b$ where a and b are real numbers.)

The clear focus of the definition of a ratio is that it establishes a relationship. A definition for ratio that zeroes in on the idea of *comparison* aligns with the idea of relationships and should be acceptable. Definitions that stray from that central idea can be incomplete or misleading for several reasons. Misleading interpretations of ratio follow a common pattern of using related terms inappropriately. Examples include definitions that treat ratio as interchangeable with a fraction as a rational number, or with division and quotients. Definitions that include a restriction that the comparison must be with the same units of measure are misleading because a ratio could be a comparison of 3 smokers to 5 nonsmokers, for example.

When going through the system, I sometimes heard the phrase "ratio and proportion" which was confusing to me. I did find definitions where the term *proportion* was used as a synonym for *ratio*. However, the two terms are not synonymous. Rather, they are closely related because the idea of a ratio is embedded within the definition of a proportion. So a simple yet deep definition of a proportion could build on an understanding of ratio, as follows: "A proportion is an equation that states that two ratios are equivalent." An example of a proportion, then, is $\frac{3}{2} = \frac{6}{4}$, and each fraction in that proportion is a ratio. Because the focus of a ratio is relationships, then by definition, the focus of a proportion is relationships as well. This key distinction is addressed later in this chapter.

Slope and Probability. Slope and probability are other types of fractions that also express relationships. In general, the definition of *slope* is "a rate of change." (See Chapter Four for a detailed discussion of the definition of slope.) In the expression $\frac{c}{d}$ ($d \neq 0$), where the context is slope, a relationship is established that assigns a certain amount of change in c (the numerator) to a specific amount of change in d (the denominator).

Probability deals with relationships in a similar way, but within a different context. Rather than a representation of the idea of change, a *probability* is "an expression of the likelihood that an event will occur." In the expression $\frac{c}{d}$ ($d \neq 0$), where the context is a probability, c represents the number of a given outcome, and d represents the total number of possible outcomes. In some ways, fractions expressing probability parallel those expressing a part of a whole because the value of d is referred to as a total. However, a $\frac{3}{4}$ probability of randomly picking a blue marble out of a jar of marbles does not necessarily mean the jar contains only four marbles. As a result, in a probability, the idea of total outcomes is slightly misleading because the relationship is usually expressed in simplified form. Although a probability does not represent an actual quantity or fall within the world of cardinal numbers, the expression can be used to determine quantities given a context with sufficient information. And with a clear understanding of the categories of fractions, students can distinguish contexts of probability and quantity.

As mentioned, Box 7.1 presents only one possible visual representation of the fraction kingdom. For the sake of simplicity, other terms that fall under the category of relationships, such as *rate*, were not included. If rate had been included, it would be shown as a type of slope, because change is the cornerstone of the definition of rate. In addition, some educators may argue that slope and probability should be shown as types of ratios. The purpose of the chart was not to try to resolve such debates. For this reason, other educators may want to revise the chart, using a different organization. If such alternatives are developed, the key is that students are provided with a visual overview of fractions and that the organization and categories of the chart reflect and align with how the terms are defined.

Fractions as Quantities

The second category in the fraction kingdom is the use of fractions to express quantities. The definition of a fraction as a quantity is as an expression of parts of a whole or parts of a set and is the most common interpretation of a fraction. Even though a fraction as a relationship and a fraction as a quantity are separate entities with different meanings, the representation is the same for both. It is the interpretation of this symbolism used for both meanings that can be especially difficult for students and teachers alike. The interpretation is dependent on context and is made even more complex with the involvement of other factors. Examine the context in Box 7.4 as an example that illustrates this issue.

Box 7.4

$$\frac{1}{2} = \frac{2}{4}$$

Is this equation true or false? Justify.

Most adults can easily identify this equation as true. Even many elementary school students will have no difficulty with the answer. But suppose one student, Jimmy, states that the equation is false and he can prove it. Curious, the teacher lets him present his case to the class. Jimmy goes to the board and draws the two images shown in Box 7.5.

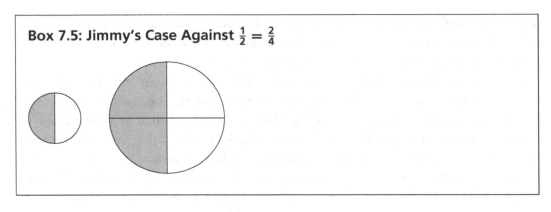

Box 7.5: Jimmy's Case Against $\frac{1}{2} = \frac{2}{4}$

Turning to the class, Jimmy asks them to imagine that the two circles are pizzas. He then explains that if he eats $\frac{1}{2}$ of the first pizza and the teacher eats $\frac{2}{4}$ of the second pizza, they will have not eaten the same amount. The teacher will obviously have eaten more. Jimmy asserts he has proved that $\frac{1}{2}$ is not equal to $\frac{2}{4}$, so the equation is false. The teacher composes herself, but before she can respond, Loretta, another student, declares that she agrees the equation is false, but for a different reason. The teacher allows Loretta to present her case to the class as well. Loretta goes to the board and draws the image shown in Box 7.6.

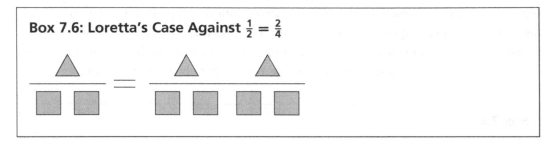

Box 7.6: Loretta's Case Against $\frac{1}{2} = \frac{2}{4}$

Loretta reminds the teacher that earlier in the year, the class learned that an equation is like a balance scale. For an equation to be true, the amount to the left of the equal sign must be the same as the amount to the right. In addition, if you add something to one side, you must add the same thing to the other side to maintain the balance. Loretta then points to her drawing and asserts that the equation is false because the amount of stuff to the left of the equal sign is less than the amount of stuff to the right. Some of the other students agree with Loretta, while others in the class agree with Jimmy.

What is the teacher to do? Both Jimmy and Loretta have presented different, yet seemingly valid, arguments that the equation $\frac{1}{2} = \frac{2}{4}$ is false. What the two students have unearthed are major problems in the symbolism used for fractions. If we review Jimmy's argument, presented in Box 7.5, he has a valid point: the two pizzas are obviously different sizes, so the problem is that we are dealing with two different wholes. Therein lies the problem. In the equation $\frac{1}{2} = \frac{2}{4}$, there is an assumption that we are dealing with the same whole on each side of the equation. Mathematics should be an exact science, but the reality is that the symbolism sometimes requires assumptions, particularly when numbers are presented without context. Is it any wonder students are confused? On top of all the definitions, properties, and algorithms, students must figure out when and where to make assumptions about the symbolism.

To provide assistance, teachers need to clearly explain to students the assumptions involved in the symbolism of mathematics. In this instance, fractions that represent quantities do not indicate the size of the whole, which renders them incomplete expressions. For example, if $\frac{2}{3}$ of a school district's staff is composed of teachers, how many teachers are on staff? We cannot determine that number unless we know the total staff employed by the district. This point may seem obvious to many adults, but it can derail students who fail to grasp the basic assumptions involved with fractions. The bottom line is that teachers need to explain to students that a fraction expressing a quantity is nebulous and incomplete, missing the applicable *whole*. Moreover, in an equation such as $\frac{1}{2} = \frac{2}{4}$, the assumption is that the fractions each refer to the same whole. One way a teacher can help students who are struggling with this concept is to clarify the mathematical context by presenting the equation as $\frac{1}{2} w = \frac{2}{4} w$, where w represents the *whole*. Written in this way, the statement is unequivocally true, no assumptions required.

Loretta's case, presented in Box 7.6, raises a related problem in interpretation. Loretta's argument states that $\frac{1}{2} = \frac{2}{4}$ is false because the amount of stuff to the left of the equal sign is less than the amount of stuff to the right. She has a valid point that the number of the items on each side of the equation is not the same, making the two sides unbalanced. The confusion is that comparing the contexts for Jimmy and Loretta is the proverbial comparison of apples to oranges. In each case, the category of the fraction, and thus its meaning, are different. Loretta's drawing is not an expression of equal quantities; rather, it depicts a proportion—a *relationship*. Thus we are now in a world of relationship, not quantity. As mentioned, a proportion is a mathematical sentence stating that two ratios are equivalent. In turn, a ratio, typically written in the form $\frac{a}{b}$, is a comparison of whatever is represented in the numerator to whatever is represented in the denominator.

When $\frac{1}{2} = \frac{2}{4}$ expresses a *quantity*, the equal sign indicates that $\frac{1}{2}$ of a whole is equal to $\frac{2}{4}$ of that same whole. But when the equation expresses a proportion, the equal sign indicates a *relationship*—that the *relationship* expressed by the ratio on the left is equivalent to the *relationship* expressed by the ratio on the right. Loretta's context will be confusing and unresolved if it is approached from a quantitative lens. Because this situation is based on an equation, the notion of equal value will tend to dominate the reasoning. This context requires a new, different interpretation of the equal sign because the definition of equality is typically based on equal amounts or values, not equivalent relationships. The equal sign in a proportion must be interpreted from a relationship lens.

Viewing Loretta's drawing as a proportion, the established relationship is two squares in the denominator for every one triangle in the numerator. The key in a proportion is that the same relationship must be expressed or maintained on each side of the equal sign. In Loretta's drawing, the relationship is expressed once on the left and twice on the right, as shown in Box 7.7. This example highlights how an understanding of the big picture of the fraction kingdom can benefit students—and teachers. By helping students understand that fractions can express relationships as well as quantities, and how to identify and interpret each type, teachers can better help students like Loretta work through their confusion.

Box 7.7: Loretta's Drawing Viewed as a Proportion

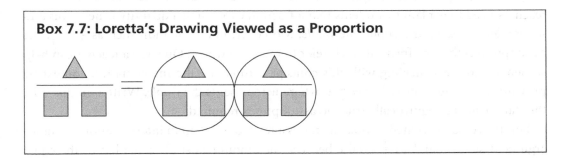

Fractions as Division

The third category in the fraction kingdom is the use of fractions to express the operation of division. This is a completely different interpretation than that of a fraction expressing a relationship or a quantity. In this context, the fraction bar is actually the operation symbol for division in much the same way as the symbol "÷." What is not inherently obvious is the embedded understanding of the accompanying grouping. The fraction bar as a symbol for division includes the understanding that all computation in the numerator and in the denominator must be done first and the division is the last step done. For example, a fraction with $3 + 7$ in the numerator and $23 - 3$ in the denominator would be equivalent to the expression $(3 + 7) \div (23 - 3)$.

Fractions as Rational Numbers

Considering the equation $\frac{1}{2} = \frac{2}{4}$, mathematicians would argue that it is true because of the definition of a fraction as a rational number, the final category in the fraction kingdom. This category falls more within pure mathematics, where rational numbers are defined as a subset of the real numbers. This use refers to the more abstract idea of a fraction as a member of the set of real numbers, typically represented as each occupying a unique point on a number line. Given this perspective, $\frac{1}{2} = \frac{2}{4}$ is unequivocally true because $\frac{1}{2}$ and $\frac{2}{4}$ occupy the same position on the number line. In other words, the representations of fractions as rational numbers do not exhibit a one-to-one correlation on the number line; rather, a point such as $\frac{1}{2}$ can be expressed as an infinite number of equivalent rational numbers, such as $\frac{2}{4}, \frac{3}{6}, \frac{4}{8}$, and so on.

In K–8 math classes, however, the typical context for a fraction is aligned and associated with the idea of cardinality in that they represent a quantity. This is ironic given that we have seen that the fraction symbol does not adequately represent a quantity unless the whole is explicitly stated. In Chapter Two, the term *number* was defined to align with the cardinal numbers because the term is typically used to designate a quantity, not the abstract idea of a number as a member of the set of real numbers or as a position on the real number line.

In the animal kingdom, location is a determining factor in the types of animals that exist in that environment. For example, I would no more expect to find pythons in Antarctica than penguins in the Mojave Desert. Knowing where I am guides and validates my expectations and judgment. It is no different with fractions. As the Fraction Kingdom chart in Box 7.1 shows, the one-size-fits-all fraction symbol has multiple possible meanings based on context, and those meanings place you in different subsets of the fraction kingdom. Traditional instruction often fails to address this fact, which is one reason fractions can be so confusing for students. Trying to interpret an equation such as $\frac{1}{2} = \frac{2}{4}$ can be analogous to turning on the television to a documentary on polar bears and deducing that the location is somewhere in or near the Arctic. I would know the environment and what to expect. To interpret a fraction, students must first decide on their location in the fraction kingdom by categorizing it based on context. If the context is about quantities, students know certain assumptions and interpretations are in effect. If the context is about relationships, then other interpretations are in effect. The same holds for the contexts of division and rational numbers. By identifying the context of how a fraction is being used, students can place it within the fraction kingdom, thereby identifying the fraction's unique traits and symbolic attributes.

INTERPRETING FRACTIONS

Interpreting fractions, then, requires a broad conceptual foundation, the skill to identify the context, and—the final critical piece of the puzzle—the skill to interpret and translate the nuances of the symbolism. These difficulties are manifested in all the fraction categories although the majority of interpretation issues are found in expressing relationships and quantities.

Interpreting Relationships

As a relationship example, consider the scenario in Box 7.8.

Box 7.8

You are attending a professional development math session on circles. During the session, the presenter uses the circumference formula for a circle: $C = d \bullet \pi$. As part of the problem-solving process, the presenter then manipulates the formula to appear as follows: $\pi = \frac{C}{d}$. An astute teacher in the room interjects and comments that the second equation is not acceptable. He asserts that π is an irrational number, and as such, by definition cannot be expressed as the rational number $\frac{C}{d}$. Thus, the equation $\pi = \frac{C}{d}$ is not valid. How should the presenter respond?

The teacher in the audience has a valid point. By definition, π is an irrational number and cannot be represented as the rational expression $\frac{C}{d}$. On the other hand, the presenter began with a valid formula and did nothing wrong to reach the new equation $\pi = \frac{C}{d}$. So what can be done to resolve this conflict? The key is to go back and determine in which area of fractions this context fits. The teacher who raised the concern is in rational number (or possibly quantity) mode. However, the presenter is using the equation $\pi = \frac{C}{d}$ as a symbolic expression of the definition of π, which is the *ratio* of the circumference of a circle to its diameter. Because ratios are about *relationships*, the context is not about quantities or the set of real numbers. Through a relationship lens, $\pi = \frac{C}{d}$ is a valid representation. Note that this resolution required a conceptual understanding of the broader fraction kingdom and the associated nuances of the symbolism.

Many students struggle both with identifying the context of fractions and interpreting the symbolism. Successful interpretation of the symbolism is an integral part of determining relationships. Refer to Box 7.9. These examples illustrate the type of progressive interpretations that students should be proficient at making, but often aren't. The issues these examples highlight build on those discussed in Chapter Six regarding the interpretation of the multiplication symbol. With fractions, students must be taught, not only to interpret the denominator as a word rather than a number, but also to identify the contexts in which that interpretation is appropriate. For example, in the first item in Box 7.9, students must learn to interpret $\frac{5}{4}$ as "$5 \cdot \frac{1}{4}$" and then to interpret that expression, in turn, as "5 one-fourths." As mentioned in Chapter Six, given a general expression such as "$c \cdot d$," students should be taught the flexibility to interpret "$\cdot d$" as a noun, not as an operation or number.

Box 7.9

a. Do students see $\frac{5}{4}$ as $5 \cdot \frac{1}{4}$? Do students see $\frac{5}{4}$ as 5 *one-fourths*? Why or why not?

b. Do students see $1\frac{1}{2}$ as $1 + \frac{1}{2}$? Do students see that $9 = 1\frac{1}{2} \cdot 6$ means that 9 is 1 and $\frac{1}{2}$ *sixes* (1 set of six and $\frac{1}{2}$ of another set of six)? Why or why not?

The second item in Box 7.9 highlights another common problem involving fractions. Many students have difficulty interpreting a mixed number, such as knowing that $1\frac{1}{2}$ is $1 + \frac{1}{2}$, as simple as that skill may seem. At the root of this difficulty is the fact that mixed numbers do not fit the idea of place value. In a number such as 315, each of the digits represents a certain place value. However, in a mixed number such as $32\frac{1}{4}$, the $\frac{1}{4}$ *has no clear place value*. Students need to understand this quirk. Fortunately, a mixed number follows the pattern that the value is determined by the sum of what each digit represents, for example, $315 = 300 + 10 + 5$. However, teachers need to use reminders and scaffolding so that students can readily interpret a number such as $32\frac{1}{4}$ into its constituent parts: $30 + 2 + \frac{1}{4}$, or simply $32 + \frac{1}{4}$. Combining this support with continuous application of the distributive property will ensure that students can interpret $1\frac{1}{2} \cdot 6$ as "1 and $\frac{1}{2}$ sixes," which in turn is "1 six and $\frac{1}{2}$ of another six," which in turn is $6 + 3 = 9$.

Contexts Involving Quantities: A Whole Other Problem

Each area of fractions has its own issues regarding interpretation. For contexts involving quantities, students must be cognizant of both the value of the *whole* and of the *units* being used. As mentioned, fractions expressing quantities require certain assumptions because of limitations of the symbolism. Teachers need to explain that the actual quantity represented by a fraction is unknown without an indication of the size of the whole. To help students grasp this concept, teachers need to provide instruction and practice in the determination of the whole as well as the difference it makes in the possible representation. As an example, refer to Box 7.10.

Box 7.10

Determine the amount shaded in the diagram.

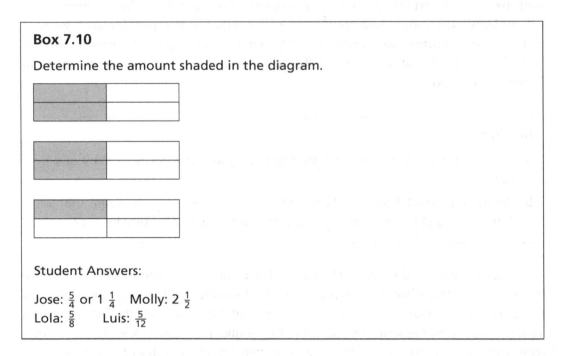

Student Answers:

Jose: $\frac{5}{4}$ or $1\frac{1}{4}$ Molly: $2\frac{1}{2}$
Lola: $\frac{5}{8}$ Luis: $\frac{5}{12}$

The task in Box 7.10 is ambiguous and subject to different interpretations. Although seemingly counterintuitive, using ambiguous tasks can be a powerful teaching strategy because such activities demand that students think, justify their reasoning, and see things from different perspectives. The power of the task in Box 7.10 is that multiple interpretations are possible, but with proper justification, all four student responses can be shown to be true. In Jose's case, he interpreted the question as asking for the *total* amount shaded to come up with his response of $\frac{5}{4}$. In addition, he interpreted the diagram as showing three rectangles, each constituting a separate whole and divided into fourths. (Refer to Box 7.11.) Thus, *fourths* became his unit of reference. Jose then added the $\frac{2}{4}$ in the first rectangle with the $\frac{2}{4}$ in the second rectangle and the $\frac{1}{4}$ in the third rectangle to get a sum of $\frac{5}{4}$.

Box 7.11

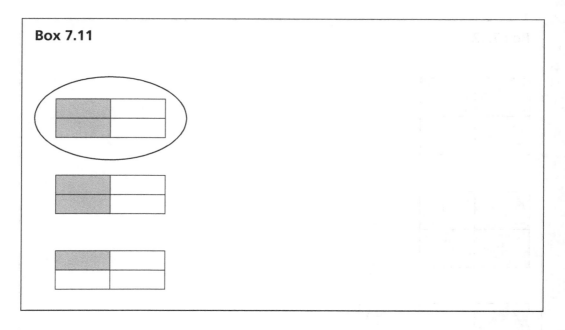

In Molly's case, she interpreted the diagram in the same way Jose did to reach her response of $2\frac{1}{2}$. However, she saw $\frac{1}{2}$ as the unit of reference, so the first rectangle has a shaded half, the second rectangle has another shaded half, and the third rectangle has $\frac{1}{2}$ of a shaded half for a sum of $2\frac{1}{2}$. In this case, though, for the answer to be clear it must include the unit: $2\frac{1}{2}$ *halves*. This example is analogous to someone claiming that 500, 50, and 5 are all equal. Because the assumed unit for any number is *ones* unless otherwise indicated, this claim requires the additional indication of units: 500 ones, 50 tens, and 5 hundreds. Thus, Molly's response needs to be $2\frac{1}{2}$ halves, with the additional stipulation that each of the larger rectangles constitutes a separate whole. Without that clarification, the diagram would need to look like the one in Box 7.12 to be a correct representation of $2\frac{1}{2}$.

Lola's interpretation, unlike those of Jose and Molly, is based on a different whole, as indicated by the circle in Box 7.13. In her interpretation, the whole equals a combination of two of the larger rectangles, subdivided into eight parts. Thus, the unit is *eighths*. The lone shaded portion not included in the whole is an additional eighth that can be mentally moved and visualized. However, Lola's interpretation of the whole is atypical, and her answer, like Molly's, requires that the units and whole be clearly stated.

Box 7.12

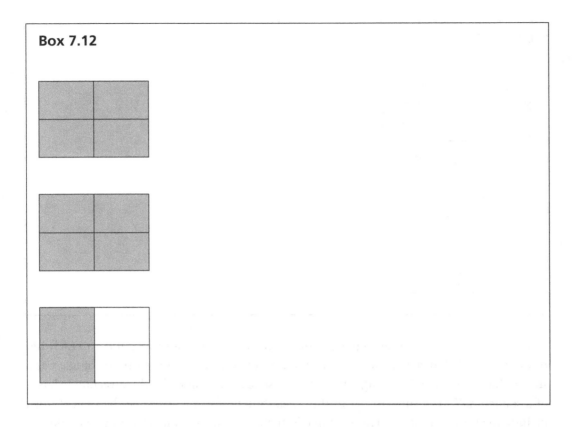

Luis's response of $\frac{5}{12}$ is probably the one most students would give. Unlike his classmates, his interpretation of the whole is a combination of all three rectangles, as shown in Box 7.14. This interpretation transforms the image into one large rectangle divided into 12 equal parts, 5 of which are shaded, for a solution of $\frac{5}{12}$.

A task such as this one, with multiple interpretations, would not likely appear on a standardized test. The directions and diagram are vague and do not clearly indicate the intended whole. In some ways, based on assumptions, traditional instruction dictates that each of the three rectangles constitutes one whole (Box 7.11), each divided into four equal parts, making *one-fourth* the unit of reference and Jose's response the most appropriate.

From an instructional viewpoint, ambiguous tasks such as this one provide the knowledge and practice students need to develop a conceptual understanding of fractions. As with other areas of mathematics, students must learn to be flexible in their interpretation of problems and symbolism and to understand the roles of key concepts such as *whole* and *unit*. To get the most out of this type of task, teachers need to provide structured

Box 7.13

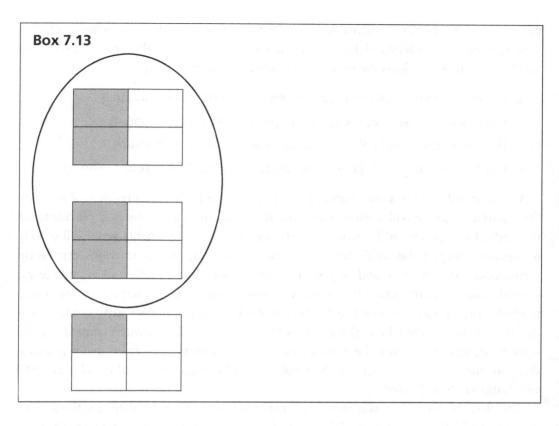

Box 7.14

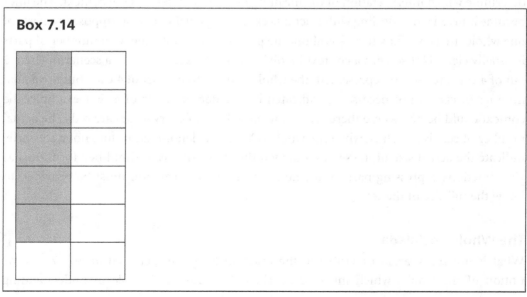

guidance to ensure that students justify their responses, consider and debate different perspectives, and understand key concepts. For example, with the task in Box 7.10, teachers might ask students the following questions to guide learning:

1. Is it possible for $1\frac{1}{4}$ to be the correct response? Justify your reasoning.

2. Is it possible for $\frac{5}{12}$ to be the correct response? Justify your reasoning.

3. Is it possible for $\frac{5}{8}$ to be the correct response? Justify your reasoning.

4. Is it possible for $\frac{5}{2}$ (or $2\frac{1}{2}$) to be the correct response? Justify your reasoning.

Working with fractions can be an exacerbating exercise in the interpretation of not only the fraction symbol but also what constitutes the whole in different cases. By focusing on this critical component of fractions, teachers can ensure that students acquire the skills to flexibly interpret the whole based on context. For example, in fractions expressing relationships, the idea of a *total* may be more appropriate than a whole and in some cases, a whole does not even exist. In fractions expressing quantities, interpreting the whole is often much easier. Because the fraction symbol ($\frac{a}{b}$) alone cannot express the actual quantity or size of the whole, the whole is frequently provided through context. At the same time, students need to be reminded that the denominator in fractions of quantity does not indicate the total size of the whole but rather the number of equal parts into which the whole is divided.

The first decision that students must make when confronted with fractions is to determine which interpretation of the meaning of a fraction best fits the context. The lines become blurred when dealing with fractions expressing parts of a set as opposed to parts of one whole. In a context where $\frac{3}{4}$ is about the parts of one whole, the total number of parts is usually clear. Not so with a context involving part of a set. Consider a scenario where 3 out of 4 cars are red. As represented, the whole appears to be a set of 4 cars, but the actual number of cars is not necessarily indicated by the denominator of 4. For example, the context could be one where there are 20 cars and 3 out of every 4 cars are red. The actual number of cars is 20. Thus, when the whole is a set, the denominator does not necessarily indicate the actual size of the set, especially if the expression is in simplified form. Just as with fractions expressing parts of a whole, additional information must be provided to know the full size of the set.

The Whole Enchilada

What is not transparent or visible in the Fraction Kingdom depicted in Box 7.1 is the notion of the whole, which must be considered because of its role in understanding the various meanings and contexts. Understanding where you are among the different categories of a fraction will help determine how to interpret the whole in each context.

Wholes in Relationships.   Interestingly, in contexts where fractions express relationships, it is possible that no real whole or total exists. Relationship scenarios are typically expressed as ratios. Suppose that a count of the cars in a parking lot reveals that there are 2 blue cars for every 3 red cars, represented by the ratio $\frac{2}{3}$. This comparison involves neither a whole nor a total, and in such a context, that information is not necessarily needed. In other instances, some ratios may constitute a part-to-part comparison, which can provide the necessary information to determine the whole or total if needed. For example, if the student count in a classroom constitutes a ratio of 18 girls to 12 boys, one can determine that the class has 30 students. But in a context where a classroom has a $\frac{3}{2}$ ratio of girls to boys, the class size may not necessarily be 5. The class size could be 25 if there are 15 girls and 10 boys, or several other equivalent combinations that adhere to the $\frac{3}{2}$ ratio. Determining the whole may or not be possible in a context, depending on the information provided.

The whole in a probability context can be similarly nebulous or complex and parallels that described for a ratio. A probability expresses the relationship involved in determining the likelihood that an event will occur. But as noted, the denominator does not necessarily represent a total, especially if the probability is in simplified form. For example, if the contents of a jar indicate a $\frac{2}{5}$ probability of selecting a blue marble, this does not necessarily mean the jar has a total of 5 marbles. Thus, students need to be flexible in their interpretation of the denominator in a probability context.

As was the case with ratio and probability, a fraction as slope focuses on relationships. The idea of a whole or a total can enter the picture, but is dependent on the context. Moreover, a context may initially focus on a relationship, then morph into one focused on quantity when an operation such as multiplication is introduced.

Wholes in Quantity Contexts.   This situation has been addressed at length. We have seen for example, that $\frac{2}{3}$ of the staff at a school is not a quantity unless the whole is known. Thus, knowing that a fraction without a whole is not quantifiable, teachers and students alike can condition themselves to the point that an internal alarm sounds off in a quantity context of a fraction.

Wholes in Division.   There is yet another confusing facet in the merger of fractions and wholes. If the fraction is being used to represent the operation of division, the dividend is typically, but not always, the whole (or total) and the divisor is usually either the size of the set or the number of sets. Refer to Box 7.15.

Box 7.15

Typical Division Context:

$$\frac{whole\ or\ total}{\#of\ sets\ or\ size\ of\ set}$$

Typical Quantity Context:

$$\frac{part}{total}$$

The typical division scenario is one where the whole or total is larger than the size of the set or the number of sets. However, the interesting twist is that in a division context, the total is typically expressed in the numerator, not the denominator. This is the exact opposite of where traditional instruction leads students. For fractions being used to represent quantities, students are led to believe that the denominator is the whole or total (which has been shown to be problematic in a *part of a whole* scenario).

CONCLUSION

The animal kingdom consists of different members that can be distinguished because of observable differences, particularly in their physical makeup. Likewise, the fraction kingdom contains members that can be differentiated because of different meanings or properties. This framework of a fraction kingdom can assist students because it not only facilitates their visualization of the big picture of fractions, but also enables them to focus on the specific properties or characteristics that make membership in each category unique. The nebulous, incomplete, and inadequate definition of fractions, coupled with the complexities of additional factors such as the symbolism, assumptions, wholes, and units can lead to nothing less than confusion and anxiety. There is a tendency for humanity to have a fear of the unknown, so it is little wonder that the mere mention of the word *fraction* elicits fear. (And you thought the reference to fractions as the "F" word in math meant something else?)

This chapter has concentrated on fractions as a concept. This still leaves out the conversation regarding the flip side of the fraction coin. The dark cloud of anxiety and confusion also appears overhead when computation of fractions enters the picture. The complexities of the same issues such as interpretation, symbolism, assumptions, wholes, and units are just as evident in the computation of fractions. These fearsome issues will be addressed in the next chapter, which focuses on operations with fractions.

Operations with Fractions

The misconceptions and assumptions that permeate fractions only multiply when computation comes into play. As in other areas, methods for teaching the operations of fractions typically rely on shallow rules and procedures. The old adage "Ours is not to reason why; just invert and multiply" is yet another example of students learning a process without any idea of the conceptual basis for it. At the same time, the procedures for computing fractions and the results they produce can seem foreign to students used to working with whole numbers. Mystified and lost, students can feel like strangers in a strange land. To help students adjust to operations with fractions, teachers need to provide both a conceptual foundation that connects to whole number operations and guidance in interpreting the language and symbolism.

ADDING AND SUBTRACTING FRACTIONS

Most teachers and students would probably consider addition and subtraction to be the easiest of the four basic operations. It is somewhat of a paradox then that many students find adding and subtracting fractions to be extremely challenging. Sometimes, though, what we know gets in the way of learning something new. The habits instilled in students when they add and subtract whole numbers, coupled with an inattention to the language and symbolism of math in instruction, can interfere with students' ability to learn the same two operations with fractions.

So What's the Problem?

Examine Box 8.1, which illustrates a common error students make when adding fractions with unlike denominators. No doubt, countless teachers have been frustrated by trying to help students avoid this mistake.

> ### Box 8.1: Incorrect Addition of Fractions
> $$\frac{2}{3} + \frac{1}{5} = \frac{3}{8}$$

The primary culprit behind this error is the lack of instructional emphasis on the property that only like items can be combined. Students are taught they can only add and subtract fractions with common denominators, but not *why*. By connecting to the role of like items in combining fractions, teachers can help students build on the conceptual foundation of whole-number addition and subtraction. Chapter Five, in the discussion on the order of operations, explains how math instruction initially emphasizes the property of like items in basic addition and subtraction. Students receive problems such as 2 apples + 3 apples = 5 apples, while also being told they can't add 2 apples to 3 oranges without converting to a common unit, such as *fruit*. Over time, though, math instruction drops such units or descriptors and presents bare equations, such as 2 + 3 = 5. This continued practice results in the disastrous erosion of the basic concept that only like items can be combined. For years, most teachers and students ignore the huge assumption about like items that's made in equations such as 2 + 3 = _____. Often, not until a formal algebra course are students reminded of this property when told they cannot combine 2b and 3c because they are not the same.

Solutions and Benefits

Because students often do not remember or understand the property of like items, they don't consistently apply the concept when adding and subtracting fractions. A simple but effective solution is to reinforce the property throughout elementary school by including units or descriptors in most expressions and equations. This approach may seem time-consuming, but the benefits (detailed later) would far outweigh the extra effort involved.

When teaching the operations of fractions, however, teachers cannot assume that students have received such reinforcement. In this situation, a solution is to connect back to students' early math instruction in adding and subtracting whole numbers. Teachers can then help students build on that foundation to apply the property of like items to the addition and subtraction of fractions.

Incorporating the Property of Like Items.   One place to start is to remind students that numbers—including fractions—represent *something*. The reality is that we use numbers primarily as cardinal numbers, and as such, in most contexts they represent a certain quantity of some item. To help students reestablish that solid foundation, teachers can present parallel expressions such as those in Box 8.2.

Box 8.2

     3 books + 7 books

     9 cows − 4 cows

     1 goose + 6 geese

     5 mice − 1 mouse

     3 textbooks + 4 trucks

     5 roses + 2 clouds

     1 seventh + 2 sevenths

     1 half + 3 eighths

     2 thirds + 4 fifths

By asking students which expressions can be simplified as is and then discussing the responses, teachers can reintroduce the property of like items with whole numbers. Several examples may be necessary to ensure that students grasp the concept. Once they do, teachers can make the connection to fractions by asking students how they think the property of like items applies to the last two expressions in Box 8.2. Again, guided discussion will be necessary to ensure that students understand that the property applies to fractions as well as whole numbers.

Because the activity involves written forms of fractions, students can more clearly see the parallel with whole numbers. For this reason, the activity must include a focus on the language and symbolism of fractions. As covered in Chapter Seven, students need to learn to be flexible in how they interpret the fraction symbol. In certain contexts, the denominator in a fraction should be interpreted as a word rather than a number, such as in the progressive interpretation of $\frac{2}{3}$ as "$2 \cdot \frac{1}{3}$" and then "2 one-thirds." This interpretation enables students to more easily see how an expression such as "3 sevenths + 2 sevenths" parallels one such as "3 pencils + 2 pencils." Likewise, students need to be able to translate written forms of fractions, such as those in Box 8.2, into symbolic forms, such as $\frac{1}{2} + \frac{3}{8}$ and $\frac{2}{3} + \frac{4}{5}$. By having students practice interpreting and translating fractions as both words and symbols, teachers can strengthen this connection—and in turn, strengthen students' understanding of how the property of like items applies to fractions.

Another practice here would be an insistence on including the unit in the resulting sum or difference because another mathematical benefit emerges that will minimize or possibly eliminate the mistake made in Box 8.1. If students are continually exposed to equations such as 9 cows − 4 cows = 5 cows and 1 seventh + 2 sevenths = 3 sevenths a solid mathematical principle will be subliminally embedded. This principle is that when items are added or subtracted, the item that results is the same item. In other words, if one adds cats with cats, the results are still cats.

Repeated practice of these skills with both whole numbers and fractions will greatly reduce students' tendency to add unlike denominators. When confronted with an expression such as $\frac{2}{3} + \frac{4}{5}$, students will know to interpret it as "2 thirds + 4 fifths." With that interpretation, students can see that the two fractions do not represent like items and, therefore, cannot be combined as is. What's more, after calculating the least common denominator and converting the fraction to $\frac{10}{15} + \frac{12}{15}$, students will be less likely to make the mistake of adding the like denominators because practice will have reinforced the idea that like units or "things" do not change when combined.

Reinforcing Like Items in Elementary School.   As noted, perhaps the most effective solution for reinforcing the property of like items is to include units or descriptors in most math expressions and equations throughout elementary school. The benefit of this repeated exposure would be to ingrain the property of like items into students' minds. Traditional math instruction in the United States insists that repeated drill and practice is critical, but we must choose wisely what we have students drill and practice. If students repeatedly practiced the inclusion of units and descriptors as part of numerical expressions, they would repeatedly see that when you add or subtract, the units or things being combined (1) must be the same and (2) do not change. Math teachers in middle school and high school would be very grateful as well.

As an added benefit, including more written descriptors in mathematics at the elementary level would help integrate English-language arts (ELA) into math instruction. For example, written descriptors can reinforce reading, writing, vocabulary, and spelling. They can aid the learning of singular and plural versions of words and emphasize adjective-noun relationships, as in expressions such as *9 cows*. This integrated ELA support would benefit English language learners as well as native speakers.

Unfortunately, the tendency of the U.S. education system is to strip mathematical expressions of context as students get older. The situation is analogous to the tale of "The Emperor's New Clothes." All the numbers are naked, but no one is willing to point it out—except our students by repeatedly making the same mistakes in math class. As a result, we are missing a great opportunity to reinforce mathematical context and the property of like items. Given that U.S. society is so enamored with acronyms, perhaps a compromise would be to include units or descriptors, such as 7 yards + 2 yards = 9 yards, until fourth or fifth grade and then transition to an abbreviated equation such as 7y + 2y = 9y. That transition would actually ease students into the world of algebraic expression and also would serve as a reminder that numerals represent *something*, that only like items can be combined, and that when combined the unit does not change.

MULTIPLYING FRACTIONS

The next step after the addition and subtraction of fractions is multiplication. Here again, students are confronted with a process that can run counter to what they learned in the multiplication of whole numbers. For example, with whole numbers, students may learn that $b \cdot c$ represents b sets each containing a quantity of c. But when covering proper fractions, some educators drop this interpretation, insisting it does not apply. However, it is possible to have $\frac{1}{2}$ of a set rather than only a whole number of sets. Likewise, can we not have sets of halves or sets that have a quantity of $4\frac{1}{3}$ in each? The visualization and representation might be more difficult, but the real world does not preclude the existence of something like $3\frac{1}{5}$ sets with $5\frac{3}{7}$ in each. In this text, the stance remains that the interpretation of $b \cdot c$ as representing groups or sets is as viable for fractions as it is for whole numbers, albeit more difficult to visualize and represent.

Multiplying a Fraction by One Is Complex?

As mentioned in Chapter Three, one of the most basic principles in mathematics is the multiplicative identity. This property states that for any real number r, $r \cdot 1 = r$. The simple English translation is that any number multiplied by 1 yields itself. In the world of natural numbers, this basic and, quite frankly, simplistic concept is one that students master with little effort. However, as is often the case with fractions, even the simple process of multiplication by 1 involves intricacies with symbolism and translation. We multiply fractions by 1 primarily when simplifying fractions and creating equivalent fractions. Unfortunately, even though the multiplicative identity is the critical foundation of both processes, the use of shortcuts and the idea of *cancel* in traditional instruction render its role invisible. Granted, from a computation perspective, multiplication by 1 is simple regardless of the numbers involved. Students can easily survive without understanding the hidden subtleties. Analogous to this context would be the knowledge that despite the calm appearance of a duck cruising by on the water, there is a lot going on under the surface. And as has been repeatedly emphasized, the goal for our students is deep, not shallow understanding.

So what is so complicated about multiplying a fraction by 1? One way to address this question is to review the entire process of simplifying a fraction, all the paddling going on under the surface that enables the duck to propel itself forward. Chapter Three detailed the damage done by the overuse of shortcuts in this process. The practice of "canceling" totally hides from students the fact that multiplication by 1 is happening as well as it being the linchpin of the process. Box 8.3 presents the same example used in that chapter (Box 3.3) to illustrate the full process of simplifying a fraction.

Box 8.3

$$\frac{6}{8} = \frac{3 \bullet 2}{4 \bullet 2} = \frac{3}{4} \bullet \frac{2}{2} = \frac{3}{4} \bullet 1 = \frac{3}{4}$$

The pivotal role of the multiplicative identity in this process is worth revisiting. Only by going through each step in the simplification process can students understand the property's key role and why the process works as it does. For instance, nothing is eliminated or "canceled." Rather, the multiplicative identity is the primary property that enables us to "drop" the "• 1" portion of the fourth expression. Note how "$\frac{3}{4} \bullet 1 = \frac{3}{4}$" parallels the expression of the multiplicative identity: $r \bullet 1 = r$.

What many students, and even some teachers, do not realize is that the process of creating an equivalent fraction is the same as the process of simplifying a fraction, just in reverse. Examine Box 8.4 and note how the process shown is the reverse of the one in Box 8.3.

Box 8.4

$$\frac{3}{4} = \frac{3}{4} \bullet 1 = \frac{3}{4} \bullet \frac{2}{2} = \frac{3 \bullet 2}{4 \bullet 2} = \frac{6}{8}$$

The specific example in Box 8.4 can be stated more algebraically to generalize the expression of creating an equivalent fraction. Box 8.5 shows this general expression, in which b, n, and c are real numbers with $c \neq 0$ and $n \neq 0$.

Box 8.5

$$\frac{b}{c} = \frac{b}{c} \bullet 1 = \frac{b}{c} \bullet \frac{n}{n} = \frac{b \bullet n}{c \bullet n}$$

Thus, the general expression for an equivalent fraction is $\frac{b}{c} = \frac{(b \cdot n)}{(c \cdot n)}$. Shortcuts for this process leave out the multiplication by 1, which can leave students wondering why we multiply the initial fraction by $\frac{n}{n}$, where $n \neq 0$. Consequently, students must recognize that $\frac{n}{n}$ is an expression for numbers such as $\frac{2}{2}$, $\frac{3}{3}$, $\frac{4}{4}$, and so on, which are all equal to 1. This should be a solid part of their mathematics repertoire. Although not initially apparent, this basic understanding and application of the multiplicative identity in computation lays the foundation for future math because it carries over to the simplification of expressions and the solving of equations in algebra.

Notice that the connection between simplifying a fraction and creating an equivalent fraction not only simplifies instruction but also reduces the amount of content students must learn. This scenario is another example that in the long run, shortcuts often create more work than they eliminate. The two processes are actually the same, only reversed. However, teachers cannot make this connection if shortcuts are being used in the two processes, because the shortcuts make them appear unrelated and different. Shortcuts do have a role and can be allowed at some point, but students must first have a thorough understanding of what really happens in this component of fraction computation. Yes, the duck can move on the water, but do we want students to accept it as some type of magic, or do we want them to know how it does it? The multiplication by 1 can be taught as something simple with shortcuts, but here easy means shallow. The alternate approach with the whole detailed process is much more involved, but the reward is depth of understanding.

Multiplying by One: Context Matters

The hidden nuances involved in multiplying fractions by 1 are not readily apparent in the computation alone. On the surface, multiplying fractions by 1 appears no more difficult than whole-number contexts. However, there is a conceptual understanding that flies totally under the radar. This understanding is not apparent until there is physical modeling of the multiplication of a fraction by 1. That context reveals a subtle yet distinct difference in the way in which a fraction $\frac{b}{c}$ is equivalent to a fraction $\frac{(b \cdot n)}{(c \cdot n)}$ depending on whether the fraction involves one whole subdivided into parts or if it represents part of a set comprised of multiple items. Multiplication by 1 is the duck on top of the water and multiplication by $\frac{n}{n}$ is the paddling going on under the surface. Multiplying by 1 is the duck ... it remains the same duck. However, multiplication by $\frac{n}{n}$ is the paddling that provides propulsion. Mathematically, in a quantity context, the multiplication of a fraction by $\frac{n}{n}$ involves changing the parts or the whole, depending on the context.

A Whole of 1. A physical model helps illustrate what actually happens when a fraction is multiplied by $\frac{n}{n}$. The more common context is one where the fraction represents *one whole* that is subdivided into parts. Box 8.6 provides a physical model for the fraction $\frac{2}{3}$, where it represents 2 shaded parts of *one whole* subdivided into 3 parts:

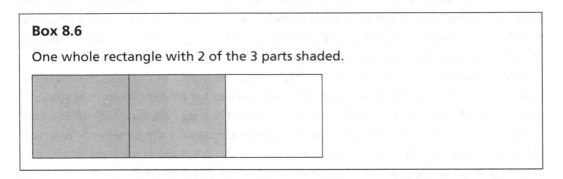

Box 8.6

One whole rectangle with 2 of the 3 parts shaded.

If we wanted to create an equivalent fraction, we would multiply $\frac{2}{3}$ by $\frac{n}{n}$. For this example, let $n = 2$. Multiplying $\frac{2}{3}$ by $\frac{2}{2}$, we get the equivalent fraction $\frac{4}{6}$. Box 8.7 indicates how the model changes to show this fraction:

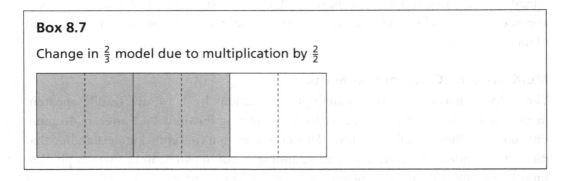

Box 8.7

Change in $\frac{2}{3}$ model due to multiplication by $\frac{2}{2}$

Note the details in the modeling. What did multiplying $\frac{2}{3}$ by $\frac{2}{2}$ actually do? It changed the number of *parts*. Each of the thirds was multiplied by 2, resulting in each third being further subdivided into 2 parts. The resulting rectangle is now divided into 6 equal parts with 4 of them shaded. Comparing the before and after models reveals that each rectangle still has the same amount of area shaded, and this effectively models that $\frac{2}{3} = \frac{4}{6}$. Note that *the size of the whole did not change*. This represents the idea that multiplying by 1 does not change the amount. However, the impact of the multiplication did result in a *change in the size and number of the parts*. This reflects the multiplication by $\frac{n}{n}$ perspective that physically involved the subdivision of the parts. In addition, from a relationship standpoint, note that the ratio of the amount of shaded to unshaded area is equivalent in each model, 2 to 1 in Box 8.6 and 4 to 2 in Box 8.7. This is true because we have the same size whole in each case. (Remember Jimmy's dilemma in Box 7.5?)

A Whole That Is a Set.   Now, consider a new context in which the fraction $\frac{2}{3}$ represents a whole composed of a set of items, versus one subdivided item. Keep in mind that this is a context (our location in the fraction kingdom) where the fraction is one that deals with quantity. Box 8.8 provides a model of this context, where $\frac{2}{3}$ represents 2 circles that are shaded out of the total set of 3 circles:

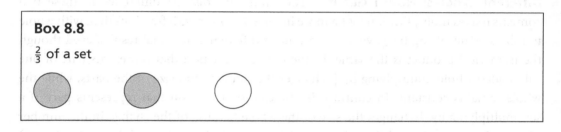

Box 8.8

$\frac{2}{3}$ of a set

As with the rectangular model, to create an equivalent fraction, we multiply $\frac{2}{3}$ by $\frac{n}{n}$. Again, let $n = 2$, where the multiplication by $\frac{2}{2}$ results in the equivalent fraction $\frac{4}{6}$. The model above transforms into the one shown in Box 8.9.

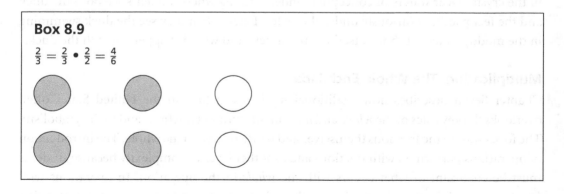

Box 8.9

$\frac{2}{3} = \frac{2}{3} \cdot \frac{2}{2} = \frac{4}{6}$

Note how the circle model changed. What did multiplying $\frac{2}{3}$ by $\frac{2}{2}$ do in this case, where a set is involved? Unlike the rectangular model, the individual size of the circles, which in this model constitute the parts, did *not* change. Instead, the number of circles increased from 3 to 6. In other words, *the size of the set—the whole—changed*. Thus, when a fraction represents part of a set of items, multiplying by $\frac{n}{n}$ increases the number of items that make up the set, which results in changing the size of the whole; the size of each part remains the same. The size of each part not changing reflects the perspective of multiplication by 1 whereas the change in the size of the whole connects to the perspective of multiplication by $\frac{n}{n}$. This context links back to the discussion of Loretta's confusion depicted in Box 7.6. What is interesting is that a quantity context where the whole is a set of multiple items can easily morph into a ratio context that involves relationships. In this case, the relationships expressed by $\frac{2}{3}$ and $\frac{4}{6}$ are equivalent because 2 shaded circles out of 3 is the same relationship as 4 shaded circles out of 6.

Different Wholes: Now I Get It!   The subtle but distinct difference in these two contexts makes multiplication by 1 a more involved process with fractions than with whole numbers. Multiplying by $\frac{n}{n}$, versus 1, produces different contextual results, even though the numerical product is the same. In the case of a fraction that represents part of one subdivided whole, multiplying by $\frac{n}{n}$ changes the number and size of the parts, while the whole remains constant. In contrast, in the case of a fraction that represents part of a set, multiplying by $\frac{n}{n}$ changes the size of the whole because of the change in the number of items in the set. In addition, the size of the individual members of the set (each part) remains constant. More often than not, this critical difference is overlooked in instruction, much to the detriment of students' in-depth understanding of the interaction of the multiplicative identity with fractions. Done correctly, the duck is initially seen swimming in the crystal-clear waters of conceptual understanding where students see both the duck and the feet paddling furiously under the water. Later, when they see the duck swimming in the muddy waters of shortcuts, they still understand what is happening with the duck.

Multiplication: The Whole Enchilada

Chapter Seven describes how traditional math instruction in the United States often overlooks the key roles of the *whole* and *units* in interpreting fractions and their symbolism. The focus was on the fractions themselves and issues related to the whole. The introduction of operations performed with fractions adds another layer of complexity because students must be cognizant of what occurs with the *whole* in the operation. In operations with fractions, multiplication in particular, there is a lot of paddling under the water that goes undetected. Box 8.10 illustrates the complex role that the whole can play in the multiplication of fractions.

Box 8.10

Trace how the *whole* changes in this scenario: Steve has $\frac{1}{2}$ gallon of gasoline in his container. He uses $\frac{2}{3}$ of the gasoline to mow the grass. How much gasoline did he use?

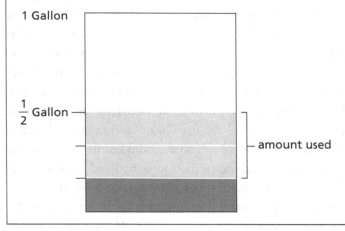

You can see that this scenario involves a quantity context and two different wholes. For the initial fraction $\frac{1}{2}$, the whole is one gallon (the whole container in Box 8.10). However, for the fraction $\frac{2}{3}$, the reference whole is the $\frac{1}{2}$ gallon of gasoline (the total shaded area in Box 8.10). When the multiplication $\frac{2}{3} \cdot \frac{1}{2}$ is performed, the *whole* for the correct solution of $\frac{1}{3}$ reverts back to one gallon again. A student can argue that, technically, $\frac{2}{3}$ "half-gallon" is a correct answer, and that's a valid point. But in a scenario without additional clarification or direction, we assume the intent is to find out how much of *one*—in this case, one gallon—a fraction represents. In essence, the multiplication of two *proper* fractions can be viewed as a transformation, where the product is a fraction where the whole is one, rather than a different whole or unit. Rather than resort to typical multiplication of 2 fractions, refer to Box 8.11 for a different approach to this problem.

Box 8.11

Changing $\frac{2}{3}$ of $\frac{1}{2}$ gallon to $\frac{1}{3}$ of 1 gallon

$$\frac{2}{3} \cdot \frac{1}{2} = \frac{2 \cdot 1}{3 \cdot 2} = \frac{1 \cdot 2}{3 \cdot 2} = \frac{1}{3} \cdot \frac{2}{2} = \frac{1}{3} \cdot 1$$

Remember the emphasis in Chapter Seven regarding the importance of translating the symbolism of fractions? This scenario serves as an example of that powerful skill. Note that the task is to convert $\frac{2}{3}$ of $\frac{1}{2}$ gallon to an expression where the whole is one. Notice that we begin by translating $\frac{2}{3}$ of $\frac{1}{2}$ to $\frac{2}{3} \cdot \frac{1}{2}$. Then we change it to a single fraction (mathematically change it from the product of 2 quotients to the quotient of 2 products). What follows is a simple change of the order of the 2 factors in the numerator using the commutative property; thus $2 \cdot 1$ becomes $1 \cdot 2$. Then we convert back to 2 factors. The simplification gives us the last expression. The "$\cdot 1$" was deliberately left in the expression for interpretation purposes. Compare the beginning and the end. Remembering the power of understanding the symbolism, $\frac{2}{3} \cdot \frac{1}{2} = \frac{1}{3} \cdot 1$ says that $\frac{2}{3}$ of $\frac{1}{2}$ gallon is the same as $\frac{1}{3}$ of 1 gallon. Wow! Pardon my exuberance, but these types of "aha" moments are cool! Note that a more complicated context such as $\frac{3}{4} \cdot \frac{5}{8} = \frac{15}{32}$ requires computation beyond that in Box 8.11. The learning is that $\frac{15}{32}$ is equivalent to $\frac{15}{32} \cdot 1$, so the conversion to a whole of one is still accomplished but not as evident because of the more involved computation. However, the true "aha" is that $\frac{3}{4} \cdot \frac{5}{8} = \frac{15}{32} \cdot 1$ says that $\frac{3}{4}$ of $\frac{5}{8}$ is the same as $\frac{15}{32}$ of 1.

The focus of this text is mathematics content, but instruction is an inseparable component if the desired outcome is increased student learning. Numerous methods exist for teaching the multiplication of fractions. The following is one such method that makes multiplication of proper fractions literally transparent by illustrating how multiplying proper fractions transforms the context to a fraction with *one* as the *whole*, unless otherwise indicated. This method uses transparent squares as an area model for the multiplication of proper fractions. A teacher selects the two appropriate transparent squares and lays one over and perpendicular to the other so that one transparency shows vertical columns and the other shows horizontal rows. The area that contains the shaded portions of *both* squares is the product of the two proper fractions. Refer to the scenario in Box 8.12.

Box 8.12

Ernesto ran $\frac{2}{5}$ of one mile. His younger brother Bobby only managed to run $\frac{3}{4}$ of Ernesto's distance. How far did Bobby run?

The task is to find the length of $\frac{3}{4}$ of $\frac{2}{5}$ of one mile. Of course, one could insist that we already have the answer—Bobby ran $\frac{3}{4}$ of two-fifths of a mile, but that solution would not be acceptable to a teacher because the expectation is a fraction with one mile as the whole. To model the context in the scenario, a teacher would select two transparencies, one illustrating $\frac{3}{4}$ and the other $\frac{2}{5}$, as shown in Box 8.13. The two figures are congruent squares.

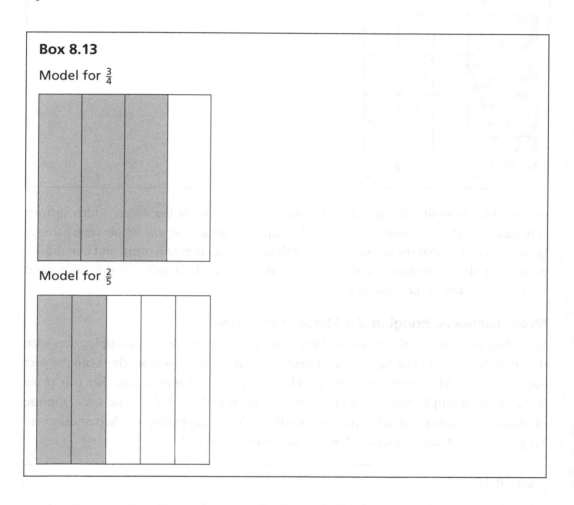

Box 8.13

Model for $\frac{3}{4}$

Model for $\frac{2}{5}$

The next step is to turn the transparency modeling $\frac{3}{4}$ sideways so that the shaded columns are horizontal. Then, the teacher would place that transparency directly over the one for $\frac{2}{5}$ so that the edges of the congruent squares align. The result is a combined image that looks like the square in Box 8.14.

The image is divided into 20 equal parts. The darker shaded area is the intersection of the two individual shaded areas. The common shaded area in turn represents $\frac{3}{4}$ of $\frac{2}{5}$, which is 6 of the 20 parts. Thus, the product is $\frac{6}{20}$. In simplest form, Bobby ran $\frac{3}{10}$

Box 8.14

$$\frac{3}{4} \cdot \frac{2}{5} = \frac{6}{20}$$

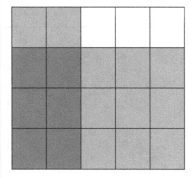

of one mile. Note that the solution is a fraction where *one* is the *whole*, which in turn is modeled by the two initial transparencies (squares) becoming one whole transparency (square). The fact that the whole is now *one* should be an intended, overt, and announced outcome in the instruction in order to deepen students' understanding of the process and the interpretation of the modeling.

Mixed Numbers: Bridging the Multiplication Gap

Just when students get the multiplication of proper fractions down, multiplication with mixed numbers comes along to present new challenges. Once again, teachers can connect back to the multiplication of whole numbers to provide a foundation that can make learning the multiplication of mixed numbers much easier. At the same time, the use of visual approaches can help students envision what is happening mathematically and support different learning styles. Refer to the scenario in Box 8.15.

Box 8.15

You have taught your students the multiplication of mixed numbers using the standard algorithm: Convert to improper fractions, multiply, and then simplify and convert back to a mixed number if applicable. You are tutoring Michael because he still doesn't get it. Using $3\frac{1}{2} \cdot 2\frac{1}{2}$ as an example, think about how you would go about helping Michael gain a conceptual understanding of mixed-number multiplication using other perspectives or approaches. Write down an explanation of how you would help Michael.

The scenario in Box 8.15 also appears in Chapter One. There, the message was that teachers tend to teach not only in the same way as they were taught but also what they were taught. If a teacher's content knowledge is limited to the standard algorithm for multiplying mixed numbers, then a student like Michael is out of luck. When he asks for help, he will just get the same approach, but on a one-on-one basis.

By expanding their repertoire of approaches, teachers can better help struggling students. Alternatives to the standard algorithm for multiplying mixed numbers include a numeracy approach using the definition of multiplication, an algebraic approach using the distributive property, and a geometric approach using an area model. The following sections describe each approach, as well as the powerful connections among them, and explain how they can deepen students' conceptual understanding of the process.

A Numeracy Approach. What does $3\frac{1}{2} \cdot 2\frac{1}{2}$ really mean? Visualizing the expression based on the definition of multiplication may enable students to have a deeper understanding of what the multiplication of two mixed numbers entails conceptually. If $3 \cdot 2$ by definition is three groups with two in each group, then $3\frac{1}{2} \cdot 2\frac{1}{2}$ means three and one-half groups with two and one half in each group. A pictorial representation (Box 8.16) would enable students to literally see what the expression looks like.

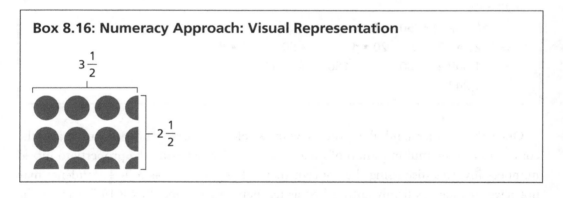

Box 8.16: Numeracy Approach: Visual Representation

Each row is one set or group of $2\frac{1}{2}$ shaded circles. Note that the first three rows show full sets, while the last row shows only $\frac{1}{2}$ of a set of $2\frac{1}{2}$ shaded circles. Students can visually determine the correct solution by combining the like items, the shaded areas in this case. By combining the 6 wholes, 5 halves, and 1 quarter, we get an answer of $8\frac{3}{4}$. Box 8.17 shows the numerical representation of this process.

Box 8.17: Numeracy Approach: Numerical Representation

$$6 + (\tfrac{1}{2} + \tfrac{1}{2}) + (\tfrac{1}{2} + \tfrac{1}{2} + \tfrac{1}{2}) + \tfrac{1}{4}$$
$$= \quad 6 + 1 + 1\tfrac{1}{2} + \tfrac{1}{4}$$
$$= \quad 7 + 1\tfrac{1}{2} + \tfrac{1}{4}$$
$$= \quad 8\tfrac{1}{2} + \tfrac{1}{4}$$
$$= \quad 8\tfrac{3}{4}$$

An Algebraic Approach.   An algebraic approach to the problem involves using the distributive property. Students may be unaware that they have been using this property since they began multiplying multidigit whole numbers. Although discussed in Chapter Six, it bears repeating that students need to see the distributive property done horizontally as well as vertically, which is the more common method. Box 8.18 shows the distributive property presented horizontally for the whole-number expression $23 \cdot 54$.

Box 8.18: Distributive Property with Whole Numbers

$$23 \cdot 54$$
$$= \quad (20 + 3) \cdot (50 + 4)$$
$$= \quad 20 \cdot 50 \quad + \quad 20 \cdot 4 + \quad 3 \cdot 50 + \quad 3 \cdot 4$$
$$= \quad 1{,}000 + \quad 80 \quad + \quad 150 \quad + \quad 12$$
$$= \quad 1{,}242$$

Once they understand the process with whole numbers, students can make the connection to the multiplication of mixed numbers. Transferring the property to mixed numbers involves discussing the concept that $3\tfrac{1}{2}$ is the same as $3 + \tfrac{1}{2}$. Students may not have this idea as firmly entrenched as teachers might hope. Box 8.19 illustrates the distributive approach to multiply the two mixed numbers $3\tfrac{1}{2} \cdot 2\tfrac{1}{2}$.

Working through each step of this process shows students exactly what is happening mathematically when they multiply two mixed numbers. Teachers can then strengthen this understanding by connecting the process to the other approaches. For example, by linking this approach with the previous numeracy approach, the critical discovery is that

Box 8.19: Algebraic Approach: Distributive Property with Mixed Numbers

$3 \frac{1}{2} \cdot 2 \frac{1}{2}$

$\begin{aligned}
&= \quad (3 + \tfrac{1}{2}) \cdot (2 + \tfrac{1}{2}) \\
&= \quad 3 \cdot 2 \quad + \quad 3 \cdot \tfrac{1}{2} \quad + \quad \tfrac{1}{2} \cdot 2 \quad + \quad \tfrac{1}{2} \cdot \tfrac{1}{2} \\
&= \quad 6 \quad + \quad \tfrac{3}{2} \quad + \quad \tfrac{2}{2} \quad + \quad \tfrac{1}{4} \\
&= \quad 6 \quad + \quad 1\tfrac{1}{2} + \quad 1 \quad + \quad \tfrac{1}{4} \\
&= \quad 8 \tfrac{3}{4}
\end{aligned}$

a common pattern of partial products develops. In the numeracy approach, the image depicts three and one-half groups of two-and-one-half shaded circles each. This depiction matches the numerical expression ($3 \frac{1}{2} \cdot 2 \frac{1}{2}$) that is the starting point of the algebraic approach, shown in Box 8.19. Students can also connect the visual "partial products" (the fully shaded or partially shaded circles) in the numeracy model with the partial products ($3 \cdot 2 + 3 \cdot \frac{1}{2} + \frac{1}{2} \cdot 2 + \frac{1}{2} \cdot \frac{1}{2}$) of the algebraic model. This translates to the 6 *wholes* resulting from $3 \cdot 2$, the 5 *halves* resulting from $3 \cdot \frac{1}{2}$ and $2 \cdot \frac{1}{2}$, and the 1 *quarter* resulting from $\frac{1}{2} \cdot \frac{1}{2}$. In addition, a comparison of the numerical representation of the numeracy model, shown in Box 8.17, and the algebraic approach (Box 8.19) reveals that both involve the same addends (6, $1 \frac{1}{2}$, 1, and $\frac{1}{4}$) which are in fact the partial products. These connections take all the mystery out of the $8 \frac{3}{4}$ solution.

A Geometric Approach.   Many math teachers are familiar with using a measurement or area model, especially with whole-number multiplication. An area model can be adapted fairly easily to fit a mixed-number example as well. This geometric approach, like the numeracy approach utilizing the definition of multiplication, encourages students to use a visual model to solve a problem. In this case, the visual tool is a rectangular grid using the idea of area and square units. Drawn to scale, each rectangle reflects the size of the fraction it represents using a 1-by-1 square as the unit of reference. Students can use the grid to solve a problem without actually doing any multiplication. The preferable approach is to use a 4-by-3 grid so that the students can more clearly see how the fractional area units of $\frac{1}{2}$ and, especially, $\frac{1}{4}$ are derived. Box 8.20 depicts this geometric model for the expression $3 \frac{1}{2} \cdot 2 \frac{1}{2}$.

Box 8.20: Geometric Approach

$3\frac{1}{2} \bullet 2\frac{1}{2}$

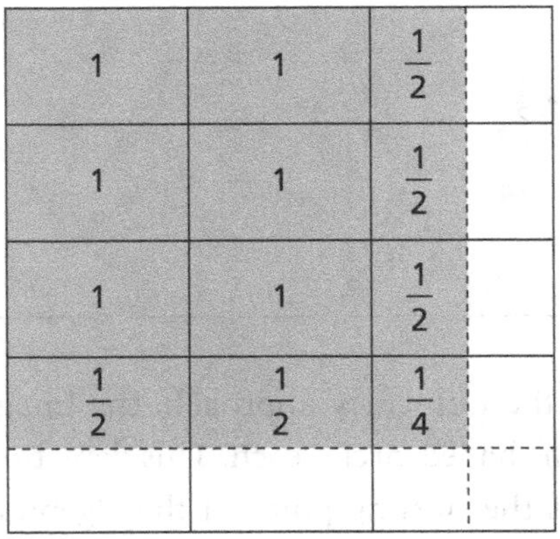

1	1	$\frac{1}{2}$	
1	1	$\frac{1}{2}$	
1	1	$\frac{1}{2}$	
$\frac{1}{2}$	$\frac{1}{2}$	$\frac{1}{4}$	

Note that the "units" in this context are 1-by-1 squares. Also, because the process of tabulating the square units is so similar to the process of determining the shaded circles in the numeracy approach, the process below is an abbreviated version to avoid repetition.

$$
\begin{array}{ll}
6 & \text{(6 whole units)} \\
2\frac{1}{2} & \text{(5 half units)} \\
+\ \frac{1}{4} & \text{(1 quarter unit)} \\
\hline
8\frac{3}{4} & \text{(1-by-1 square units)}
\end{array}
$$

Units in the Visual Models: There Is a Difference. On the surface, the geometric approach, shown in Box 8.20, appears to connect well to the numeracy approach, shown in Box 8.16. The horizontal rows in the rectangle shown in Box 8.20 illustrate $3\frac{1}{2}$ groups of $2\frac{1}{2}$ each, just as with the horizontal rows of shaded circles in Box 8.16. (And vertically, each image depicts $2\frac{1}{2}$ groups of $3\frac{1}{2}$ each.) The total is tabulated using basically the same counting process. However, it is important to ensure that students understand that there is a subtle but important difference regarding how the units in each approach are interpreted because they are in fact different in the two models. To explore this issue, examine the two figures in Box 8.21.

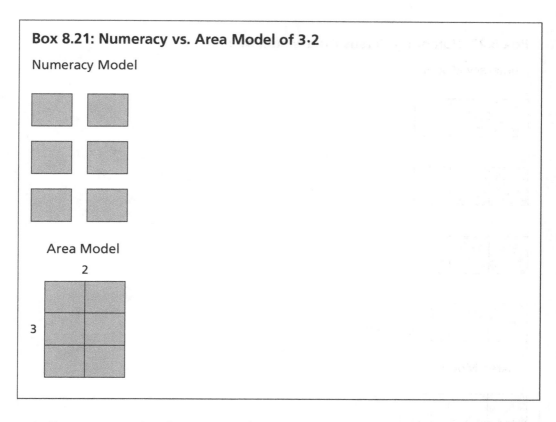

Box 8.21: Numeracy vs. Area Model of 3·2

Numeracy Model

Area Model

In Box 8.21, merging the pieces in the numeracy model produces the geometric area model. Herein lies the danger of using manipulatives and rectangular arrays to model multiplication. Invariably, little attention is paid to the units involved. In the numeracy model, each square actually represents a physical or concrete block, modeling 3 sets of 2 blocks each, which results in a total of 6 blocks. However, in the area model, the context is different. Here, the image represents, not 3 sets of 2, but linear (one-dimensional) measures of 3 linear units and 2 linear units, which when multiplied become square (two-dimensional) units.

Teachers need to make this distinction clear and explain the differences in the units that the numbers represent in each context. The key difference is that in the numeracy model, the units are the physical blocks. The context is 3 groups composed of 2 physical blocks in each group. However, in the area model, the two-dimensional units are a result of the multiplication of 2 one-dimensional units. These differences apply to the mixed numbers depicted in Box 8.22 in the same way. The next section examines unit-related issues in multiplication in further detail.

Box 8.22: Numeracy Versus Area Model of $2\frac{1}{2} \cdot 3\frac{1}{2}$

Numeracy Model

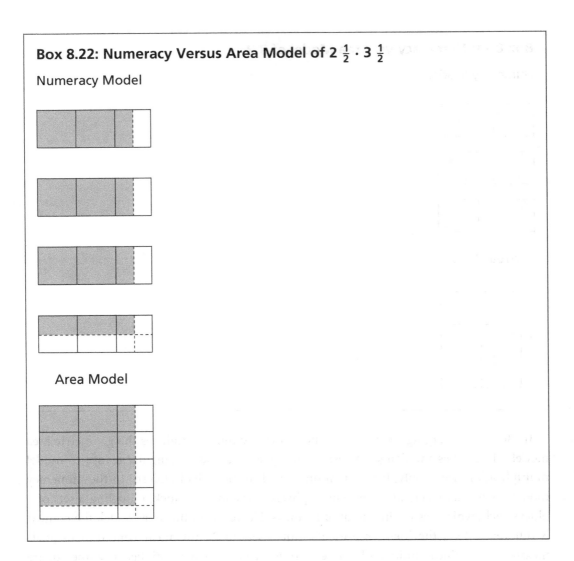

Area Model

The Standard Algorithm: A Conceptual Perspective. Obviously, not all mixed-number multiplications are as simple as $3\frac{1}{2} \cdot 2\frac{1}{2}$. For example, students would probably not be inclined to draw diagrams to find the area of a room $12\frac{5}{6}$ feet by $15\frac{7}{16}$ feet. For this reason, we need standard algorithms, particularly for contexts that involve more complicated numbers. Students need to understand the purpose of algorithms, however, as well as how to use them. In many cases, algorithms are preferred because they are either the most efficient method or can be applied universally. But without a conceptual understanding of multiplication, gained through various models and perspectives, students often see the standard algorithm for multiplying mixed numbers as just another procedure to be memorized—and easily forgotten because it has no meaning. As mentioned, algorithms and similar procedures teach efficiency, not mathematics. It is not enough for students to memorize an algorithm or procedure. Remember our paddling duck? Moreover, because students learn differently, they need to view, explore, and understand processes such as the multiplication of mixed numbers from multiple perspectives.

How can the standard algorithm for multiplying mixed numbers be taught *conceptually* to go beyond mere memorization? The key lies not in the mathematics itself, but in the mathematical language and representation used. For example, emphasizing context, symbolism, and the role of units can illuminate and reinforce for students what naked numbers cannot. As noted, in a fraction, the denominator is not really a numeric value, a concept that can easily confuse students because it differs from whole numbers. Students can easily see the descriptors or units in the statement "2 thirds plus 4 fifths," but in the expression $\frac{2}{3} + \frac{4}{5}$, seeing the denominators as descriptors and not as quantities is more difficult. By reinforcing units and symbolism, such as the nuances of the denominator, teachers can help students conceptually grasp the standard algorithm.

Consider our example problem, $3\frac{1}{2} \cdot 2\frac{1}{2}$. In the standard algorithm, the initial step is to convert the mixed numbers to improper fractions: $3\frac{1}{2}$ becomes $\frac{7}{2}$, and $2\frac{1}{2}$ becomes $\frac{5}{2}$. At this stage, a long neglected question arises—why convert to improper fractions? Do we ever address this question when teaching the standard algorithm? If we combine the area model and the standard algorithm, the answer lies in merging the symbolism, the numerical representation, and the idea of units. In this context, $3\frac{1}{2}$ represents $3\frac{1}{2}$ whole linear units. The improper fraction $\frac{7}{2}$ can be represented as $7 \cdot \frac{1}{2}$, which in turn can be interpreted as a quantity of 7 linear units that are each $\frac{1}{2}$ the length of a whole linear unit. Thus, $\frac{7}{2}$ represents 7 halves, with the understanding that each one is a half linear unit, as shown in Box 8.23.

Box 8.23

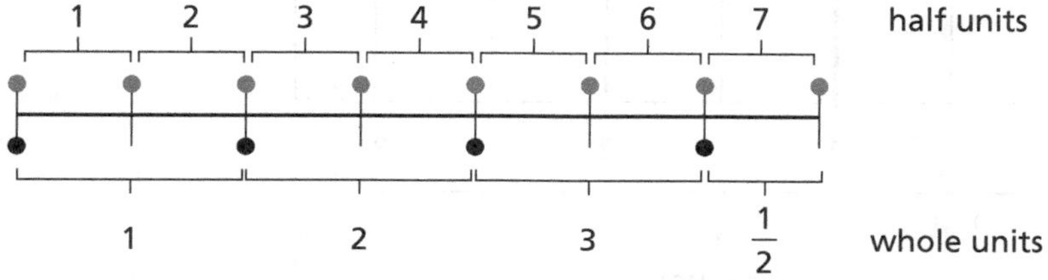

Likewise, $\frac{5}{2}$ is actually 5 halves, or half linear units. This context aligns with the area model, which depicts 7 linear half-units vertically and 5 linear half-units horizontally, as shown in Box 8.24. This unit terminology can get confusing, so let's consider the context to be that of a rectangle with dimensions $3\frac{1}{2}$ inches by $2\frac{1}{2}$ inches. Through the improper fraction conversion, we get $\frac{7}{2} \cdot \frac{5}{2}$, which in this context is a rectangle 7 half-inches by 5 half-inches (the equivalent of a rectangle $3\frac{1}{2}$ inches by $2\frac{1}{2}$ inches). When we multiply, we get a product of $\frac{35}{4}$, but what does that mean? We cannot ignore what happens to the units because they hold the secret to the standard algorithm in an area context!

Box 8.24

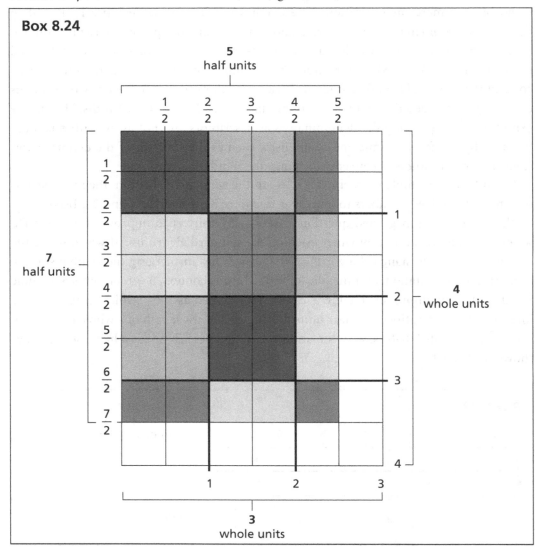

By examining the figure in Box 8.24, students can determine that the rectangle is subdivided into 35 small squares. But what does the 4 in the denominator mean? Note the shading in the diagram: each shade indicates a full or partial unit of 4 smaller squares. We can connect back to the figure in Box 8.20 and determine that in both diagrams, we have a quantity of $8\frac{3}{4}$ "whole" units of 1 square inch, or 1-by-1 squares. Within each 1-by-1 square, each of the 4 smaller squares has a linear dimension of $\frac{1}{2}$ inch by $\frac{1}{2}$ inch. Thus, the 35 small squares are each $\frac{1}{4}$ of a 1-by-1 square, or $\frac{1}{4}$ of a square inch. By seeing $\frac{35}{4}$ as $35 \cdot \frac{1}{4}$ and then as 35 one-fourths, the picture begins to become clearer.

Unit Conversion in an Area Context. By understanding that the linear units are half-inches, we can see how that interpretation produces a 7-by-5 rectangle, as shown in Box 8.24. The rectangle does not have an area of 35 square inches, but rather 35 "quarter-square inches" which are smaller squares that are each $\frac{1}{4}$ the area of one square inch. The algorithm will make sense if students understand that in an area model, it is the *numerators* (7 • 5) that undergo the *quantitative computation*. The multiplication of the two denominators does not result in an actual quantity. Instead, the multiplication of the *denominators* determines the *resulting unit* and actually involves the metamorphosis of the initial units from single-dimensional (linear) to two-dimensional (area) ones. In this example, the multiplication of the denominators, 2 • 2, is really $\frac{1}{2} \cdot \frac{1}{2}$, which equals $\frac{1}{4}$. But keep in mind, the $\frac{1}{4}$ is now a two-dimensional square unit, not a single-dimensional linear one.

Students need to understand that in an area model, the conversion of the unit of measure is actually built into the process in the standard algorithm. The solution, $\frac{35}{4}$, derived from 7 • 5 in the numerator and 2 • 2 in the denominator, makes perfect sense when students interpret the symbolism as 35 square units that are each $\frac{1}{4}$ of 1 square inch. From a symbolic perspective, the typical equation would not make this clear. Examine the equations in Box 8.25.

Box 8.25

$$8\frac{3}{4} = \frac{35}{4}$$

$8\frac{3}{4}$ 1-inch-by-1-inch squares = 35 squares that are $\frac{1}{4}$ the area of a 1-by-1 square

---

As a means to describe the result of the multiplication in our area context, the first equation is nebulous because it is a naked number that leaves us wondering what it describes. The second one shows the actual meaning by providing the units, albeit in a more descriptive fashion than normal. Thus, connecting to units and mathematical symbolism is critical to the effective instruction of the algorithm for multiplying mixed numbers.

Connecting the Dots

In mathematics, using multiple perspectives and making connections among them benefits students in several ways. A student who understands a concept or process from one perspective can leverage that knowledge to explore the concept or process from other perspectives. In turn, linking different perspectives deepens a student's understanding and supplements the learning of related concepts. A simple problem such as $3\frac{1}{2} \cdot 2\frac{1}{2}$ may not look like a rich source of instruction on the surface. But by examining the problem from multiple perspectives, an expert teacher can use it as a powerful vehicle for explaining concepts and linking ideas. In this example, a key learning opportunity was the common pattern of partial products across the three models. This pattern enables students to literally see the $8\frac{3}{4}$ solution without any of the calculations in the standard algorithm. For visual learners, seeing what's happening can help explain where and how a solution "magically" appears.

A mixed approach helps ensure that students understand the mathematical language and symbolism as an integral part of learning the standard algorithm for multiplying mixed numbers. The result should be a deeper knowledge of the algorithm, one that is not so standard. The algorithm will mean something to students because they will understand why it works. Taught alone, none of these approaches may give students a clear picture of what it means to multiply two mixed numbers. However, by examining several perspectives together, students will find it easier to see the big picture and make critical connections that reinforce each other. In addition, teaching from different perspectives increases the probability that each student will master the topic, because one of the alternative approaches may be better suited to his or her learning style. The power lies in the multiple perspectives and their ability, when combined, to elevate procedural fluency to conceptual understanding.

DIVIDING FRACTIONS

For many people, division with fractions is the calculus of arithmetic because it involves not only what is typically the most difficult of the four operations but also rational numbers, arguably the most problematic subset of the real numbers. Unfortunately, division with fractions is yet another topic that is often treated as a magical process in traditional math instruction. Students are taught to invert and multiply, with the understanding that the process is performed that way because of some ruling decreed long ago. And, as should be no surprise, a number of acronyms and memory aids have been invented to pile on another layer of content for students to learn. As we've seen, in mathematics, more is often less. We give students ever more things to remember, but it does not ensure greater understanding and can result in less. For example, one of the acronyms to help remember how to divide fractions is KFC: **K**eep the dividend, **F**lip the divisor over, and **C**hange the sign from division to multiplication. Based on the fried chicken chain, the acronym is cute and can be quite helpful. However, it doesn't provide students with a single clue as to why the process works or what concepts are involved. For real conceptual understanding, students need to see what is going on under the water with this duck.

Division Contexts

In Chapter One, the problem $10 \div \frac{1}{2}$ was used to illustrate the immense language problem involved in the interpretation of the popular expression *goes into*. In the absence of any context, it is almost incomprehensible that a student could realistically make sense of the question, How many times does $\frac{1}{2}$ go into 10? To address this issue, one of the basic ideas teachers need to explain is that division can model different contexts, even though the process may be the same. *Partitive* (sharing) division occurs when the total and the number of groups or sets are known, and the task is to find the unknown size of each group or set. A possible context would be if you have $15 and you want to figure out how to divide it equally among 3 people. *Quotative* (measurement) division occurs when the total and the size of the groups or sets are known, and the task is to find the number of groups. A possible context would be if you have 20 cookies and you want to figure out how many gift bags of 4 cookies each you can make.

Many people consider quotative division to be the easier context. For example, consider the problem $10 \div \frac{1}{2}$ in response to the question, How many half-pizzas are there in 10 whole pizzas? In this case, we know the total and size of each set and need to find the unknown number of sets. The problem could be solved visually by drawing 10 pizzas, cutting each in half, and then counting the halves to get 20 half-pizzas. Because the units are included in the solution, students are less likely to be confused, as they often are more familiar with the typical whole-number scenario in which the quotient is smaller than the total. In addition, this visual approach indicates that $10 \div \frac{1}{2}$ somehow transformed into $10 \cdot 2$. However, how this transformation occurred remains a mystery.

Why Invert and Multiply?

Understanding the process of division by a fraction is based on answering two key questions:

1. Why do we change the division to multiplication?

2. Why do we invert and multiply by the reciprocal and not by some other number?

Using a Pattern Approach. Teachers often use patterns as a strategy to uncover meaning or provide understanding. Box 8.26 lists several quotative division problems for students to solve with pictorial models.

Box 8.26

Solve using pictures:

Problem	Dividend	Divisor	Quotient
$4 \div \frac{1}{3}$	4	$\frac{1}{3}$	12
$2 \div \frac{1}{5}$	2	$\frac{1}{5}$	10
$6 \div \frac{1}{4}$	6	$\frac{1}{4}$	24
$5 \div \frac{1}{2}$	5	$\frac{1}{2}$	10
$3 \div \frac{1}{7}$	3	$\frac{1}{7}$	21

Over the course of the problems, students should notice the pattern where the solution is a product of the dividend and the reciprocal of the divisor. For example, $4 \div \frac{1}{3}$ resulted in 12, which can be expressed as $4 \cdot 3$. The problems all used divisors where the numerator of the proper fraction was one.

Does the pattern continue if the numerator of the proper fraction is a number other than 1? Obviously the answer is yes, and teachers can lead students through several examples. Box 8.27 provides one sample problem, $4 \div \frac{2}{3}$, and a possible visual representation. The drawing consists of 4 equal-sized rectangles, each divided into 3 equal parts of which $\frac{2}{3}$ is shaded. The shaded areas are labeled to count each set of $\frac{2}{3}$. However, four unshaded $\frac{1}{3}$s remain. Combining the 2 unshaded $\frac{1}{3}$s from the first two rectangles (e + e) with the 2 unshaded $\frac{1}{3}$s from the last two rectangles (f + f) and then adding those to the other 4 sets of $\frac{2}{3}$ produces a solution of 6. The relationship here is more difficult to see than in

152 The Problem with Math Is English

Box 8.26, but the pattern remains that the dividend should be multiplied by the reciprocal of the divisor.

Box 8.27

$4 \div \frac{2}{3}$

Draw a picture to solve. Explain your results.

$$4 \div \frac{2}{3}$$

$$a + a = \frac{2}{3}$$

$$b + b = \frac{2}{3}$$

$$c + c = \frac{2}{3}$$

$$d + d = \frac{2}{3}$$

$$e + e = \frac{2}{3}$$

$$f + f = \frac{2}{3}$$

Testing the Hypothesis.   Once students understand the pattern, the next step is to test the hypothesis. In this case we need to see if we get the same result from $4 \cdot \frac{3}{2}$ (Box 8.28) as we did from $4 \div \frac{2}{3}$ by using a visual approach (Box 8.27). The answer derived from the computation in Figure 8.28 is the same, showing that dividing a number is equivalent to multiplying by the reciprocal of the divisor.

Box 8.28

$$4 \cdot \frac{3}{2} = \frac{4}{1} \cdot \frac{3}{2} = \frac{4 \cdot 3}{1 \cdot 2} = \frac{12}{2} = 6$$

The hypothesis seems to be true, but from a mathematics standpoint, it must be proven algebraically to work for all numbers, as shown in Box 8.29. In this process, the initial expression is changed to a complex fraction. The primary reason for multiplying by $\frac{d}{c}$ in the next step is to simplify the denominator to 1. The initial expression was $\left(\frac{a}{b}\right) \div \left(\frac{c}{d}\right)$ and the expression that resulted was $\left(\frac{a}{b}\right) \bullet \left(\frac{c}{d}\right)$ which algebraically says that dividing a number is equivalent to multiplying by the reciprocal of the divisor.

Box 8.29

$b \neq 0,\ c \neq 0,\ d \neq 0$

$$\frac{a}{b} \div \frac{c}{d}$$

$$= \frac{\frac{a}{b}}{\frac{c}{d}}$$

$$= \frac{\frac{a}{b} \bullet \frac{d}{c}}{\frac{c}{d} \bullet \frac{d}{c}}$$

$$= \frac{\frac{ad}{bc}}{\frac{cd}{dc}}$$

$$= \frac{\frac{ad}{bc}}{1}$$

$$= \frac{a}{b} \bullet \frac{d}{c}$$

The Reciprocal Secret Revealed.   The informal proof using patterns and computation along with the formal algebraic proof seem to justify that dividing is the same as multiplying by the reciprocal. However, there is still that lingering question of why the reciprocal? I kept pondering this question and took my own advice; investigate the language and relationships involved and do not be overly concerned about the types of numbers involved. Start with the very general case of a division problem. Refer to Box 8.30.

Box 8.30

t = dividend d = Divisor q = Quotient

$t \div d = q$

$t \bullet \frac{1}{d} = q$

$\frac{1}{d} = \frac{q}{t}$

Because the quest for relationships centers on the reciprocal of the divisor, the equation is converted in such a way as to get $\frac{1}{d}$. As the focus is on relationships, the resulting equation should be interpreted as a proportion. The result is one of those "aha" moments. The reciprocal of the divisor turns out to be the ratio of the quotient to the dividend, which is typically the total. A ratio is not meaningful unless we know what is being compared, so enter the role of language! In this case, the items or units being compared constitute the language involved. It usually takes numeric examples and context to solidify the understanding of an abstract idea, so an examination of typical division contexts is in order.

Refer back to the problem and solution for Boxes 8.27 and 8.28. The solution, 6, is a naked number. The unit of measure was deliberately omitted (which should not happen in an instructional setting!). For simplicity, consider the new problem $4 \div \frac{1}{3}$ in a quotative context of division. Box 8.31 provides a visual representation.

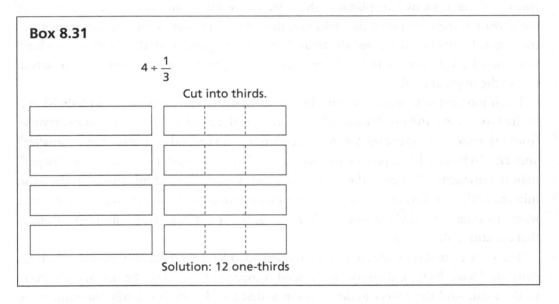

Box 8.31

$4 \div \dfrac{1}{3}$

Cut into thirds.

Solution: 12 one-thirds

Note that the figure includes two sets of 4 rectangles. The set on the left has *ones* as the unit of reference, while the set on the right has *one-thirds* as the unit of reference. In comparing the right-hand set to the left-hand set, we get a ratio of 12 one-thirds to 4 ones. This is the ratio of the quotient to the dividend, which in simplified form is a ratio of $\frac{3}{1}$. In terms of this context, there are three ($\frac{3}{1}$) times as many *one-thirds* as *ones* in a quantity of 4. Notice that the ratio $\frac{3}{1}$ is the reciprocal of the divisor, $\frac{1}{3}$. Repeating this process with other numbers will produce the same pattern.

Now, refer to the expression $4 \div \frac{2}{3}$ in Box 8.27. Again, given a quotative context of division, simply by inspecting the expression, we know there are one-and-one-half times ($\frac{3}{2}$) as many two-thirds in 4 as ones. The ratio of quotient to dividend gives a ratio of $\frac{6}{4}$, which in simplest form gives $\frac{3}{2}$ which is the reciprocal of the divisor. However, the key is to make note of the units. In this scenario the ratio was 6 *two-thirds* to 4 *ones*. This relationship should hold true in quotative division contexts that involve whole numbers. For example, in the expression $30 \div 5$, the quotient-dividend ratio ($\frac{6}{30}$) in simplest form is $\frac{1}{5}$.

To generalize, in a quotative division context, the typical quotient-dividend comparison would be the number of groups to the total. And the covert understanding is that the divisor is actually the size of the group, which will be the unit associated with the number of groups. Revisit the problem $10 \div \frac{1}{2}$ that models the task to find how many (number of groups) half-pizzas (size of the group) there are in 10 whole pizzas (total with a unit of one). Without a visual model as before, students already know that there will be two ($\frac{2}{1}$) times as many half-pizzas as there are whole pizzas. In essence, the reciprocal of the divisor is the *scale factor* that tells you the ratio of the new units for the quotient to the original units that described the total. This is true regardless of the numbers involved. For example, if the divisor is $2\frac{1}{2}$ ($\frac{5}{2}$), we know we will have $\frac{2}{5}$ as many sets of $2\frac{1}{2}$ as sets of one in the original total.

It is important to focus on the units involved. Students' early experience with division is limited to whole numbers. Those will typically be with naked numbers; thus one carryover from this experience is the mistaken impression that division always results in a "smaller" answer. Division with a proper fraction is confusing because the quotient is "larger" than the dividend. However, the continuous inclusion of units eliminates or at the least, minimizes that confusion. Cutting 10 whole pizzas into 20 half-pizzas makes sense because when a whole is subdivided into smaller pieces, the result is a greater number of pieces that constitute that whole.

The same notions of scale factor and quotient-dividend ratio apply in partitive division contexts. Here, the typical quotient-dividend comparison would be the size of each group to the total. And the covert understanding is that the divisor is actually the number of groups. A whole number example would be a context where 20 cookies are to be shared equally by 5 persons, and the task is to find how many cookies each person would get. The expression here would be $20 \div 5$ and the quotient would yield the size of the group, the equal share of 4 each. The reciprocal of the divisor is the *scale factor* that tells you the ratio of the number of groups for the quotient to the number of groups in the total. The quirk is that the total is composed of *one* group, so the total is also the size of the group. Thus, a sensible interpretation in a shared division context is that the reciprocal of the divisor is the scale factor that compares the size of each new set to the size of the total. For this problem, students would already know that the size of each group will be $\frac{1}{5}$ as large as the total. If we wanted to divide a quantity of 20 into $2\frac{1}{2}$ sets, then the size of each set needs to be $\frac{2}{5}$ the size of the total.

A Partitive Warning.   Understanding division is problematic in a partitive division context when the divisor is a *proper fraction*, as opposed to a whole number. A real-life scenario would be one in which a person has \$10, but that amount is only $\frac{1}{4}$ of what is needed to buy a desired object. In such a context, the correct mathematical expression is $10 \div \frac{1}{4}$, where 10 is the total and $\frac{1}{4}$ is the number of sets. Intuitively, we know we need 4 times the amount of money that is on hand, translating the expression to $10 \cdot 4$ that results in 40. The interpretation in a partitive division context is that the reciprocal of the divisor is the scale factor that compares the size of each new set to the size of the total. However, we have a scenario where the size of the new set is 40 and the size of the total is 10 which understandably causes confusion as to what exactly is the *total*.

In a partitive division context, the divisor represents the number of sets or parts. If that divisor is a proper fraction, it indicates that the dividend, which is normally the total, constitutes less than one full set. But we typically think of the total as one full set. One argument is that this is really a quotative context because the $\frac{1}{4}$ is the size of each set, not the number of sets. But the resulting \$40 in a quotative context is the number of groups, not the total—confusing indeed. A more mathematically correct quotative division scenario for $10 \div \frac{1}{4}$ would be one where you have \$10 and you wanted to know how many quarters that would be. In that case the \$10 truly is the total, the size of each set is $\frac{1}{4}$, and the number of sets is 40. The most sensible approach to the original context is to consider the \$10 as a partial total in the same way that $\frac{1}{4}$ is a partial set. Thus, the quotient of \$40 is actually the total, not the original \$10. When the divisor is a proper fraction, seeing the dividend as a partial total and the divisor as a partial set is somewhat of a departure from other partitive division contexts, but it does make those contexts more clear for students.

The quandary in a partitive division context with a proper fraction as the divisor can also be resolved by altering our perspective and focusing on the relationship, which leads to a proportion. For example, in a partitive division context modeled by $12 \div \frac{3}{4}$, the 12 constitutes a quantity that is $\frac{3}{4}$ of a whole set. To avoid confusion, it may be appropriate to model this context with a proportion, such as that shown in Box 8.32, where each ratio is the quantity in the set (numerator) compared to the number of sets (denominator), making Y the quantity in one full set as indicated by 1 in the denominator.

Performing the computation above results in $\frac{48}{3}$, which simplifies to a full set of 16. The quotient–dividend ratio ($\frac{16}{12}$) is equivalent to the reciprocal of the divisor ($\frac{4}{3}$) which in turn is the scale factor that says the size of a full set (16) is $\frac{4}{3}$ the size of $\frac{3}{4}$ of a set (12).

Yet another twist would be to combine the scale factor with the idea of a whole. Given that the scale factor of $\frac{4}{3}$ is greater than 1, we can visualize starting with a smaller whole and building to a larger one. Refer to Box 8.33 and let the shaded area be the original whole divided into 3 parts. By adding another third, the new larger whole will be $\frac{4}{3}$ of the original. The original whole was 12, so we can calculate that each third is 4. Knowing that all the parts must be 4, we get 4 • 4, which is 16.

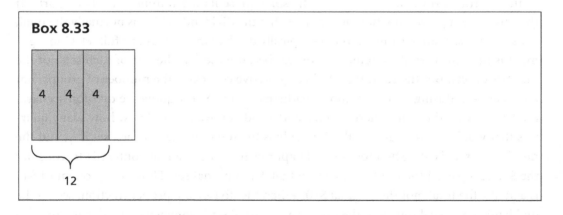

Box 8.33

The knowledge of the reciprocal being the scale factor also aids students' proficiency at estimation and evaluating the reasonableness of a solution. In the above context, realizing that 12 constitutes only part of a whole set enables students to recognize the fallacy of using $12 \cdot \frac{3}{4}$ to model the problem because that expression will yield a solution that is less than 12, not larger. By combining the knowledge in this chapter with an understanding of the language of math and a flexible interpretation of the symbolism, a student has multiple approaches for solving fractions in different contexts.

Making It Real.   To focus on the concepts being discussed, the division examples up to this point have all had whole numbers as dividends for simplicity. Once students gain a solid understanding of these concepts, however, teachers can begin using more complex examples that include proper fractions and mixed numbers as dividends. At the same time, students need to practice with real-life models or contexts. Repeated practice will enable students to take on tasks such as explaining the difference between dividing by 2 and dividing by $\frac{1}{2}$, or the difference between multiplying by $\frac{1}{2}$ and dividing by $\frac{1}{2}$. Box 8.34 lists some real-life problems that will help students build proficiency and understanding:

Box 8.34

A. Quotative Model of Dividing by a Fraction

1. How many $\frac{1}{2}$-foot lengths are in an object $5\frac{3}{4}$ feet long?

2. Given $\frac{1}{3}$ apple per serving size, how many servings will $4\frac{1}{2}$ apples provide?

3. A team of workers can construct $1\frac{2}{5}$ miles of road each day. How many days will it take them to construct $6\frac{3}{10}$ miles of road?

B. Partitive Model of Dividing by a Fraction

4. A construction site has $1\frac{1}{4}$ tons of bricks on hand, which is $\frac{2}{3}$ the amount needed for a job. What is the total amount of bricks needed for the job?

5. A train goes uphill from station A to station B and downhill from station B to A. The train takes $1\frac{3}{4}$ hours to go from station B to A. This amount of time is $\frac{3}{5}$ the amount it takes to go from station A to B. How long does it take to go from station A to B?

6. A farm has $15\frac{1}{4}$ acres planted in corn. The corn field is $\frac{3}{4}$ the size of the cotton field. How big is the cotton field?

CONCLUSION

Operations with fractions, especially multiplication and division, can frustrate and bewilder students until their heads spin. However, mastery of these operations is possible when a strong understanding of the concept of fractions is coupled with a knowledge of the nuances of the symbolism, the units of reference, and the contextual variation of the whole. Making connections among these factors is critical. These connections enable students to understand concepts such as why division by a fraction is equivalent to multiplying by the reciprocal of the divisor. Without such connections and without a focus on the symbolism and language, students have only a handful of meaningless acronyms such as KFC and rhymes, such as "yours is not to reason why, just invert and multiply." The duck does not magically float across the water because of the wind. Students need the aquarium view where they understand what happens under the surface.

Unlocking the Power of Symbolism and Visual Representation

Mathematics involves the extensive use of symbolism and visual representation. Therefore, being able to interpret and translate these elements is essential for conceptual understanding. In a way, mathematics is like a treasure map. Students must decipher the symbols, follow the hidden clues, and read between the lines to find the buried meaning. The eyes provide the means to read the map in the same way as conceptual understanding provides the vision to read the math landscape. But this ability to interpret the concept map does not come easily or naturally. Fluency with mathematical symbolism and visual representation is a learned skill, requiring focused instruction and repeated practice. In students' quest for understanding, symbols and visuals can serve as signs leading the way—or as pitfalls of confusion and misdirection. This chapter examines some common problems related to symbols, graphs, and geometric figures and explores how to help students develop skillful interpretation of these elements, thereby unlocking their full power.

SYMBOLISM

Although people tend to associate mathematics more with numbers, symbols beyond numerals are clearly a major component as well. In fact, one of the more daunting tasks in math education is changing the perspective of mathematics to a discipline that is dependent on language, and this language includes a wide array of symbols that require focused instruction and practice for skillful interpretation. Much to students' loss, however, K–12 instruction in the United States has not traditionally emphasized symbolism to the extent needed. As previous chapters have mentioned, shallow knowledge limits the interpretation of symbolism which can lead to numerous problems for students. The following examples delve into some of these problems, including how the inappropriate use of symbols can make them worse. The text then illustrates how developing a deep understanding of mathematical symbolism is bolstered by in-depth understanding of concepts. This combination gives students greater power to make conceptual connections, interpret mathematical language, and view concepts and processes from multiple perspectives.

Weak Symbolism = Weak Understanding

One problem that leads to a shallow knowledge of concepts is the tendency of traditional math instruction to resort to shortcuts even with the use of symbols. Repeated use can erode symbols' meaning or lead to misconceptions. For example, consider the Pythagorean theorem, which describes the relationship among the three sides of a right triangle. An informal survey of U.S. adults would likely indicate that many people understand this theorem as $a^2 + b^2 = c^2$ (see the left-hand triangle in Box 9.1). This standard symbolic representation of the theorem—a shortcut, really—is well-intended but is a representation that neither provides nor promotes conceptual understanding. What's more, the equation involves several assumptions. Given that equation alone, how do we know it refers to a right triangle, or to any type of triangle for that matter? And how do we know that the variables represent the exact context in the left triangle of Box 9.1? Simply rearranging the a, b, and c in that triangle would make it a false statement. What is a student to do if confronted with a triangle that has different labels, such as y, z, and g, as shown on the right in Box 9.1? Because of the multiple limitations, $a^2 + b^2 = c^2$ as an explanation of the Pythagorean theorem can seriously harm understanding.

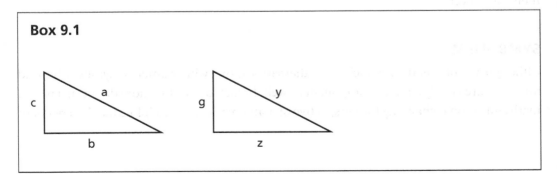

Box 9.1

To establish a strong conceptual foundation of the Pythagorean theorem, and its standard symbolic representation, a teacher should start with a simple but deep definition: "In a right triangle, the square of the hypotenuse is the same quantity as the sum of the squares of the two legs of the triangle." Although symbols are essential components of mathematical language, they must be used in such a way as to not erode meaning or understanding. Teachers need to provide students with a clear definition and solid understanding of the Pythagorean theorem. The only reason to ever introduce $a^2 + b^2 = c^2$ would be to emphasize that it is not a valid definition, to ensure that students are aware of how others might refer to the Pythagorean theorem, and to recognize that the left triangle in Box 9.1 is the only context where that equation holds true. In addition, defining the Pythagorean theorem as $a^2 + b^2 = c^2$ totally disregards the fact that the Pythagorean theorem is applicable only to a *right* triangle. That limited equation virtually eliminates students' recognition and utilization of the converse of the Pythagorean theorem, which states that if the square of the hypotenuse of a triangle is the same quantity as the sum of the squares of the two legs, then that triangle must be a right triangle. Note that recognition of the fallacy of $a^2 + b^2 = c^2$ is possible only because of the in-depth understanding of the concept.

Symbolism and Conceptual Connections

A second problem related to symbolism involves the complex interaction of knowledge in mathematics. This interaction requires students to make connections among many concepts and processes—including the symbolism. In some cases, if students have a shallow understanding of a given concept and the nuances of the associated symbols, they will not be able to make some key interpretations. The result can be a domino effect of limited understanding that can seriously hamper students later in higher-level math classes such as Algebra 2 or Calculus. Two examples include the pi symbol (π) and the equal sign ($=$).

Pi: More Than a Number. In Chapter Seven, a scenario illustrated how the circumference formula for a circle ($C = d \cdot \pi$) can be rewritten as $\pi = \frac{C}{d}$. Understanding π conceptually as the relationship of the circumference to the diameter enables students to recognize that $\pi = \frac{C}{d}$ symbolically expresses the definition of π. A conceptual understanding of π as more than the number 3.14 is essential to grasp this connection. With such an understanding, students can recognize that π as an irrational number that is approximated by 3.14, by definition, cannot be expressed as the rational number $\frac{C}{d}$ if it is a *quantity*.

Thus, the equation $\pi = \frac{C}{d}$ as the definition is actually an alternate interpretation of the equal sign as expressing an equivalent relationship.

Thus, having a conceptual understanding of π as a relationship, versus just being a number, is a powerful tool that can help students bridge fundamental topics. As always, developing this type of understanding begins with a simple yet deep definition. Examine Box 9.2, which shows one common visual representation of π.

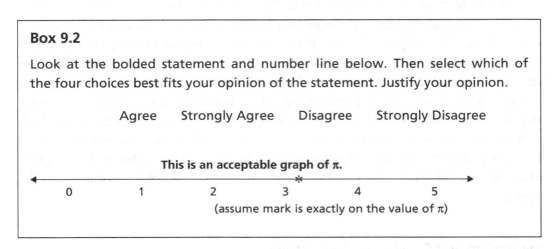

Box 9.2

Look at the bolded statement and number line below. Then select which of the four choices best fits your opinion of the statement. Justify your opinion.

Agree   Strongly Agree   Disagree   Strongly Disagree

This is an acceptable graph of π.

0   1   2   3   4   5

(assume mark is exactly on the value of π)

Teachers should disagree with the statement if they want their students to develop a conceptual understanding of π. The number line focuses on the numeric value of 3.14, which unfortunately, is the only meaning many people have of π. However, a deep understanding of π has at its core the simple yet deep definition that "π is the *relationship* of the circumference of a circle to its diameter." Therefore, a better visualization for π is a two-dimensional graph, because it can visually represent a *relationship* between two variables. Box 9.3 presents π shown on a coordinate graph, with the circumference as the dependent variable and the diameter as the independent variable. The result is a line that has coordinates with approximate values such as (1, 3.14), (2, 6.28), (3, 9.42), and so on. The line has a slope of $\frac{c}{d}$, which numerically is approximately 3.14. There is a connection here to the fraction kingdom discussed in Chapter Seven. Notice the merger of the ideas of ratio and slope because they both express relationships, with the slope expressing the relationship relative to the change in the circumference to the change in the diameter.

Box 9.3

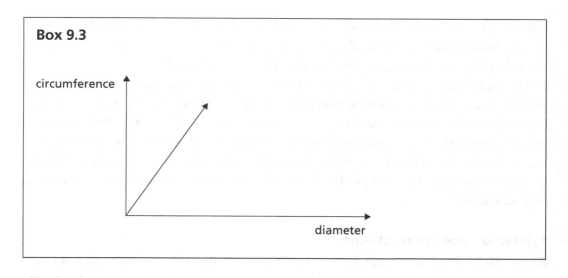

Equal Sign: Reading Between the Lines.   The equal sign can also serve as a powerful link to other mathematical concepts, but only with a conceptual understanding of the symbol. As an example, think back to Chapter Four, where a logarithm was defined simply yet deeply as an exponent. An aspect not explored at that time was how this definition is hidden within the equation that represents a logarithm. Consider an exponential equation such as $2^x = 30$. This same equation when converted to logarithmic form reads $\log_2 30 = x$. If we temporarily disregard the numeric values, we can focus on the bolded fundamental components, $\mathbf{\log_2}\ 30 = x$. Thus, the equation basically says that the logarithm $= x$. Because x represented the exponent in the original equation, the basic translation can be made that the logarithm *is* the exponent, in simple terms. This reasoning, however, required that we read between the lines and understand that an equation can actually be the symbolic version of a relationship, as was the case with $\pi = \frac{C}{d}$, or the symbolic representation of a definition as shown with a logarithm.

Equations are sentences in mathematics that can communicate important messages, but those messages arise only from skillful interpretation of the symbolism. But just as a sentence has little meaning if one does not know the definitions of the words that constitute it, an equation has little meaning without an astute knowledge of the symbols involved. Chapter Four noted that younger students often read an equation such as $a - b = a + (-b)$ with no understanding. With insight and practice, students can learn to interpret the equation as stating that subtracting two numbers ($a - b$) is the same as ($=$) adding the opposite of the second addend [+ (−b)] to the initial addend (a). However, the linchpin to that understanding is the flexible interpretation of the symbol "−" as subtracting on one side of the equation and as "the opposite of" on the other side.

The equal sign is also an integral component in the symbolic expression of the multiplication process. Astute teachers and students realize that the reason the two expressions in an equation such as 4 • 5 = 2 • 10 are equivalent is that they both represent the same quantity. At the same time, internalized in that realization is the understanding that although the totals are the same, each expression physically represents a different grouping or context. For example, the given equation could represent a context involving four nickels and two dimes.

Symbolism and Interpretation

Superficial knowledge of a concept can also prevent students from interpreting nuances in the associated symbol's meaning and from distinguishing subtle but distinct differences in its use. Chapters Seven and Eight illustrated a multitude of problems involving fractions as a result of confusion arising from the symbolic representation. To avoid such problems, students (and teachers alike) need to develop flexibility in their perspectives and interpretations of fractions. For example, Chapter Eight examined the problem $\frac{3}{4} \cdot \frac{2}{5}$ (see Box 8.12). Students need to recognize that this type of context, involving the multiplication of two proper fractions, results in the product of a fraction that has a *whole of 1*.

One critical facet of fraction symbolism not explored yet is the confusion that can result because of the fraction bar. Examine Box 9.4.

Box 9.4

$$\frac{a+b}{c+d} \qquad \frac{a}{c} + \frac{b}{d}$$

The two expressions shown in Box 9.4 are not equivalent, but the similarity in the symbolism can easily cause students to miss the subtle difference. To help students gain a deeper understanding of the symbolism and how these expressions differ, teachers can apply an alternative perspective by using different symbolism to represent the two expressions. For example, the expression on the left can be rewritten using the division sign (÷) rather than the fraction bar, producing the following: (a + b) ÷ (c + d). This approach clearly indicates that the expression involves only *one division*, with a dividend of (a + b) and a divisor of (c + d). From a mathematical perspective, this expression will yield the quotient of the two sums. Using the same approach with the expression on the right, we get the following: (a ÷ c) + (b ÷ d). Clearly, this expression involves *two divisions*. From a mathematical perspective, it will yield the sum of the two quotients.

To further illustrate how the two expressions are not equivalent, a teacher can substitute values for the variables. This process will yield a different result for each, clarifying the critical distinction in the symbolism for students. Box 9.5 illustrates this less algebraic approach.

Box 9.5

$$\frac{2+2+2}{3+3+3} \quad \text{versus} \quad \frac{2}{3} + \frac{2}{3} + \frac{2}{3}$$

Using the same process as in Box 9.4, the left-hand expression becomes $(2 + 2 + 2) \div (3 + 3 + 3)$, while the right-hand expression becomes $(2 \div 3) + (2 \div 3) + (2 \div 3)$. Solving the two new expressions reveals they are not equivalent. The first equals $\frac{6}{9}$, while the second equals $\frac{6}{3}$. Exercises such as these will serve as computation drill; but more important, they will instill in students the distinct differences in the symbolism. Unless teachers focus on interpreting nuances and subtle distinctions in symbolism, as shown in this case, students' confusion regarding these nuances and distinctions may not become apparent or ever be addressed.

Symbolism and Perspective

A shallow understanding of concepts can also deny students the power to view the symbolism from alternative perspectives that in turn alter the interpretation. As shown in Chapter Eight, understanding a topic from multiple viewpoints provides several benefits, such as enabling students to understand different meanings and contexts for the associated symbolism and to make connections that might not otherwise have been clear. The converse is also applicable in that alternate perspectives of the symbolism or visual representations can affect the understanding of a topic.

Focusing on symbolism, one example is the simple interest formula. This formula is expressed as $I = P \cdot R \cdot T$, where I is the simple interest, P is the loan principal, R is the annual interest rate as a decimal, and T is the time in years. Most adults are familiar with this common financial formula. But the standard order of the variables in this formula, which may or may not be deliberate, has the unintended result of masking the full amount paid in interest. Consider a car loan at 7% annual interest for 5 years. A borrower may pay little attention to the full cost of this interest over time. But suppose a student has the foresight to manipulate the formula, changing the order to $I = R \cdot T \cdot P$. With the known variables computed, the formula now becomes $I = 35\% \cdot P$. This perspective more clearly shows borrowers that they are actually paying 35% interest, not 7%, when time is factored in with the interest rate! Being able to see this perspective, though, requires the knowledge that the formula can be manipulated in this way by applying the commutative property; and that knowledge, in turn, requires a deep understanding of the meaning of each symbol in the formula. Indeed, students gain real power when they understand mathematics symbolism, even if all it involves is changing the order of the symbols to gain a different perspective.

VISUAL REPRESENTATION

In addition to language and symbolism, mathematics has a third major component: visual representation. Invariably, students will be faced with mathematical problems or tasks that necessitate interpreting visual representations, such as graphs and geometric figures. These visuals are often an integral part of the problem or context, and students must be fully fluent in their use and interpretation. As with symbolism, teachers need to provide focused instruction and repeated practice to ensure that students gain visual fluency in mathematics.

Interpreting Graphs

Graphs are a common but critically important form of visual representation in mathematics (as well as in many other disciplines). To progress successfully in math, students must master the major types of graphs, including their specialized symbolism. This mastery includes not only reading graphs but also creating them by presenting mathematical ideas in graphical form. And just as with symbolism, graphs carry certain subtleties and nuances that students must fully understand to accurately interpret and present graphical information. Many resources are available that cover graphs. As a result, the following examples focus on how to help students develop a conceptual understanding of some of the key nuances and subtleties related to graphs.

Graphing Real-Life Contexts. Mastery of two-dimensional graphs using the coordinate plane is a non-negotiable skill if students are to be successful in algebra. Creating these types of graphs, which is the more common task students face, requires the skill to identify the dependent and independent variables, determine the proper scale for each axis, and ensure that equal intervals are maintained on each axis. Box 9.6 presents a typical graphing activity students might receive as well as a typical student response.

Box 9.6

You have just put a bag of popcorn in the microwave. Sketch a simple, single quadrant graph that tells the story of the popcorn and the "pops" heard as time elapsed in the process.

Sample Student Response:

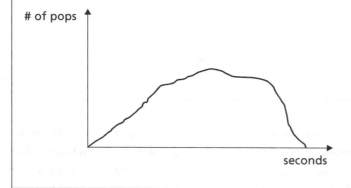

On the plus side, the student's graph is correctly labeled regarding the variables. Also, in general, it illustrates the popping process accurately. The kernels begin to pop at a slow rate, crescendo to a faster rate, drop to a slower rate, and then decline until they eventually stop, as indicated by the data line intersecting the x axis.

However, the graph includes two critical mistakes that illustrate a failure to understand some of the nuances involved. First, the data line begins at the origin, which indicates that the popping began immediately after turning on the microwave. In actuality, a few seconds pass before the first pops occur. Second, the data line is solid. The use of solid lines in coordinate plane graphs is commonplace, and from a pure mathematical standpoint, solid lines represent an equation or function. However, from the perspective of what happens in real life, the solid line in this scenario indicates continuous time and that the pops occurred at infinitesimally small increments—which is not realistically possible.

Box 9.7 presents a more accurate graph of the popcorn popping process. Time is allowed to pass before the first pops are heard, and a discrete line provides a more realistic depiction of the number of pops heard over the time shown. These are not insignificant details because everything in a visual communicates something. Students need guidance and experience to be attuned to all that a graph communicates.

Box 9.7

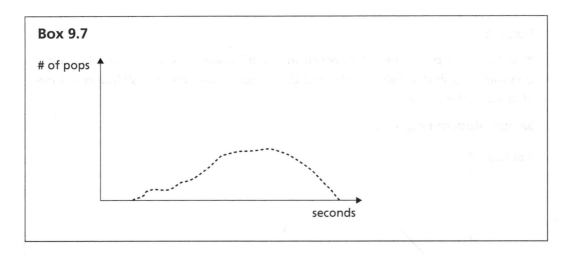

Students can avoid the types of errors in the previous example if they develop an understanding of what each specific part of a graph communicates mathematically and connect those ideas with real life. For example, suppose a man weighs 240 pounds and decides to diet with the goal of losing 8 pounds per month. An equation that models this context would be W = 240 − 8M, where W is the new weight and M is the number of months. A common practice is to graph this context as a single equation resulting in one line segment. However, this is problematic. First, it is highly unlikely that the man's weight loss will be exactly 8 pounds every single month. Second, the diet cannot go on indefinitely. If we substituted 20 for the number of months, the man would weigh 80 pounds, truly a skeleton of his former self! And just like the popcorn context, the graph should actually be a discrete line to reflect reality.

Such issues can be learning opportunities that teachers can utilize, such as more clearly defining the weight-loss goal as an *average* of 8 pounds per month. The reality that the man could not lose weight indefinitely would be an opportunity for a teacher to introduce the notion of restricting the domain or range of a function. In this case, that equation would be applicable to the point where he reaches his target weight, thus the need to restrict the possible values for the x (time) and y (weight) variables. After the ideal weight is reached, the equation would become a constant such as y = 180 and the graph would be a horizontal line from that point onward.

What is important is that students know that sometimes graphs in math will not be a true reflection of reality. Math instruction in such courses as Algebra typically focuses on abstract mathematics that involves real numbers as the set of numbers used. In the weight loss scenario, having an infinite number of possibilities results in the graph in Box 9.8 even though the reality might be better expressed by the graph in Box 9.9. Students are expected to provide mathematically founded solutions or visuals, but students who truly understand what the visuals communicate will understand the distinctions and differences that a reality-based representation would look like.

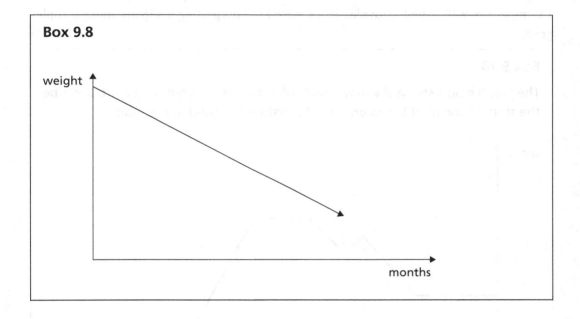

Box 9.8

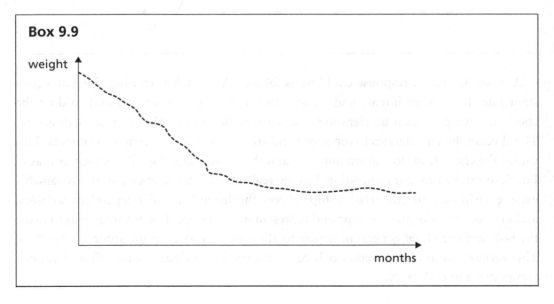

Box 9.9

Graphing in Reverse: The Devil Is in the Details. Students also need to get adequate experience with the reversed process of interpreting the information in a graph in order to "tell the story" that the visual communicates. In addition, teachers need to ensure that younger students learn to interpret more complex graphs because textbooks tend to use simple graphs that consist of one line or curve rather than multiple line segments or curves. Examine Box 9.10, which provides an exercise for interpreting a slightly more complex graph.

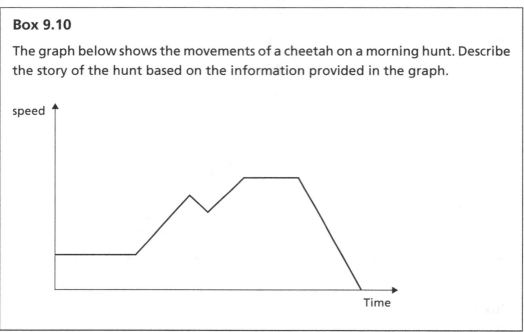

Box 9.10

The graph below shows the movements of a cheetah on a morning hunt. Describe the story of the hunt based on the information provided in the graph.

A possible student response could be as follows: A cheetah is trotting along at a constant rate. It spots an impala and chases after it. The impala swerves and so does the cheetah, having to stop accelerating and slowing because of the change in direction. The cheetah then accelerates to top speed and after a few seconds catches the impala. This causes the cheetah to slow down abruptly and then come to a stop. Tasks such as that in Box 9.10 can be fun and motivating, but the real value is that they give students valuable experience in analyzing the relationship between the dependent and independent variables, and in understanding the meaning and representation of slope. It is advantageous to make the task and the visual general in nature to allow more variety in the student responses. This variety can in turn generate rich conversation that includes justification of various components of each story.

The following tasks depicting job scenarios (Boxes 9.11, 12, and 13) are offered as additional examples of details of graphical representation that must be addressed. The focus is again the mining and interpretation of the information contained in the graphs. The contextual information that is provided combined with every component of the graphs assist students in their quest to see both the big picture and the details. A main objective of these exercises is to bring out details about graphs that textbooks often neglect. Note that once the graphs are interpreted, the conversations in these contexts that involve interpreting the graphs merge with those such as the weight loss and popcorn problems where students did the reversal and created graphs based on written information. In addition, note how deep understanding of concepts such as slope is essential in order to make sense of the information ingrained in the visual.

Box 9.11

The two jobs shown pay hourly wages by the week. Use the graph to answer the questions below.

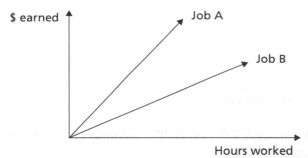

1. Job A and Job B are basically the same job with the same responsibilities and work shift. Which job would you prefer? Explain why.
2. Is it realistic for the job earnings graphs to be solid lines? Explain why or why not.
3. Why are the lines for the two jobs straight?

The first question is focused on students' understanding of slope. As the jobs are basically the same, Job A is the obvious better choice because for the same amount of hours worked, Job A pays more than Job B. An additional observation is that Job A must pay more per hour because the slope is steeper, which indicates a faster rate of change (in this case, hourly wage) than Job B. The second question was addressed in the prior popcorn scenario. In this context, a solid line indicates that workers' time is being measured in increments much smaller than seconds, and that the possible wages could be paid in increments much smaller than pennies. The solid line, thus, does not reflect the realities of time measurement and monetary denominations. The third question addresses a topic that is often neglected in mathematics instruction. Students need to understand that the graph of a linear equation is a straight line for a critical reason. A straight line symbolizes that the slope, or rate of change, is *constant*. In this context, if the slope of Job A was $\frac{15}{1}$, then a worker in that job would get paid the same amount ($15) for each hour worked, not $10 one hour, $18 the next hour, $16 the next, and so on.

Box 9.12

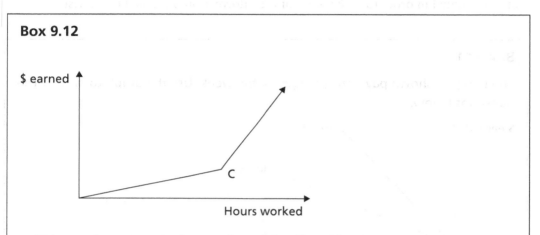

This graph represents the pay for a job offered by the company. Answer the questions below based on this representation.

1. Why is the line not entirely straight? Mathematically, what happens at Point C?
2. What is a possible real-life explanation of Point C?

In this graph, the slope changes at Point C. As a result, the line segment from that point on has a different equation than the initial segment. The most likely real-life explanation is that Point C is the number of hours (such as 40 hours) at which the job starts paying overtime. From that point forward, a worker would get paid a higher hourly rate, which meshes with the graphical representation.

Box 9.13

The two jobs shown are sales jobs at a car dealership.

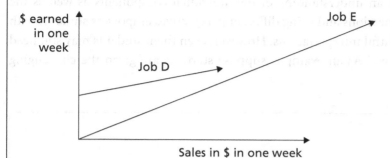

1. How does Job D get paid? Explain.
2. How does Job E get paid? Explain.
3. How do the two jobs differ, and what could explain the differences?
4. Which job is better in terms of earnings?

A rich scenario such as this one gives students experience with interpreting visual information from a coordinate graph and drawing conclusions based on that information. In deciphering Job D, students can realize from the y-intercept that this job pays the employee a certain amount per week plus a sales-based commission. In contrast, Job E begins at the origin, so this job is paid on commission only. However, Job E involves a higher percentage of commission on sales because it has a steeper slope. Which job is better depends on the sales made that week. The intersection of the two graphs would represent where the pay would be the same for the two jobs. For sales amounts less than the point of intersection, Job D would pay more. For sales amounts more than the point of intersection, Job E would pay more.

Interpreting Geometric Figures

Geometric figures, like graphs, communicate information symbolically. Each requires interpretation that is dependent on understanding concepts. In the case of geometric figures, the concepts are primarily the definitions of the figures and the associated properties of each. Those properties can sometimes be expressed as formulas; thus interpretation can become more complex in connecting definitions to visuals to properties and then the formulas that represent them. Contexts can include figures that are a combination of basic polygons, which require an understanding of the individual components as well as the big picture. Making connections and using different perspectives empowers students with the ability to make insightful interpretations. However, even then, students may still need to think "outside the box." As an example, suppose students are given the challenging problem in Box 9.14.

Box 9.14

Given: AD = 12

BC = 20

$\overline{BC}$ is perpendicular to $\overline{AD}$

AM = MD

Find: The area of the kite figure ABDC. Explain the process used.

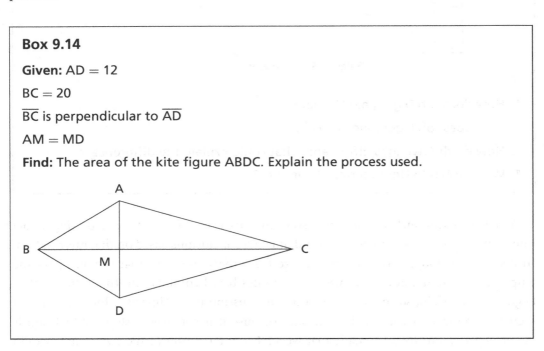

In a problem like this, the typical solution process is to start with the formula for the area of a triangle. After determining 6 as the length of $\overline{AM}$, one would find the area of triangle ABC using 6 as the height and 20 as the base ($\frac{1}{2} \cdot 6 \cdot 20 = 60$). Then, one can determine that triangle DBC is congruent to triangle ABC, so the area of triangle ABC (60 square units) is doubled to calculate the area of the kite figure (120 square units).

A student who knows the definitions and connections among triangles and quadrilaterals would have the vision to see beyond the given diagram and use a unique solution process. This process involves adding four line segments to the original diagram to form a rectangle that encloses the kite, as shown in Box 9.15.

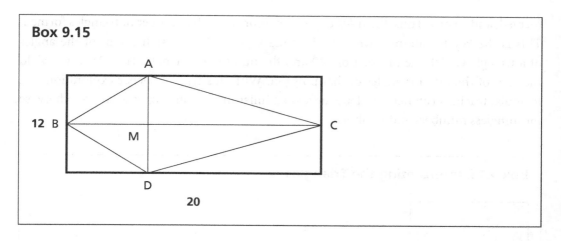

Box 9.15

The student truly went outside the box with this approach. Because the rectangle is 12 by 20, its area is 12 • 20 = 240. Each of the matching pairs of triangles appears to be congruent, so the area of the kite should be half of the area of the rectangle. This yields a solution of 120 square units. Depending on the grade level and experience, there are various methods to show congruence in this context. For example, if a student knows from basic geometry that a diagonal cuts a rectangle in half, he or she could justify the equal areas of the pairs of triangles in each of the four smaller rectangles.

Using Figures to Interpret Formulas

Traditional instruction often demands that students memorize formulas that are nothing more than numbers and letters to them. As with any type of written communication, students must understand what the written information means or says. As an example, examine the formula for the sum of the interior angles of a polygon (triangles, quadrilaterals, pentagons, and so on). The formula states $S = 180 • (n - 2)$, where S is the sum of the interior angles and n is the number of the sides of the polygon. Most students do not understand what this formula means. However, an informal proof can be done to make sense of the meaning of the symbols.

Refer to the three polygons in Box 9.16. Note that diagonals have been drawn from one of the vertices of each polygon. The sum of the angles of the triangles formed by those diagonals is equivalent to the sum of the angles of that polygon. For example, in the pentagon, the sum of the five angles of the pentagon is the same as the sum of the nine angles of the three triangles formed. A pattern is established where the number of triangles formed is two less than the number of sides of each respective polygon (the quadrilateral has 4 sides, and 2 triangles were formed; the pentagon has 5 sides, and 3 triangles were formed, and so on). Thus, the n – 2 expression represents the number of triangles formed. This is the key to interpret what the formula says. And because the sum of the angles of a triangle is 180, the product of 180 and the number of triangles (n – 2) would yield the sum of the interior angles of that polygon. With this type of deeper exploration of a formula, teachers can help students develop a fuller understanding of what are otherwise meaningless numbers and symbols.

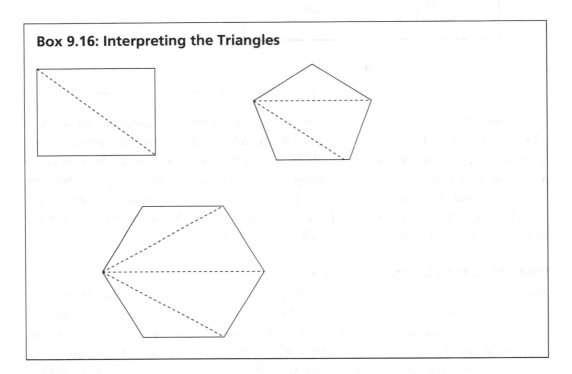

Box 9.16: Interpreting the Triangles

THE POWER OF INTERPRETATION: THREE PERSPECTIVES OF TRAPEZOIDS

The ability to read visual representation and the associated mathematical symbolism can lead to interesting perspectives that can guide the reasoning process. Multiple instances exist in mathematics that exemplify the power of interpreting symbols and visuals, but few are more compelling than the formula for the area of a trapezoid. How one reads the formula can actually guide the proof or justification of it. This section explores three perspectives for interpreting the trapezoid formula to illustrate the conceptual understanding each one provides. Note that several related concepts must be understood to arrive at these perspectives and interpretations. For this reason, the parallelogram formula, which connects closely to the trapezoid formula, has been provided as well. Box 9.17 presents the two formulas.

Box 9.17: Area Formulas for Trapezoids and Parallelograms

Area of a trapezoid: $A = \frac{1}{2} \bullet h \bullet (b_1 + b_2)$

Area of a parallelogram: $A = b \bullet h$

Trapezoid Perspective I

This activity is one where the initial trapezoid is manipulated and transformed to a parallelogram. This perspective is illustrated by using trapezoid figures cut out of card stock. As a class activity, the task works best if students form small groups. Each group needs a pair of safety scissors, a ruler, a pencil, and a drawing of the figure in Box 9.18 on card stock.

Box 9.18

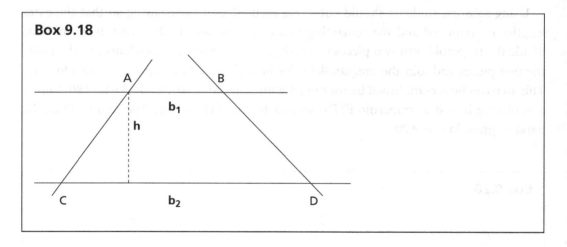

In the figure, transversals intersect parallel lines, and *h* represents the height. Although extending past the points of intersection, the transversals and parallel lines form a trapezoid ABDC with bases b_1 and b_2. Have students find the midpoint of each of the two *nonparallel* sides ($\overline{AC}$ and $\overline{BD}$), ensuring that measurement is done from the vertices, not from the ends of the line segments beyond the trapezoid. Next, have students connect the two midpoints with a line segment. This segment is a median parallel to b_1 and b_2 that connects the two nonparallel sides and also bisects the height. Students should then label all the matching pairs of segments that have equal measures. These actions should result in a figure similar to the one shown in Box 9.19.

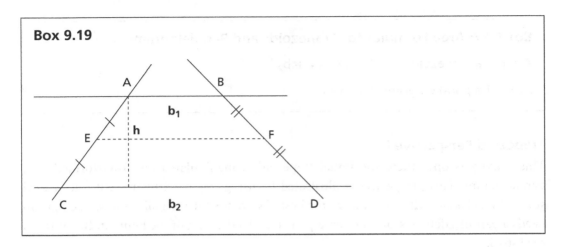

Box 9.19

Using scissors, students should cut along each edge of the drawing so that the extra lengths are removed and the remaining figure is trapezoid ABDC. Next, have students divide the trapezoid into two pieces by cutting along the median. Students can then take the two pieces and join the *nonparallel* sides in such a way as to form a parallelogram. This step can be accomplished by rotating the top trapezoid, ABFE, clockwise 180 degrees and placing it next to trapezoid EFDC so that $\overline{BF}$ and $\overline{FD}$ overlap. The result will be the parallelogram in Box 9.20

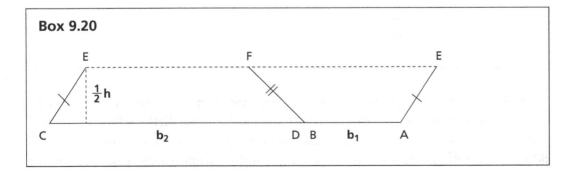

Box 9.20

The assertion that the resulting quadrilateral is a parallelogram can be proved, an activity that would be appropriate in a secondary-level mathematics class. The area of the new parallelogram is equivalent to the area of the original trapezoid because no area was eliminated nor any additional area created. The original figure was a trapezoid, and an important observation for students is that the height of the new parallelogram is half that of the height of the original trapezoid. In addition, the base of the parallelogram is the sum of the two bases of the original trapezoid.

All of this information in conjunction with the labeling of the original trapezoid and the resulting parallelogram can now be used to show the equivalence of the two area formulas. Begin with the area formula for a parallelogram where A = area, b = base, and h = height. Most textbooks express the formula for the area of a parallelogram as $A = b \cdot h$. Using the commutative property, change the formula to read $A = h \cdot b$. Using the values of the parallelogram that students have created (Box 9.20), substitute the appropriate values into the formula $A = h \cdot b$. The result will be $A = (\frac{1}{2} \cdot h) \cdot (b_1 + b_2)$.

Now compare this result to the general formula for a trapezoid $A = \frac{1}{2} \cdot h \cdot (b_1 + b_2)$. Note that the only difference between the formulas is in how the values are organized, which corresponds to what happened in the activity. The height of the parallelogram formed is half that of the height of the original trapezoid, and the base of the constructed parallelogram is composed of the sum of the two bases of the original trapezoid. The thought process in the activity parallels how the formula is read and interpreted based on the transformation to a parallelogram. The benefits are founded on the connections that can be made, both in the labeling of the figures and the generating of an equivalent form of the trapezoid formula from the parallelogram formula.

Trapezoid Perspective II

This second activity also involves connections between parallelograms and trapezoids. This perspective is illustrated by using parallelogram figures cut out of card stock. Again, this class activity works best with students in small groups. Provide each group with safety scissors, a ruler, a pencil, and a drawing of parallelogram ABCD (Box 9.21) on card stock.

Have students measure the length of the top base ($\overline{AB}$). Then, having students mimic your actions, pick a point along that base ($\overline{AB}$) that would divide it into 2 unequal segments. For example, if $\overline{AB}$ is 7 inches long, the point might divide it into a 2-inch and a 5-inch segment. Label the point P_1, the segment on the left as b_1, and the segment on the right as b_2. Because the figure is a parallelogram, AB and DC are equal lengths. Repeat

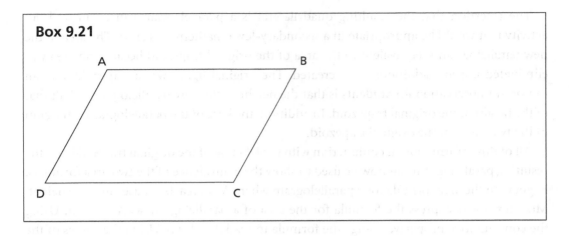

Box 9.21

the previous process on $\overline{DC}$ using the same lengths, but *reverse* the position of the two pieces. Based on the example above, on $\overline{DC}$ the positions of the 2-inch segment and the 5-inch segment would be reversed. Label the point on $\overline{DC}$ as P_2; then label the segment on the right of that point as b_1 and the segment on the left as b_2. Next, draw a segment that connects points P_1 and P_2. Mark all the matching segments that have equal measures. The result should now look like the figure in Box 9.22.

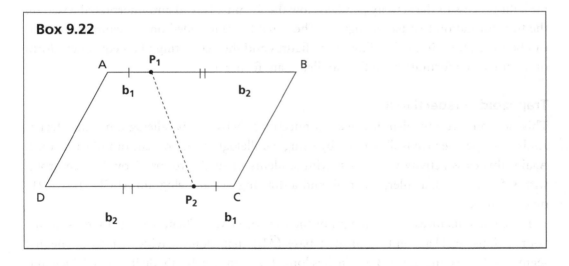

Box 9.22

Note that each of the two bases $\overline{AB}$ and $\overline{DC}$ has been subdivided into two pieces. As a result, students can see that $AB = b_1 + b_2$ and $DC = b_1 + b_2$. Now have students cut the parallelogram into two pieces along the segment that connects points P_1 and P_2. The two newly formed figures will be congruent trapezoids. To help younger students realize this fact, have them place one of the new smaller trapezoids on top of the other to see that one fits exactly over the other. More advanced students might be expected to do a more formal proof using matching pairs of congruent angles and matching pairs of congruent sides.

Because the two smaller figures are congruent trapezoids, they have equal areas. As a corollary, the area of each of the new smaller trapezoids is $\frac{1}{2}$ the area of the original parallelogram. Similar to the Trapezoid Perspective I activity, teachers can use this information, combined with the labeling of the original parallelogram and the new trapezoids, to illustrate the symbolic transformation and derivation of a different interpretation of the trapezoid area formula.

Starting with the standard area formula for a parallelogram ($A = b \cdot h$), use the commutative property to restate it as $A = h \cdot b$. The base of the parallelogram was renamed as ($b_1 + b_2$). Through substitution, the area of the original parallelogram becomes $A = h \cdot (b_1 + b_2)$. Because each of the trapezoids had an area half that of the parallelogram, the area of either trapezoid could be expressed as half of $h \cdot (b_1 + b_2)$, which written mathematically would be $A = \frac{1}{2} \cdot [\, h \cdot (b_1 + b_2)]$. Compare that reorganized version to the standard formula $A = \frac{1}{2} \cdot h \cdot (b_1 + b_2)$.

As with the first activity, the only difference between the formulas is in how the values are organized, which corresponds to what happened in this second activity. In the first activity, the height of the parallelogram formed was half the height of the original trapezoid and the base of the parallelogram was the sum of the two bases of the original trapezoid. In the second activity, the area of the trapezoid formed was half the area of the original parallelogram. In each case, how the standard area formula is reorganized and read parallels the process and the new figure that resulted. Combined, the two activities reveal the power of different interpretations of mathematical symbolism and the new perspectives that can result.

Trapezoid Perspective III

This third perspective relies on making connections to conceptual knowledge of an average (or the mean) and is not as dependent on the manipulation of geometric figures as the two prior activities. However, diagrams are necessary in order to visualize the bridging of numeric and geometric perspectives. As with the previous two activities, this task is best done with students in small groups. Give each group a drawing of trapezoid WXYZ (Box 9.23) on card stock.

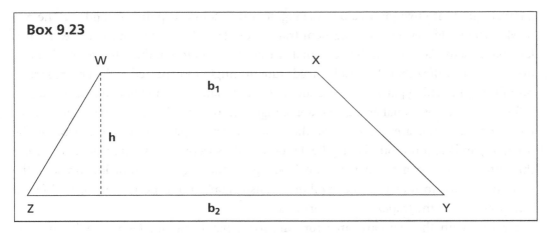

Box 9.23

Start the activity by investigating what happens when we average *two* numbers. As an example, compute the average of 8 and 12, which is 10. In the original context, the numbers are 8 and 12 and in the other the numbers would be 10 and 10. Each of the two addends in the second context is the mean. If other pairs are averaged, students will see the pattern and realize that when two different numbers are averaged, we essentially make the two addends the same number. For instance, averaging 6 and 24 produces two 15's. Students must internalize this critical understanding before continuing the activity.

In trapezoid WXYZ, what would be the result if we averaged the lengths of the two bases, b_1 and b_2? The lengths of the two bases are numbers, so averaging the two bases would result in two new lengths that are the same values. Using the numerical examples, we would reach a parallel conclusion from a geometric perspective. We have changed the figure to one where WX = ZY as shown in Box 9.24. Give this new version of WXYZ to students on card stock.

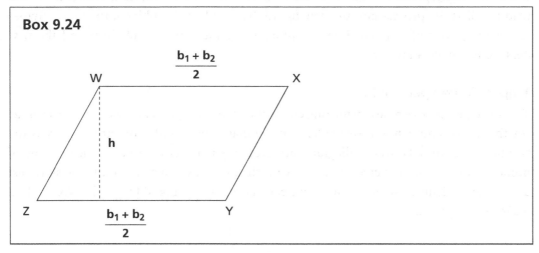

Box 9.24

There is a geometric theorem which states that if a quadrilateral contains a pair of sides that are both equal and parallel, then that quadrilateral must be a parallelogram. Have students examine the figure in Box 9.24 to see if it meets those conditions. First, the two bases were averaged, so WX and ZY are equal lengths. Second, $\overline{WX}$ and $\overline{ZY}$ were also the bases of the original trapezoid, and by definition, the two bases of a trapezoid are parallel. Thus, $\overline{WX}$ and $\overline{ZY}$ meet the two conditions required by the theorem to establish WXYZ as a parallelogram. (The formal proof that WXYZ is a parallelogram is better suited to a geometry class.)

Next, have students compare the areas of trapezoid WXYZ and parallelogram WXYZ. Students should realize that both figures have an equal area because the height and the sum of the bases remained the same in transforming the trapezoid into the parallelogram. Students need to realize that they could apply the standard trapezoid formula to the parallelogram and get the same result. For example, if the two bases in the original trapezoid were 7 and 9, their sum $(b_1 + b_2)$ would be 16. If averaged, the bases would be 8 and 8, resulting in the same sum of 16. Applying the trapezoid formula to each figure the area in each case would be $\frac{1}{2} \cdot h \cdot (16)$.

Although slightly more tedious, the area of a parallelogram could actually be found using the formula for the area of a trapezoid. This third perspective shows how closely related the two formulas are and how, with the proper manipulation, the averaging of the two bases of any trapezoid actually converts it to a parallelogram! In a sense, the area formula for a parallelogram is a special case of the trapezoid formula where the bases are the same length, which of course makes the trapezoid a parallelogram. Box 9.25 presents the transformation process in this activity symbolically.

Box 9.25: Connecting the Trapezoid and Parallelogram Area Formulas

1. The process begins with the area formula for a trapezoid:

   $A = \frac{1}{2} \cdot h \cdot (b_1 + b_2)$

2. The order of the formula is rearranged using the commutative property:

   $A = h \cdot \frac{1}{2} \cdot (b_1 + b_2)$

3. The expression $\frac{1}{2} \cdot (b_1 + b_2)$ is rewritten using one fraction bar: $\dfrac{b_1 + b_2}{2}$

4. Substituting the expression above into the formula in step 2 results in the following:

   $A = h \cdot \left(\dfrac{b_1 + b_2}{2} \right)$

In this form, the trapezoid area formula parallels the area formula for a parallelogram as depicted in Box 9.26.

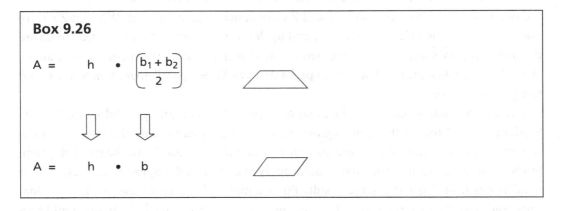

Box 9.26

$$A = h \cdot \left(\frac{b_1 + b_2}{2} \right)$$

$$A = h \cdot b$$

In this reorganized format, the "plain English" reading or interpretation of the formula would be that the area of a trapezoid is given by the height multiplied by the average of the two bases. This reasoning may seem simple enough, yet students might not make the connections and realize how profound this interpretation of the generic formula truly is. Because traditional math instruction focuses on memorizing formulas instead of exploring why they work, this lack on students' part is not surprising. Activities like this one that merges perspectives can help ensure that students get these connections.

Trapezoid Summary

Box 9.27 depicts a mathematically expressed summary of the different perspectives of the area formula of a trapezoid. The different perspectives in the trapezoid activities illustrate the depth of understanding that can be attained via the convergence of multiple interpretations. In this case, rearranging the components of the area formula enabled students to make these interpretations and realize key connections. A constant bridging of the area formulas for a trapezoid and parallelogram throughout the activities helped emphasize these connections and led to enlightened thought processes.

When adapted for classroom use, activities such as this trapezoid exercise have implications for student learning. Rather than simply memorizing a meaningless formula, students would use mathematical vocabulary to explain the formula orally and in writing. In this case, that explanation would include the attributes of trapezoids and parallelograms, as well as foundational concepts such as transversals and parallel lines. To build on that foundation, students can then use solid models to illustrate, examine, and discuss formulas for geometric figures. Here, students worked in cooperative groups to discuss and construct area formulas for two related polygons. In addition, students are given opportunities to examine how their thinking and perspectives can be expressed as, and transcribed to, mathematical statements such as formulas.

Box 9.27

Generic Formula $\;\; A = \frac{1}{2} \bullet h \bullet (b_1 + b_2)$.

Perspective I $\qquad A = (\frac{1}{2} \bullet h) \bullet (b_1 + b_2)$

Perspective II $\qquad A = \frac{1}{2} \bullet [\, h \bullet (b_1 + b_2)]$.

Perspective III $\qquad A = h \bullet \left(\dfrac{b_1 + b_2}{2} \right)$

CONCLUSION

The tasks and activities in this chapter serve as prime examples of the power of conceptual-level understanding of not only mathematical concepts, but also of mathematics language and representation, which in turn build a capacity to make enlightened connections. To read a map correctly, a student needs a map legend to understand the meaning of all the symbols and figures used. Understanding the meaning of the symbols and visuals in mathematics is no different. The legend in math is in-depth knowledge of concepts, which enables fluid and meaningful interpretation of symbols, graphs, and geometric figures that are inescapable components of the language of mathematics. With an outstanding legend, the route to the mathematical destination becomes clear and the necessary connections become more like interstate highways rather than bumpy country roads.

Language-Focused Conceptual Instruction

In mathematics you don't understand things. You just get used to them.

—Johann von Neumann

T he above statement is an indication of the frustration that some students may encounter in mathematics classrooms. If students "don't understand things," part of the reason must be the quality of classroom instruction. The early chapters in this book detail language issues in mathematics and how traditional instruction often overlooks and even exacerbates them. Chapter Four begins the conversation on what conceptual understanding should look like and the need to address not only how we teach but also what content we teach. Understanding requires a foundation of deep yet simple definitions of key concepts. These definitions, in turn, shape the types of statements and questions used in classroom instruction.

Even when teachers have a thorough knowledge of the concepts, though, it can be a challenge to bring them to life in the classroom. What methods help differentiate traditional instruction from conceptual instruction focused on language? These methods include going beyond definitions, dissecting word problems from a language perspective, and utilizing strategies such as ambiguity, advanced fundamentals, hard-to-see connections, and manipulatives to deepen understanding. The result is instruction to help ensure that von Neumann's statement no longer applies to our students.

LANGUAGE FOCUS: BEYOND THE DEFINITIONS

As you've seen, the foundational blocks for conceptual understanding in mathematics are simple yet deep definitions. Such definitions are an integral part of language-focused conceptual instruction, which focuses first on the *what* and the *why* of concepts, saving the *how-to* procedures for an appropriate later time. This focus includes not only current concepts but also related ones taught in earlier grades. Teachers cannot assume previous content knowledge, which some educators refer to as committing *assumacide*.

Merely presenting simple yet deep definitions is not enough to build a strong conceptual foundation, though. Instruction needs to go beyond the definitions themselves. The typical classroom scenario for teaching key terms has students memorizing a definition in a textbook, followed by working through an associated procedure or process, the infamous how-to. This approach results in only a shallow knowledge. So what is a better approach?

When teaching vocabulary, some other disciplines such as language arts employ the Frayer Model, shown in Box 10.1. Examine the model to see how it goes beyond teaching just a definition.

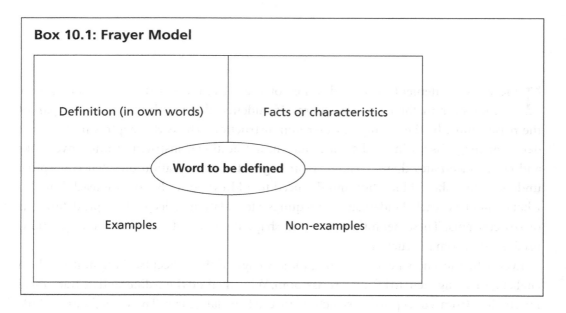

Box 10.1: Frayer Model

| Definition (in own words) | Facts or characteristics |
| Examples | Non-examples |

Word to be defined

The Frayer Model uses four techniques to teach vocabulary. Although more rigorous than the traditional math approach, this model still falls short of the mark, however. The language of mathematics is extremely complex and interconnected. As Chapter Four shows, terms may be used differently in math from their use in everyday English, and understanding one term often depends upon understanding another. What's more, terms may be closely linked to symbolism or visual representation. As a result, mathematics requires a vocabulary model that goes even further to ensure understanding.

Refer to the suggested model in Box 10.2. This organizer presents multiple factors to clarify and deepen the meaning of a key math term. The model serves only as a basic framework; teachers can simplify or expand it as needed to ensure they address a specific term's factors. Some educators may consider this approach too complex or time-intensive. The benefits in understanding far outweigh the costs in time, though. By using such a framework, instruction goes beyond *definitions*. Students are learning *mathematics*. With this deeper understanding of terminology, students have a strong mathematical foundation on which to build, enabling them to make powerful connections and to grasp other concepts. Teachers may want to expand and adapt this version of the framework by replacing *Word to be defined* with a phrase such as *Concept or process to be taught*.

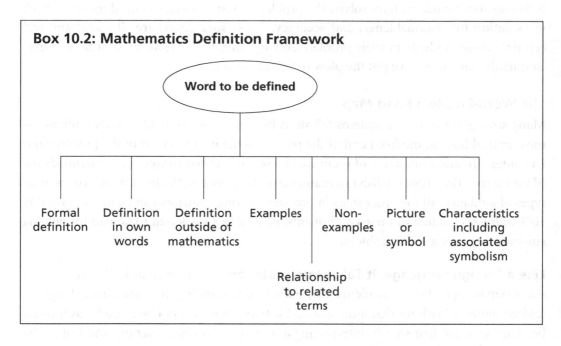

Box 10.2: Mathematics Definition Framework

Word to be defined

- Formal definition
- Definition in own words
- Definition outside of mathematics
- Examples
- Relationship to related terms
- Non-examples
- Picture or symbol
- Characteristics including associated symbolism

Once students have a strong grasp of terminology, the next step in language-focused instruction is to address the issues inherent in the combination of words in mathematics. Knowing the pieces of the puzzle is only a start; students must be able to make sense of the pieces when they are combined to see the bigger picture. Such is the case with word problems.

THE SECRETS TO SOLVING WORD PROBLEMS

The difficulty of mathematical language is most apparent in word problems. A common lament heard in teacher lounges throughout the country is, "My kids aren't good problem solvers." Despite numerous resources that propose problem-solving strategies, the difficulties and lamentations persist. This text does not try to solve this dilemma or give teachers a magic bullet for transforming their students into word-problem-solving machines. But it does bring attention to a critical component that most problem-solving strategies invariably ignore—the actual language of the problem.

Common threads run across most problem-solving strategies, with slight variations. The majority begin with suggestions to read the problem carefully, identify key words, organize the facts, and determine what is being asked. Next, many suggest that students draw an appropriate figure or diagram, if applicable. This step is usually followed by a generic direction that students develop a plan (such as what operations to use) and apply it. Finally, once students have solved the problem, most strategies remind them to check the solution for reasonableness and accuracy. These suggestions are all useful and will certainly assist students in their problem-solving endeavors. However, as a farmer may eloquently state, they have put the plow before the horse.

The Word-Problem Road Map

Many strategies for word problems fall short because they fail to adequately address the most critical issue at the front end of the process—the *interpretation* of the problem and its context. In addition, many of them slight a second related component, the *translation* of the information from English to a mathematical expression. Without these two essential types of guidance, all the other steps in problem-solving strategies can be for naught. Box 10.3 addresses the first of these components, providing a suggested road map for helping students interpret a word problem.

Like a Foreign Language: It Takes Interpretation.   Not inherent in Box 10.3 is that every step is dependent on students' conceptual understanding of mathematical language and symbolism. Without that foundation, this framework will not be as useful as it could be. That said, the first step in interpreting a word problem is to identify and isolate the question from the other information. A key trap that can occur at this stage is when pertinent information is integrated into the question itself. For example, the question might include information such as the price of an item, which would be needed to find the solution. The next task is to examine the information and, on the basis of the question, determine what information is relevant and what is extraneous. Elementary students

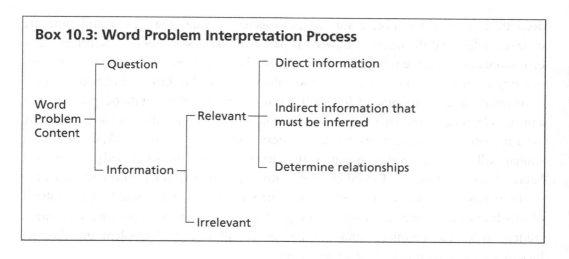

Box 10.3: Word Problem Interpretation Process

Word Problem Content
- Question
- Information
  - Relevant
    - Direct information
    - Indirect information that must be inferred
    - Determine relationships
  - Irrelevant

sometimes struggle with this task because they don't have any experience with word problems with irrelevant information. Teachers at the earlier grades must collaborate across grade levels to coordinate the transition to problems that contain information extraneous to the solution.

In all likelihood, the most problematic phase in the interpretation process is deciphering the relevant information. The far-right section of the diagram lists the three parts of this phase. The easiest of the three is to interpret the information provided *directly*. For example, a problem might state that the price of an item is $14.95 or that a car is traveling at 60 miles per hour. The difficulty lies in the *indirect* information that students must infer. Here is where students must apply critical thinking and have a solid foundation in mathematical definitions and concepts. Being told that a farmer's field is rectangular in shape (direct information) also provides indirect information about the field's sides, angles, and diagonals. In fact, providing information in an indirect fashion is actually a method used to transform a one-step problem into a multistep problem. Because multistep problems can give students fits, teachers need to ensure younger students get enough practice with ferreting out indirect information. The students will reap the benefits later as they face increasingly complex word problems.

The last task in the diagram, determining the relationships among the facts and information, can often be the hardest—and the most overlooked. Once again, students' depth of content knowledge plays a key role in accomplishing the task. Sometimes, the relationships in a word problem are obvious or provided directly. A problem that states a woman bought two items, one costing $10 and another $5, indicates a relationship regarding money amounts. Other relationships must be inferred or discovered through deep thought. For instance, a student is expected to infer that speed and time are inversely related (if the distance traveled is held constant). Still other relationships must be reasoned, such as the parallel between the number of games and the number of losers in a single-elimination playoff series in football, as described in Box 1.7 in Chapter One.

As mentioned, the framework in Box 10.3 is not a magic bullet, but it does give students a process to understand the information in a word problem. Students can use this process, in turn, to develop a plan to answer the question. This guidance framework, or something similar, will be an asset to students and with repetition will become ingrained processes and habits. Two components of word problems, finding indirect information and seeing the relationships, are typically the most troublesome for students and should be the emphasis of this framework. Having a map to interpreting the problem is important. Otherwise, students will wander aimlessly and find the correct path in a word problem only through luck or after much more work than necessary.

Of course, the most accurate interpretation of a word problem is of little use if students do not then develop an appropriate plan of action to correctly answer the question being asked and to justify the solution. This step involves the second key skill students need—to translate the problem from English into a mathematical expression.

Interpretation Done: Now What?   Determining which operation(s) to use to reach a solution often proves to be a can of worms. Traditional instruction sometimes exacerbates the process with well-intended strategies such as "clue words." Teachers at the elementary level often pass along this strategy, which they learned as students, and some resources suggest using it as well.

True, key words provide important clues, but these should be used to determine *relationships*, and not as a means to decide which *operation* to use to solve the problem. There is a huge difference between the two. Students need guidance to become critical thinkers. Using clue words to determine the operation to use is a mistake because it can lead to mindless, incorrect decisions. For example, elementary students might be taught to add if they see the word *sum* in a problem. But for every problem where that strategy works, an astute teacher or test developer can make up a problem where it does *not* work.

Suppose students are given the test question in Box 10.4. Students who blindly follow the strategy will add 15 and 8 to get 23, which is obviously incorrect. And of course, on a multiple-choice exam, test developers would ensure that 23 is an answer choice. In addition to possibly leading students to the wrong choice of operations, used inappropriately, the clue words strategy is counter to developing students' thinking skills because it can inhibit rather than promote thinking. In fact, as used, the clue words strategy is actually a *shortcut* that eliminates thought and reasoning!

Box 10.4

Solve the following:

I have two numbers whose **_sum_** is 15. One number is 8. What is the other number?

Translation into Mathematics. Clue words are critical, but the proper use for them is based on finding the *relationships* in a problem context. This strategy will promote the student thinking and reasoning that teachers desire in their protégés. As an example, consider Box 10.4 in light of what a student should do with clue words. The key is to use the clue words in the translation and understanding of the context and relationships in the problem. Students should then write those out in such a way that the English statement can be translated into mathematical representation. The clue word uncovers the relationship, which in turn serves as the basis for the key statement.

In the problem in Box 10.4, the word *sum* would guide the student to write: "One number plus another number is 15." In many contexts, such a statement represents the relationships in the problem. Translated into mathematical representation, the statement would be ＿＿＿＿＿＿ + ＿＿＿＿＿＿ = 15. The additional information in the problem tells the student that one of those numbers is 8. Logic then dictates that the statement becomes 8 + ＿＿＿＿＿＿ = 15. The student reasoned and thought critically rather than making an automatic, uniform and incorrect decision. All that is left to do is what other problem-solving strategies suggest—solve and check for reasonableness and accuracy.

Box 10.5

Solve the following:

At a local toy store, you buy 4 toys at $1.50 each. You must pay a 6% sales tax on the cost of your purchase. How much change should you get back if you give the cashier $10?

Refer to Box 10.5. Students often hit a brick wall when they transition from single-step to multistep problems. Although not patently obvious, the reality is that the process here is basically the same as in the problem in Box 10.4. Often, the additional steps in a multistep problem are embedded in the main expression describing the primary relationship, which in this task is as follows: "The amount of money I provide the cashier minus the total cost of my purchase is the change I should get back." As teachers, having students write the primary relationship in words is nonnegotiable. Students must do it!

The next steps in the translation process may sometimes require intermediate statements that mix English and math. The next statement could look something like this: *$10 − total cost = my change.* (In real life, the cashier determines and tells you the cost first, which informs you as to how much money to provide. However, providing that information here would make it a simple subtraction problem!) Notice that the total cost was not provided directly, but rather indirectly. This step connects back to the last phase of Box 10.3. Determining the total cost is a smaller problem within the larger problem. The additional steps will determine the cost of the 4 toys with the 6% sales tax included (4 • $1.50 • 1.06). The resulting total cost of $6.36 can then be substituted into the primary statement to read: *$10 − $6.36 = my change.* The calculation can be finalized and the result then checked for reasonableness and accuracy.

Promote and Visualize Thinking

At the elementary and middle school levels, the logic in most word problems is fairly simple, as the problems in Boxes 10.4 and 10.5 show. Unfortunately, this logic does not enter students' minds through osmosis. Young students must learn some basic logical ideas (such as "the change I get back is what I give minus the cost") by experience and practice. The initial steps of having students interpret the information in a problem and then develop a word statement of the primary relationship are key. Those actions must be coupled with a deliberate process to translate the English to mathematical symbolism.

It bears repeating that students must physically write out the primary relationship in the problem in English and then transform it to a mathematical expression. This step must be made mandatory. By writing out the question and the relationships involved, students will literally *see* their thinking. As an added benefit for teachers, students' thinking would no longer be a mystery, which would enable teachers to see students' errors in reasoning and adjust instruction accordingly. From an assessment perspective, that written information shifts the focus to gauging students' thinking rather than their computation skill. The extent of harm done because of shortcuts was detailed in Chapter Three. Those assertions most definitely apply to word problems as well. Shortcuts in writing translate to shortcuts in thinking. The development of students into problem solvers and insightful thinkers will not occur via shortcuts or haphazard approaches any more than it will via wishful thinking or divine intervention. If we as educators allow student work that consists only of a numeric answer or do not provide guidance in interpreting and translating word problems, we will only have ourselves to blame for the results.

Language-focused conceptual instruction helps students understand what various pieces of the puzzle mean by using simple yet deep definitions to interpret problems, find relationships, and translate that information into viable solution strategies. Also, by dissecting word problems, they have a better idea of how those pieces fit together to create a bigger picture. But there is no rote recipe for putting a puzzle together in mathematics. Besides, different puzzles yield different pictures. Students need additional guidance and experience in recognizing how those pieces connect and, in time, the ability to see the bigger picture even before it is completed. The next section discusses a number of strategies and tools to help students build this next level of conceptual understanding.

SUGGESTED INSTRUCTIONAL STRATEGIES

In many ways, a good teacher is like a good taxicab driver. It is not enough to know only the most direct or fastest route. A taxi driver needs to be able to picture all of a given area, be flexible, and adapt with different routes when necessary. For example, if an area is under construction or a passenger requests to be taken on a scenic route, a driver needs a memory bank of alternate routes from which to draw. The same applies to effective teachers. They need a memory bank of multiple approaches or perspectives from which to draw to build understanding, strengthen connections, and help struggling students. Several chapters have highlighted the benefits of alternative approaches. The following is a smorgasbord of strategies teachers can use to put such approaches into action.

Ambiguity: Make It an Asset, Not a Liability

One of the problems with language noted in Chapter Two was ambiguity. In mathematics, ambiguous statements and terms that have more than one definition that can be applied to a specific context can be problematic. However, much like the taxi driver with knowledge of multiple routes to the same destination, effective teachers can transform ambiguity into an asset by using it as another route to understanding. As a strategy, ambiguous questions can help teachers solicit student thinking and use the language of mathematics as an instructional tool. The following tasks illustrate three ways to make ambiguity an asset rather than a liability in classroom instruction.

Ambiguity Task 1: Before and After.   The question in Box 10.6 illustrates how a teacher can strategically use ambiguity in teaching the mathematical concept of similarity. A teacher might ask this question prior to an instructional unit on similarity and then again at the end of the unit. Without prior knowledge, most students will answer the question based on the standard English definition of *similar*, stating that the figures are similar because they share attributes such as four right angles and matching pairs of parallel sides. After studying the mathematical definition of similarity, students should realize that squares and rectangles are not similar except when both figures are squares. By comparing student responses to ambiguous questions from the start and end of a unit, teachers can generate interesting dialogue that could deepen students' knowledge of the concept while also helping students develop an awareness of the language issues in mathematics.

Box 10.7

Denise claims that Figure B has more area shaded than Figure A. Alberto claims the opposite. He thinks Figure A has more area shaded. Who is correct? Explain your assertion.

A

B

Ambiguity Task 2: Different Interpretations.   The scenario in Box 10.7 deliberately utilizes the ambiguous interpretation of the word *more*. Because of this ambiguity, each student in the scenario can effectively argue his or her case. Denise sees the term *more* from an absolute or actual-quantity perspective. In support of this interpretation, visual inspection does reveal that a greater quantity of area is shaded in Figure B. Alberto sees the term *more* from a proportional perspective. Assuming that the entire figure in A is considered the "whole," it appears that about 75% of A is shaded and only about 25% of B is shaded. Alberto has a valid justification as well. Given their interpretations, both students are correct. However, this scenario provides an opportunity to help middle school students make the critical shift from absolute reasoning (Denise) to relative or proportional reasoning (Alberto). This shift is critical because proportional reasoning is an integral part of algebra and algebraic reasoning. The instructional implication is that the ambiguous nature of the term *more* allows different yet valid conclusions that teachers can leverage to prompt rich classroom conversations and help students develop new perspectives.

Box 10.8

Given a 1-by-1 square, what would the square look like if you made it twice as big? Draw and label the original and the larger square. Justify your reasoning.

Ambiguity Task 3: Vague Meaning.　The task in Box 10.8 would leave many students, as well as adults, wondering what exactly is meant by the phrase *twice as big*. The figures in Box 10.9 represent the quandary faced by students and teachers alike.

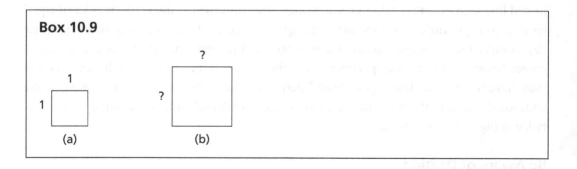

Box 10.9

For the majority that attempt this task, the choices narrow down to the sides of the larger square being either 2 or $\sqrt{2}$. Those who assert that $\sqrt{2}$ is the correct length argue that because the original 1-by-1 square has an area of 1, the new square must have an area of 2 to be twice as big. Thus, because the length times width needs to equal 2, the side must be $\sqrt{2}$ ($\sqrt{2} \cdot \sqrt{2} = 2$). The counterargument for the contingent on the other side of the fence is that the length of the side should be 2 because 2 is twice as big as 1.

The correct answer is the latter: The new side should be a length of 2. However, the reason is different than the one proposed above. This third task illustrates the use of ambiguity not only as a way to explore vague expressions but also as a way to address a problem referred to in earlier chapters—*drifting*. For one reason or another, people can drift from an appropriate definition or perspective to another, often erroneous, one. So why and how do students commonly drift in their understanding of squares? The reason ties back to instruction. To represent a square, teachers often use solid objects, such as square cutouts of cardboard or prefabricated models made from plastic. With continued exposure to these solid models, students' (and even teachers') perspectives of a square can drift to the one illustrated in Box 10.10.

Box 10.10

Students drift to the erroneous interpretation that a square is a solid, as shown in Box 10.10, and therefore includes the interior area. However, by definition, a square is four joined line segments that exhibit certain properties (intersect at the vertices, sides of equal length, all right angles, and so on). The figures in Box 10.9 are actually more accurate depictions of squares because the focus is on the four segments. In essence, a square is somewhat synonymous with perimeter. The distinction is that a square is the set of points that make up the four line segments and perimeter is a numeric value that represents the combined length of those segments. Thus, a square with each side the length of 2 is in fact twice as big as a 1-by-1 square.

Be Aware of Drifting

The previous task highlighted the need for teachers to be cognizant of traps caused by drifting and to be vigilant in addressing them. Some drifting occurs because of a tendency to flow to plain-English definitions of terms that have different meanings in mathematics. One such example is drifting from the mathematical meaning of *slope* to the English meaning of an incline.

Repeated patterns also promote drifting to erroneous perspectives. For example, students' idea of division can easily drift to the mistaken belief that the answer must be smaller than the dividend. Likewise, their interpretation of an equation can drift to a belief that it must contain a variable. Another common drift is the idea of $-y$ being a negative number when in fact it could be positive. The culprit in this case is students' repeated interpretation of the "$-$" sign as *negative* rather than *the opposite of*. Still another drifting example due to repeated patterns is the mistaken notion that the height of a geometric figure must be vertical because the majority of pictorial representations in teaching materials depict the height as vertical rather than horizontal or another orientation. Students need experiences with examples that illustrate the more precise definition of height as a segment drawn from a vertex so that it is perpendicular to the opposite side. Refer back to Box 10.2. That framework can serve as a reminder to address drifting via appropriate components such as examples, non-examples, and definitions of a given term outside of mathematics.

Teach Place Value with Other Bases

Another common mathematical issue similar to drifting is one where a topic not only drifts but erodes to a simplistic version, which is usually never revisited. Perhaps the most important example is the critical concept of place value. Students and teachers lose sight of the multiplicative nature and exponential growth of place value because of the computational ease of the base 10 system. With the ease of adding zeroes or moving decimal points, students can lose sight of what really happens in base 10 place value.

Teachers and curricula do not often reinforce the concept of place value by using other base systems. This tendency is unfortunate because working in other base systems enables students to dig deeper into the underlying foundations of place value. Because using other place-value systems is by and large a forgotten practice, revisiting the topic may create anxiety for teachers, requiring them to leave their base 10 comfort zone. However, by brushing up on the subject and using an activity with the proper context and connections, teachers can give students an opportunity to use another base to gain insight into the base 10 system. Box 10.11 shows an activity using a base 4 system.

Box 10.11: The World of Transportia

In the world of Transportia, a strict law governs the transportation system. This system is run by the government, which also owns all transportation vehicles. Due to limited fuel resources, vehicles are utilized according to need and efficiency. Transportia uses bicycles, compact cars, vans, buses, and monorails (trains) as transportation vehicles. A number code represents each type of vehicle's capacity to transport people, with each digit signifying the number of vehicles used. This code is structured as follows:

| _____ | _____ | _____ | _____ | _____ |
| trains | buses | vans | cars | bicycles |

The Transportia number system is analogous to place value. A bicycle has the capacity to transport 1 person and is, thus, in the normal "ones" place. A car is used to transport 4 people and is the unit in what would be the "tens" place. A large van is used to transport 16 people and occupies the "hundreds" place. A bus holds 64 people, and a train carries 256 passengers, occupying the "thousands" and "ten thousands" places respectively. Transportia law mandates that all vehicles can only be operated at maximum carrying capacity and used to the utmost efficiency to transport people from point A to point B. For example, a van cannot be used to transport only 10 people, and a bus must be used rather than four vans to carry 64 passengers.

From an instructional perspective, Transportia opens up interesting possibilities. Students can construct cutouts of the different vehicles as hands-on manipulatives and play different roles in the transportation system. Teachers may also choose not to tell students they are learning a base 4 system. To them, it is just the Transportia code. This code, through the use of concrete manipulatives, enables students to *see* the base 4 system and make sense of how it works through context. The context of this scenario enables teachers to devise activities and problems that mandate conversions from the decimal system to base 4, or vice versa. Box 10.12 gives two examples of possible tasks.

In Task 2, look at the place values for the Transportia code and determine which one is the largest that is 483 or less. The largest carrying capacity (place value) is 256, so that is the place value with which we start. How many 256s can we get out of 483? Or better yet,

Box 10.12: Transportia Tasks

Transportia Task 1

You are the transportation liaison for your company. You are given the Transportia code 3123. How many people are being transported with this combination of vehicles?

Solution: The task here is to convert the 3123 Transportia code (3 buses, 1 van, 2 cars, 3 bicycles) to a "regular" number (base 10).

3	1	2	3	Transportia digits
64s	16s	4s	ones	place "value"

The solution might be easier to see if done vertically.

$3 \cdot 64 = 192$ (3 buses • 64 people each)
$1 \cdot 16 = 16$ (1 van • 16 people each)
$2 \cdot 4 = 8$ (2 cars • 4 people each)
$3 \cdot 1 = 3$ (3 bicycles • 1 person each)
219 (total people)

Transportia Task 2

You are the transportation liaison for your company. Today you have 483 people (decimal system) that must be transported home. Find the Transportia code that will tell you the vehicles that will be needed to get the job done.

Solution Strategy: Use Transportia digits place "value" (vehicle capacities):

256	64	16	4	1

how many trains can 483 people completely fill? The answer is 1 because $1 \times 256 = 256$ and $2 \times 256 = 512$, and we cannot use a vehicle with any empty seats. The next step is to subtract the 256 people on the train from the total to determine the number of people left to transport: $483 - 256 = 227$. We now look at the next place value, which is 64s. How many 64s can we get out of 227, or how many buses can 227 people fill? Using division, we can get 3 full sets (buses) of 64 people each out of 227, with 35 people left over. The next place value is 16s. We can take 2 full sets of 16 out of 35 (or fill 2 vans), with 3 people left over. The next place value is 4s, but because the 3 people remaining do not create a full set of 4, we cannot use a car. The last place value is 1s, so we have to use 3 bicycles. In looking at the process, we see that the necessary vehicles to transport 483 people would be 1 train, 3 buses, 2 vans, 0 cars, and 3 bicycles, creating the Transportia code 13203.

We can reverse the process to check the solution:

$$
\begin{array}{rcl}
1 \times 256 &=& 256 \\
3 \times 64 &=& 192 \\
2 \times 16 &=& 32 \\
0 \times 4 &=& 0 \\
3 \times 1 &=& \underline{3} \\
& & 483
\end{array}
$$

Elementary or middle school teachers might be apprehensive about using an activity such as The World of Transportia, considering other place value systems to be upper-level mathematics. For example, third grade teachers may think their students do not need to know "all that algebra stuff" because it has nothing to do with what they are teaching. However, introducing base systems to deepen and reinforce understanding of place value lays a foundation for later concepts essential to algebraic reasoning. What's more, this type of activity can easily be adapted to various grade levels. In addition, Transportia demonstrated that understanding place value using a context simplifies conversions and adds clarity to the multiplicative nature of a number system, which can alleviate teacher anxiety. For teachers who are apprehensive about using different base systems because they are rusty with the mathematics, a key message of this book is the importance of teachers' content expertise. Elementary and middle school teachers must have a profound understanding of mathematics because otherwise, countless learning opportunities fail to become realities. And students are the ones who pay the price.

Teach Advanced Fundamentals

The majority of mathematics resources and textbooks use the phrase *elementary math*. Even this publication falls into that trap. However, *elementary* is not actually a fitting descriptor because it implies *simple*, and nothing could be further from the truth. Perhaps *fundamental* mathematics is a better descriptor of the content taught in elementary and middle schools. In examining that content, something interesting happens where fundamental mathematics intersects upper-level mathematics. At that intersection, the two merge to form an intermediary level we can refer to as *advanced fundamentals*. One perspective is that advanced fundamentals facilitate the metamorphosis of arithmetic into mathematics. By focusing on this deeper-level grasp of fundamentals, elementary and middle school teachers can help students develop a much stronger foundation in both arithmetic and mathematics. At its roots, *advanced fundamentals* are advanced in that a fundamental topic is taken to new depths and advanced in that the instruction on a fundamental topic simultaneously provides learning experiences that establish foundations for related, often more advanced concepts. That deeper level of understanding is a must-have for students if we are to narrow the math performance gap between the United States and its global competition. The following examples illustrate how advanced fundamentals bridge fundamental and upper-level topics and what instruction in these fundamentals looks like in the classroom.

Multiplication and Inverse Proportion. Examine the question in Box 10.13. Teachers who focus on multiplication only as repeated addition may struggle to answer this question. This fact highlights the importance of teacher expertise in fundamental mathematics.

Box 10.13

How can a conceptual understanding of multiplication be used as a powerful tool to establish an early foundation for students' understanding of inverse variation?

The key to answering the question is a knowledge of multiplication as a process for faster addition based on using *equal-sized groups*—the simple yet deep definition presented in Chapter Six. Building on that knowledge, experience with factors and products should provide a pattern in the relationship between the number of groups and the size of the groups. Take the factors of 24, for example. The expression $4 \cdot 6$ indicates that we have 4 groups of 6 each. If we *increase* the number of groups to 12, to still have a product of 24, we must *decrease* the size of the groups to 2 each. If we then go in the opposite direction and *decrease* the number of groups from 12 to 8, we must *increase* the size of each group from 2 to 3. Thus, an *inverse relationship* exists between the number of groups and the size of each group in multiplication.

Depending on the grade level, teachers can extend this pattern beyond whole numbers to contexts involving fractions. Using the same product of 24, suppose that 24 students each get one full bag of chips. But for whatever reason, the number of students increases to 48. Because the number of groups *increased*, the size of each group must *decrease*. Because $48 \cdot \frac{1}{2}$ is 24, each student will get $\frac{1}{2}$ bag of chips.

Fractional parts and wholes can also be used to help students understand that when one whole is portioned into pieces, the *larger* the number of pieces, the *smaller* each piece becomes. This critical inverse relationship with fractions connects directly with grouping in multiplication. With sufficient experience, an understanding of the fraction relationship will prevent students from mistakenly thinking a fraction such as $\frac{1}{3}$ is less than $\frac{1}{4}$ (assuming the same-sized whole) because 3 is less than 4.

Note that in all of these cases, and in any inverse or direct variation, there are actually *three* components, one of which must remain constant so that the relationship between the other two can be determined. For example, in the scenario with the factors of 24, the product of 24 must remain constant to determine the inverse relationship of the two factors. This context is no different from that of a fraction where the whole, just like the 24, remained constant. And just like more slices meant smaller slices, more groups meant smaller groups.

Division as a Proportion.   Consider Box 10.14. Teachers often ask students to do computations similar to the one shown. The students get an answer, in this case 1.25, but teachers leave the story unfinished. By not examining the deeper meaning, the computation becomes yet another tedious "drill and kill" activity with no real learning or purpose. How can teachers address this issue through advanced fundamentals?

Box 10.14

How can this division problem be interpreted as a proportion?

$4\overline{)5}$

What was the purpose of the task above in the first place, and what does the result truly mean? These are the types of questions teachers should ask themselves when assigning such tasks. The typical purpose for a problem such as the one in Box 10.14, is to provide more computational practice in division. But there can be a lot more, deeper math that can be mined from such a problem. This depth begins with a connection to a simple yet deep definition of a proportion. In Chapter Seven a proportion was presented as an equation stating that two ratios are equivalent. The other piece of the puzzle is finding relationships. As a model for the above problem, consider a wage scenario. In discussing wages, employees do not normally say they make $80 every 4 hours. Instead, they say they make $20 per hour. We have a propensity to compare to one, which is logical because comparing to one is the easiest and most comprehensible of comparisons. This tendency is the basis for a unit rate, such as the comparison of hourly pay to one hour. Mathematically, the thought process for the wage scenario would look like this:

$$\frac{80}{4} = \frac{20}{1}$$

If a student were to express the problem in Box 10.14 as an equation, it would probably look something like the one below:

$$\frac{5}{4} = y$$

Once the computation is completed, the equation then becomes the following:

$$\frac{5}{4} = 1.25$$

Unfortunately, this limited process completely masks the idea of comparing to one. If we focus on the idea of a proportion, however, students can take the expression written in the typical form with the division symbol and convert it to the proportion below:

$$\frac{5}{4} = \frac{y}{1}$$

Avoiding shortcuts and laziness, the solution should be expressed as:

$$\frac{5}{4} = \frac{1.25}{1}$$

By expressing the solution in this manner, students can see what the result truly communicates. The purpose for doing division is no longer a drill, but to show how in some contexts, the purpose and result is expressing a relationship as a comparison to one, versus some other amount. When using an approach like this one, teachers need to inform students at the start what the purpose of the task is and what connection is being made. In this case, that explanation would help students understand they need to set up the equation as a proportion.

Merge and Connect Seemingly Unrelated Concepts

Interesting things happen when two seemingly unrelated topics in mathematics merge. And, once again, such connections are dependent on the content expertise of the teacher.

The Multiplication Chart: Hidden Gold.   Upon first inspection, it would not seem that the typical multiplication chart should be used in the instruction of fractions. A cross-country tour of elementary and middle schools would find thousands of multiplication charts (Box 10.15) hanging on classroom walls. Although rich with potential, the very name of these charts often limits their focus and utilization to *multiplication*. An old adage states that sometimes we cannot see the forest because of the trees. In this context, we cannot see the forest because of the multiplication.

Box 10.15: Typical Multiplication Chart

	1	2	3	4	5	6	7	8	9	10
1	1	2	3	4	5	6	7	8	9	10
2	2	4	6	8	10	12	14	16	18	20
3	3	6	9	12	15	18	21	24	27	30
4	4	8	12	16	20	24	28	32	36	40
5	5	10	15	20	25	30	35	40	45	50
6	6	12	18	24	30	36	42	48	54	60
7	7	14	21	28	35	42	49	56	63	70
8	8	16	24	32	40	48	56	64	72	80
9	9	18	27	36	45	54	63	72	81	90
10	10	20	30	40	50	60	70	80	90	100

It is regrettable that the times table, preferably referred to as a grouping table or a multiplication chart, more often than not collects dust on classroom walls. However, by connecting the dots, we can transform this dusty chart into a Chart of Hidden Gold, as shown in Box 10.16. This chart takes advantage of the multiplication chart's focus on factors and multiplication. *Equivalent fractions* also involve multiplication and factors. There must be a connection or overlap somewhere. Although not readily apparent, the multiplication chart contains almost every set of equivalent fractions that elementary or middle school students would ever need. Someone once said that beauty is in the eye of the beholder, and in this context, the revamped chart glitters like gold.

Box 10.16: Equivalent Fraction Chart (aka Hidden Gold)

	1	2	3	4	5	6	7	8	9	10
1	1	2	3	4	5	6	7	8	9	10
2	2	4	6	8	10	12	14	16	18	20
3	3	6	9	12	15	18	21	24	27	30
4	4	8	12	16	20	24	28	32	36	40
5	5	10	15	20	25	30	35	40	45	50
6	6	12	18	24	30	36	42	48	54	60
7	7	14	21	28	35	42	49	56	63	70
8	8	16	24	32	40	48	56	64	72	80
9	9	18	27	36	45	54	63	72	81	90
10	10	20	30	40	50	60	70	80	90	100

So where is the gold in Box 10.16? Basically, the chart is the same as the one in Box 10.15, except presented from a new perspective. Notice that two rows are highlighted. Those two rows were selected arbitrarily as an example. Let the top row that contains the multiples of 3 be the numerator of the fraction and the bottom row that contains the multiples of 5 be the denominator. Pairing the numbers on the same vertical columns results in fractions such as $\frac{3}{5}$, $\frac{6}{10}$, $\frac{9}{15}$, and so on. It is definitely not a coincidence that the fractions formed by the matching numbers in those two columns are all equivalent fractions. The simplest of the fractions is $\frac{3}{5}$. All the others along that pair of rows are the result of multiplying both the numerator and denominator of $\frac{3}{5}$ by some factor. In fact, the factor that is used for that multiplication appears on the top row of the chart. For example, $\frac{12}{20}$ is the result of multiplying both the numerator and denominator of $\frac{3}{5}$ by 4. Students can use the chart in both directions as well. They can start at $\frac{3}{5}$ and find that $\frac{21}{35}$ is an equivalent fraction. Or students might be given the fraction $\frac{24}{40}$ and find that it is $\frac{3}{5}$ in simplest form. Notice that patterns of equivalent fractions also run vertically along the columns. However, it is more advantageous to use the horizontal rows because they parallel the representation of fractions.

The chart contains the majority of fractions that students will need in fundamental mathematics. If students were interested in fractions equivalent to $\frac{2}{7}$, they would select the rows containing the multiples of 2 and 7. If $\frac{3}{4}$ was the fraction of interest, students would highlight the rows containing the multiples of 3 and 4. The key to deeper understanding is to use the chart as a tool that visually represents what happens in the process of finding equivalent fractions. The information that is needed to help understand *why* the process works as it does is contained in the chart. For example, if the task is to simplify $\frac{42}{60}$, find a column that contains both the 42 and the 60. By looking at the top of the column, we notice that the common factor is 6. Now we know that both the numerator (42) and the denominator (60) must be divided by 6, resulting in $\frac{7}{10}$. Scrolling to the left along both rows will land us at $\frac{7}{10}$, but that constitutes a shortcut. Teachers may want to use this shortcut to assist struggling students, but the chart should not become a crutch that students use without deep thinking. And it is up to the teacher to ensure this proper use.

Used appropriately, then, the chart is not about making computation easier but about helping students make conceptual connections. For example, when two numbers are in the same vertical column, those two numbers must have a common factor, which is the one at the top of that column. This realization can then help students better understand that to simplify a fraction, the numerator and denominator must have a common factor. This type of conceptual understanding is the hidden gold in the chart.

An Adapted Addition Facts Chart: A Hidden Gem. What happens when you cross-pollinate a basic addition chart with the coordinate plane? You find a hidden gem. I have been in countless classrooms and gone to numerous websites looking for different types of addition fact tables, but all I have found are charts similar to the one in Box 10.17.

At first glance, the likelihood of the convergence or intersection of the two disjointed topics of a basic addition facts chart and coordinate geometry seem unlikely. However, pondering the initial question more seriously, we can see a common feature that this chart and the coordinate plane share. If we consider the vertex at the bottom left of the chart to be the origin, the chart would be the first quadrant of a coordinate plane. The addition facts could then be rearranged to fit the labeling of the x- and y-axes of the coordinate plane. The merger results in the chart in Box 10.18.

Box 10.17: Addition Facts Chart

+	1	2	3	4	5	6	7	8	9	10
1	2	3	4	5	6	7	8	9	10	11
2	3	4	5	6	7	8	9	10	11	12
3	4	5	6	7	8	9	10	11	12	13
4	5	6	7	8	9	10	11	12	13	14
5	6	7	8	9	10	11	12	13	14	15
6	7	8	9	10	11	12	13	14	15	16
7	8	9	10	11	12	13	14	15	16	17
8	9	10	11	12	13	14	15	16	17	18
9	10	11	12	13	14	15	16	17	18	19
10	11	12	13	14	15	16	17	18	19	20

The merged chart is the result of using strong content expertise to connect two seemingly unrelated topics, thereby bridging fundamental and higher-level mathematics. The bridging of a supposed gap between basic addition and the coordinate plane was accomplished through a deep, *advanced* knowledge of those two *fundamental* concepts, and the chart in Box 10.18 is the result of that merger. A close examination of the transformed chart unearths a storehouse of possibilities and connections that take students much further than deep knowledge of only one or the other could have.

Students are experienced with horizontal number lines, but need much more experience with number lines that are vertical rather than horizontal. The original addition facts chart actually *inhibits* that learning because that vertical number line is the reversal of normal contexts. The adapted chart, on the other hand, simulates a vertical number line that corresponds to real-life contexts, such as a thermometer, height, or altitude. Both addition facts charts present the sums of different combinations of addends and share some common patterns, but the modified version has the tremendous advantage in that it also lays the foundation for navigating the x- and y-axes in a two-coordinate plane. By using this chart, students at a much younger age can get the idea that numbers get larger if you go to the right or up and smaller if you go to the left or down. In other words, computation practice using the chart has the added benefit of simultaneously ingraining the fundamental aspects of navigation on the coordinate plane. Imagine the pleasant surprise secondary math teachers will get when students arrive with the skills to read the coordinate plane already embedded in their minds!

Box 10.18: Addition Facts and Then Sum

10	11	12	13	14	15	16	17	18	19	20
9	10	11	12	13	14	15	16	17	18	19
8	9	10	11	12	13	14	15	16	17	18
7	8	9	10	11	12	13	14	15	16	17
6	7	8	9	10	11	12	13	14	15	16
5	6	7	8	9	10	11	12	13	14	15
4	5	6	7	8	9	10	11	12	13	14
3	4	5	6	7	8	9	10	11	12	13
2	3	4	5	6	7	8	9	10	11	12
1	2	3	4	5	6	7	8	9	10	11
+	1	2	3	4	5	6	7	8	9	10

Focusing on addition, the adapted chart enables students to go beyond simply finding the sum of two addends on the horizontal and vertical axes. Students can start at any number in the chart and move in the appropriate direction for one single addition or subtraction. Students can also do various combinations of addition and subtraction. For example, if students start at any of the 7s and go right 1 and up 3, they will be at 11. Expressed mathematically, the computation is $7 + 1 + 3 = 11$, which is equivalent to $7 + 4 = 11$. Note that to achieve maximum benefit from the chart, students *must* take this extra step of expressing the movement mathematically in writing.

Repeated practice using this process but with examples that start at different locations can yield alternate computation strategies. For example, if n represents different starting points, repeated application of $n - 10 + 2$ will result in the realization that this expression is equivalent to $n - 8$. In plain English, students will realize that an alternative way of subtracting 8 is to subtract 10 (which is often easier) and then add 2.

A huge bonus of the improved chart—and another pleasant surprise for future teachers—is that when used appropriately, it opens up a whole world of combinations that can lay the foundation for operations (addition and subtraction) with *integers*. For example, if students start at any 8 and go left 3 and up 1, the result is 6. The mathematical expression for that navigation would be $8 - 3 + 1 = 6$, which is equivalent to $8 - 2 = 6$. Students should notice that the $-3 + 1$ resulted in -2 and begin to see those patterns. Such repeated observations will result in students intuitively doing integer combinations before they even learn what an integer is!

This foundation in integer combinations can go as far as teachers choose to take it. With the appropriate tasks, students can discover that the sum of two negatives is still a negative. For example, if students start at any 12 and go left 3 and down 2, the mathematical expression would be $12 - 3 - 2 = 7$, with the equivalent expression being $12 - 5 = 7$. With assistance from the teacher, students can notice that the -3 and -2 are equivalent to -5. Additional experiences will lead to students' discovery that no matter where they start, going left 1 and down 2 results in subtracting 3. If teachers provide the mandatory symbolism at the same time, showing that -1 and -2 result in -3, students will begin to intuitively realize that the sum of two negative numbers is another negative number while noting the parallels of $-1 + (-2)$ and $1 + 2$.

Teachers can facilitate further discovery by helping students notice patterns of cells connected diagonally. For example, in the chart, the numbers in the diagonals with a positive slope (/) have a difference of 2. This pattern results from navigating from one number to the other along that diagonal—you either go right one and up one ($1 + 1$) or left one and down one ($-1 + -1$), accounting for the difference of 2. Of course, teachers should not point out such patterns and their causes directly but rather guide students in discovering and justifying them.

Another pattern is found in the chart cells connected along diagonals with a negative slope (\). These diagonals repeat the same numbers. The reason is similar to the one for the diagonals with the positive slope. To navigate from one number to the other along the diagonals of negative slope, you either go right one and down one ($1 - 1$) or left one and up one ($-1 + 1$). This movement accounts for a difference of 0, which leaves the number unchanged. Teachers should not be surprised if students notice that the navigation could have been -2 and $+2$ along that diagonal, or that every other number along the positive sloped diagonal has a difference of 4 because of navigations such as right 2 and up 2.

Depending on the grade level and the maturity of the students, an astute teacher can expand the chart beyond the first quadrant to one that includes all four quadrants, as in the chart in Box 10.19. This expanded chart takes the integer combinations to a new level, where negative results are possible. Note that these are *addition* charts, so one limitation is they cannot model subtraction of a negative integer. Teachers might be tempted to create imaginative rules such as modeling $5 - (-2)$ by reflecting the -2 in the opposite direction. However, such teacher-created rules can cause too much confusion for students, and perhaps another tool should be used to model that situation.

Box 10.19: Addition Facts Beyond the First Quadrant: Combining Integers

0	1	2	3	4	5	6	7	8	9	10	11	12	13	14	15	16	17	18	19	20
−1	0	1	2	3	4	5	6	7	8	9	10	11	12	13	14	15	16	17	18	19
−2	−1	0	1	2	3	4	5	6	7	8	9	10	11	12	13	14	15	16	17	18
−3	−2	−1	0	1	2	3	4	5	6	7	8	9	10	11	12	13	14	15	16	17
−4	−3	−2	−1	0	1	2	3	4	5	6	7	8	9	10	11	12	13	14	15	16
−5	−4	−3	−2	−1	0	1	2	3	4	5	6	7	8	9	10	11	12	13	14	15
−6	−5	−4	−3	−2	−1	0	1	2	3	4	5	6	7	8	9	10	11	12	13	14
−7	−6	−5	−4	−3	−2	−1	0	1	2	3	4	5	6	7	8	9	10	11	12	13
−8	−7	−6	−5	−4	−3	−2	−1	0	1	2	3	4	5	6	7	8	9	10	11	12
−9	−8	−7	−6	−5	−4	−3	−2	−1	0	1	2	3	4	5	6	7	8	9	10	11
−10	−9	−8	−7	−6	−5	−4	−3	−2	−1	0	1	2	3	4	5	6	7	8	9	10
−11	−10	−9	−8	−7	−6	−5	−4	−3	−2	−1	0	1	2	3	4	5	6	7	8	9
−12	−11	−10	−9	−8	−7	−6	−5	−4	−3	−2	−1	0	1	2	3	4	5	6	7	8
−13	−12	−11	−10	−9	−8	−7	−6	−5	−4	−3	−2	−1	0	1	2	3	4	5	6	7
−14	−13	−12	−11	−10	−9	−8	−7	−6	−5	−4	−3	−2	−1	0	1	2	3	4	5	6
−15	−14	−13	−12	−11	−10	−9	−8	−7	−6	−5	−4	−3	−2	−1	0	1	2	3	4	5
−16	−15	−14	−13	−12	−11	−10	−9	−8	−7	−6	−5	−4	−3	−2	−1	0	1	2	3	4
−17	−16	−15	−14	−13	−12	−11	−10	−9	−8	−7	−6	−5	−4	−3	−2	−1	0	1	2	3
−18	−17	−16	−15	−14	−13	−12	−11	−10	−9	−8	−7	−6	−5	−4	−3	−2	−1	0	1	2
−19	−18	−17	−16	−15	−14	−13	−12	−11	−10	−9	−8	−7	−6	−5	−4	−3	−2	−1	0	1
−20	−19	−18	−17	−16	−15	−14	−13	−12	−11	−10	−9	−8	−7	−6	−5	−4	−3	−2	−1	0

Use Manipulatives

Research on instruction shows that the use of manipulatives and models is an effective strategy. This finding seems logical because no matter how accurate, insightful, and well crafted a teacher makes the language and symbolism, some students will still not get it. For some students, they must literally *see* a mathematics idea or concept in 3-D. The use of manipulatives or models has been illustrated through activities such as the trapezoid case study in Chapter Nine.

Two caveats are needed when using manipulatives for instruction. First, teachers must ensure that the activity is hands-on, brains-on—rather than hands-on, brains-off. In other words, teachers must ensure that the focus does not drift from the intended mathematics concept to the solid manipulatives themselves. A second related problem is the need at the end of such hands-on activities to bridge the chasm between the abstract and the concrete. Teachers can sometimes forget to do this essential step and must ensure that students make the connection between the physical model and the abstract concept.

Rather than provide more examples of the use of manipulatives, the following activity is meant to provide motivation for readers to use manipulatives in instruction whenever feasible or applicable. Suppose you are a participant in a professional development session.

> **Step One.** The presenter announces that an object will be shown to the audience. Participants are told to pretend they have never seen the object before and to wipe out any knowledge they have of it. Working in small groups, participants are to make a list of all they can determine about the object based entirely on the use of their five senses (sight, touch, and so on). The object shown is a real pear.

> **Step Two**. When the groups have completed their lists, the presenter announces that the audience will be shown a second object. The instructions are similar. Participants are, once again, to pretend they have never seen the object before and know nothing about it. The new task is to eliminate or strike through any items on the group's list that are no longer true about the object or that members cannot determine about it based on their five senses. The new object is a plastic model of a pear.

> **Step Three**. When that task is complete, the presenter announces that the audience will be shown a third object. The instructions are the same as the previous step. The new object is a picture of a pear.

Step Four. This step repeats Step 3. This time, the new object shown to the audience is a sheet of paper with the written word *pear*. By this point, each group's list should almost be wiped out.

Step Five. The pattern continues with the presenter providing one last item. The presenter orally states *pear* and that is the only clue. At this point, every item on the list should be eliminated because participants do not know if the word is *pear*, *pair*, or *pare*.

The lesson of this exercise regarding the importance of using manipulatives and models in math instruction should be fairly transparent. Traditional instruction relies heavily on oral lectures supported by written words and symbols, with occasional utilization of visuals/pictures. Although teachers in the early grades often incorporate manipulatives and models, their use dwindles as the math becomes more abstract. Experienced observers of classroom instruction can validate that they are more likely to see manipulatives used in grade 3 than in grade 9. However, as the exercise shows, the richness of information increased as the source of information went from oral to written to visual sources and culminated in physical models or the real thing. Oral and written sources do not provide much information or data to process. They can't match the value of the physical and the real, particularly when students know little about a topic.

CONCLUSION

The instructional methods and strategies in this chapter focused on the language of math, and how to interpret that language, as a way to build and deepen students' conceptual understanding. As mentioned, *language-focused* in this context does not imply instruction geared to English language learners. All students share these language-based difficulties and can benefit from this type of instruction. In summary, the following actions can help transform your teaching into language-focused conceptual instruction:

- Emphasize both symbolism and academic language
- Use a simple yet deep approach to define key terms and examine those terms with a variety of techniques
- Organize thinking and processes with graphic organizers
- Use ambiguity in the language as an instructional asset
- Use the deep knowledge of one topic to make connections to and leverage the learning of both related and seemingly unrelated topics
- Use concrete models or manipulatives to the fullest extent possible

These strategies should not occur in isolation. They are far more effective and powerful when blended and used in combination. In addition, they require that teachers provide students with multiple experiences and practice to instill understanding—such activities must become an integral part of teachers' daily instruction. However, the real driving force behind these methods is a deep content knowledge of mathematics. Only by continuing to develop and expand their own conceptual understanding can teachers take full advantage of strategies such as employing advanced fundamentals. But with all the puzzle pieces in place, a language-focused conceptual approach can help instructors move beyond teaching arithmetic and efficiency to teaching *mathematics* to *all* students.

One key piece of the puzzle is still missing, however. This strategy, which is important enough to warrant its own chapter, focuses on how instructors can bridge fundamental and advanced mathematics through the use of relationships.

Mathematics: It's All About Relationships!

Arithmetic is about computation. Mathematics is about relationships.

—Unknown

In a whodunit, discovering one key relationship can sometimes cause all the clues to fall into place, revealing the identity of the perpetrator and solving the case. Mathematics is similar. Determining the key relationships in a problem often reveals the solution or at least the best way to obtain it.

Learning to approach mathematics from a relationships perspective can be a powerful tool. Yet, despite the critical role of relationships in math, few problem-solving strategies specifically include this as a critical step of the process. As a result, teachers need to ensure they help students find and understand the relationships in mathematical contexts as an integral part of instruction.

The focus on relationships was saved as the last major topic for discussion because it builds on much of the previous information. Unlike human relationships, which are based on emotion, mathematical relationships are based on reason. However, similar to relationships among humans, relationships in math are not independent entities. Uncovering and understanding relationships in math is dependent on content expertise as well as a deep understanding of the language and symbolism. In essence, relationships are the by-product of making connections among concepts, with all these factors being interdependent and

219

supportive of each other. Because of the complexity of these relationships, illustrating how they can manifest in various contexts can be helpful. These contexts involve factors such as language and proportional reasoning, which in turn are influenced by thought processes such as interpretation, assumptions, and multiple perspectives. Among humans, some relationships last even though contexts may change. Math is no different. Included in this chapter are example problems where teachers can see how the same relationships in fundamental math emerge later in more sophisticated scenarios.

LANGUAGE AND SYMBOLISM: VEHICLES FOR RELATIONSHIP RECOGNITION

Learning to recognize relationships in mathematics starts with a focus on the language. This focus is essential because, regardless of context, students can make sense of mathematics only if they understand the language, be it words, symbols, or visuals.

Precision in Language

Refer to Box 11.1, which provides examples of how students must be cognizant of minute details to successfully interpret language and contexts in mathematics.

Box 11.1

Comment on the following pairs of statements/questions:

Standard English context:

1. Today, I saw a man almost get run over by a car.
2. Today, I almost saw a man get run over by a car.
3. Slow children at play.
4. Slow, children at play.

Mathematics context:

5. If you take 3 apples from 5 apples, how many apples would you have?
6. If you take 3 apples from 5 apples, how many apples would be left?

Examination of the first pairing reveals that the reader would be well advised to be the pedestrian in statement 1 rather than statement 2. This pairing illustrates how word order can make a significant difference. The second pairing highlights how a small detail such as a comma can completely alter meaning. With no contextual clues, each statement conveys a different message. The third pairing indicates the importance of word choice and specificity. The answer to question 5 is 3 because the question asks for the apples *in your possession* after stating that *you took 3*. True, 2 apples are left, but that result matches the solution requested in question 6.

When the idea of precision is mentioned in mathematics, most people immediately think of numbers and computation or measurement. Precision in those areas is extremely important, but it's not enough. It may seem counterintuitive, but *precision in language* is equally important in mathematics, perhaps even more important than in many other disciplines. The third pairing in Box 11.1 illustrates this point, as well as being an example of how repetition of common phrases (such as that in statement 6) can dull students' awareness to the subtle changes in similar statements (such as in statement 5).

Being cognizant of precision in mathematical language helps students make accurate interpretations, a prerequisite for uncovering and understanding relationships. For example, the repeated use of loose interpretations can lead to detrimental habits, such as reading $-d$ as *negative d* rather than *the opposite of d*. This point may seem like a minor detail, but the former interpretation of the negative symbol (which is a misnomer, by the way!) can seriously hinder students' recognition of relationships in algebraic expressions, which are so common in secondary mathematics.

Do Not Forget the Symbolism

Understanding relationships starts early in mathematics with such concepts as conservation, one-to-one correspondence, cardinality, ordinality, and place value. These basic concepts all focus on number, numerical representation, and numerical contexts. Students need to realize that much of fundamental mathematics involves taking things apart, putting things together, and rearranging things. Integral to these processes is recognizing the relationships among these groupings—and integral to recognizing those relationships is an accurate interpretation of the symbolism.

Refer to the scenario in Box 11.2. This scenario illustrates how misinterpreting symbolism and what it represents can lead to misunderstanding the relationship in a problem. The problem's context connects to place value in that each digit has an associated value determined by its descriptor, which may or may not be overtly expressed. One of the fundamental facts students must commit to long-term memory is the realization that with or without context, each numeral and digit represents *something*. The interpretation of the symbolism, then, is a critical first step in the relationship discovery process. Not focusing on the *meaning* of the digits in this subtraction problem led to the student error of using relationships in the base 10 system, resulting in "regular" subtraction as the solution process. The student needed to realize that the digits have a unit of measure assigned to each. This then is the basis for the relationships in that context. Thus, the relationship between the 8 and 3 is that of feet to inches, not tens to ones as in place value. When one foot must be decomposed to inches, the result is 12, not 10, inches added to the 3 inches. The conversion results in 7 feet 15 inches. Performing the subtraction correctly obtains the correct solution of 5 feet 8 inches.

Box 11.2

Examine the following subtraction problem.

> 8 feet 3 inches
> - 2 feet 7 inches
> ——————————
> 5 feet 6 inches

What mistake did the student make? What could be the reasons for the mistake?

As mentioned previously, early mathematics focuses on separating, rearranging, and combining things. Inherent in those processes are relationships, which in turn are expressed symbolically in some fashion. For instance, when students first learn the number 7, they actually learn it as *one full set* of 7 things. In conjunction with this idea, students should learn that this one set of 7 can also consist of different *combinations, sets, or groups*. Solid manipulatives should be used to show not only all 7 things together but also other combinations, such as a set of 5 + a set of 2, a set of 4 + a set of 3, and so on. By attaching unit descriptors, teachers can inject these examples with even more meaning. With this perspective, students are following a relationship-based path, rather than a procedural process for memorizing addition facts.

Language and Symbolism: The Bridge to Relationship Recognition

Language and symbolism provide the bridge to recognizing relationships in mathematics. However, traditional instruction's inattention to and imprecise use of language and symbolism can weaken or even destroy that bridge. For students, the ultimate cost is a lack of conceptual understanding. Although this point has been made several times, the magnitude of its importance warrants another example.

> **Box 11.3**
>
> You have 7 boxes with 4 toys in each. How many total toys do you have?

Do Not Blow Up the Bridge. The careless use of language in traditional instruction is the antithesis of what is needed for conceptual understanding. Refer to the problem in Box 11.3. To solve this problem, we multiply 7 • 4 and get 28. The 7 represents the number of sets, the 4 represents the size of each set, and the 28 represents the product. Teachers sometimes make statements in this type of scenario such as "when we multiply, the answer is larger." In this context, is the "answer" of 28 really *more* or *larger*? Of course it is not! The mathematical expression for this context would be 7 • 4 = 28, so 7 sets of 4 toys each *is the same quantity* as 28 toys! We are not comparing 28 with the 7 or the 4. The 28 simply expresses the total amount of toys, but teachers for some reason unknowingly interject the idea of *comparison*. The lexical mistake in this scenario is the incomplete statement that *28 is more*. Even if there was a comparison, 28 is more than what? In mathematics, in making a comparison, one must always state all the items being compared. (The paradox is that a portion of mathematics is about making comparisons, yet the discipline actually does a poor job of expressing those comparative relationships, especially in the area of number and operations.)

Perhaps this concern may seem frivolous to some, but such careless language can inadvertently help erode students' understanding of the mathematical idea of equality. Moreover, research such as that cited in Chapter Four (Falkner, Levi, & Carpenter, 1999) indicates that a problem does indeed exist with students' interpretation of the equal sign.

Do We Really Need *Answers*? In multiplication, the correct academic term for the solution, the 28 in this scenario, is the *product*. However, teachers often revert to plain English and refer to the product as the *answer*. Either description masks what has really happened in Box 11.3, which is that 7 smaller sets of 4 each have been converted to one large set of 28. Symbolically, what happens in a context such as this might be better expressed as 7 • 4 = 1 • 28. The previous section on symbolism highlighted the need for students to learn numbers from a grouping and relationship perspective. With this foundation, students can understand that sometimes the process of multiplication actually involves converting a number of smaller equal-sized sets into one larger set. This understanding then connects to division as a process of taking one large set and subdividing it into a larger number of smaller equal-sized sets. Unfortunately, without an understanding of these relationships, a product such as 28 can drift from the idea of one large *set* of 28 to an *answer* of 28.

We have to consider if we really need answers in mathematics. And by *answers,* I mean the term and how its careless use can distort meaning. The term is often an integral part of the language associated with students' blind manipulation of naked numbers, which provide no real understanding of what the symbols or the ultimate answer represent. Even in a contextual situation, the term *answer* ultimately can replace the descriptor that should be used with the numeric result, losing whatever relationships may have emerged in the process. We need to adjust our perspective regarding the use of this term in mathematics. Insightful reflection might reveal that the use of *answer,* combined with miscues from either content or instructional practices, culminates in ludicrous assertions such as, "When we divide, the answer is smaller."

Two chapters have been devoted to fractions because of the many issues they present involving language and symbolism. Those issues, in turn, have a bearing on the relationships represented. By exploring these relationships, teachers can help students better navigate through the fraction kingdom.

RELATIONSHIPS AND FRACTIONS

The revelation of relationships in mathematics often takes place within the boundaries of the symbolism or representation. The symbolism of fractions is especially problematic, and given the amount that students struggle with the topic, recognizing relationships in fractions is an area in need of more attention.

Box 11.4

Find another true relationship in each of the two proportions below.

$$\frac{1}{2} = \frac{3}{6} \qquad \frac{a}{c} = \frac{b}{d}$$

Unearthing Relationships in Fractions

Refer to Box 11.4. The two tasks are essentially the same, with the primary difference being the level of justification required. The first task would be appropriate at an elementary school level, whereas the second would better fit a junior high school class or algebra course. The key is that students understand that in any fraction, regardless of where it falls in the fraction kingdom, a relationship exists between the numerator and denominator. Refer to the proportion on the left. By looking across the equal sign, one of the more obvious derivations of the given proportion would be for students to compare the numerators to each other and the denominators to each other (see Box 11.5). Through computation, students could informally show that this equation is a valid new proportion. However, the focus of the task should be to show how, based on the initial relationships, other relationships also exist in a proportional situation.

Box 11.5

$$\frac{1}{2} = \frac{3}{6} \implies \frac{1}{3} = \frac{2}{6}$$

The second proportion in Box 11.4 is stated more algebraically and at higher grade levels would include a more demanding justification as to validity. The same general relationships should be noted as in the first proportion. However, the expectation for a more formal proof must be met. One such approach is modeled by the process illustrated in Box 11.6. The missing component in the illustration is the explanation of the properties or logic used to arrive at the second and third proportions.

Box 11.6

$$\frac{a}{b} = \frac{c}{d} \implies \frac{a}{b} \bullet \frac{b}{c} = \frac{c}{d} \bullet \frac{b}{c} \implies \frac{a}{c} = \frac{b}{d}$$

Teachers can create a multitude of scenarios with fractions where students can explore possible relationships. For example, what happens if one takes a proportion and adds the denominator to the numerator in each ratio, as shown in Box 11.7? The level of sophistication for the justification in such scenarios would depend on the grade level and content expertise of the students.

Box 11.7

$$\frac{1}{2} = \frac{3}{6} \implies \frac{1+2}{2} = \frac{3+6}{6}$$

Previous attention has been focused on the importance of understanding the relationship of operations and the fraction bar. Students are taught to divide fractions by following a rote process that involves multiplying by the reciprocal. To discover other alternatives, students need to be allowed to explore the symbolic representation. The flow shown in Box 11.8 illustrates how division by a fraction can actually be done via division only rather than by multiplying by the reciprocal. Understanding the relationships in the symbolism is a necessity to make the transition from the second to the third expression in Box 11.8. That type of interpretive skill is not possible without expert teacher guidance, however.

Box 11.8

$$4\frac{4}{9} \div \frac{2}{3} \implies \frac{40}{9} \div \frac{2}{3} \implies \frac{40 \div 2}{9 \div 3}$$

Warning: Hidden Relationships

Like traditional instruction, textbooks can lead students to loosely interpret relationships in mathematics. This practice often happens when a figure is representing something in real life. One common example is a frequent style used for map scales: 1 inch = 20 miles. Interpreted literally, this assertion is a blatant error. One inch never has and never will be equal to 20 miles! A map scale is actually a comparison, a relationship of the size of the map to what it represents in real life. Because the scale is a ratio, it should be presented that way to ensure precision in language and mathematics (Box 11.9).

Box 11.9

1 inch (on map)
20 miles (in real life)

Teachers need to ensure that a false statement such as 1 inch = 20 miles is clarified with the more appropriate ratio shown in Box 11.9. The confusing equation is an instance of a relationship that is hidden because there was no fraction (ratio) that enables students to unearth it. The expression as a proportion provides the information students need to understand the relationship is a comparison, not an equality.

PROPORTIONAL REASONING

Understanding the relationships inherent in the symbolism of fractions is inextricably linked to proportional reasoning, which involves ratios and proportions. By definition, a ratio is an expression of a relationship, so it stands to reason that this chapter would at some point address the idea of proportional reasoning. This topic begins to garner emphasis at the middle school level, which coincidentally is when student performance in math frequently begins a precipitous decline. In addition, research indicates that proportional reasoning is a critical prerequisite to learning higher mathematical concepts. For these two reasons, highlighting the connection between relationships and proportional reasoning is in order.

Transitioning from Absolute to Relative Comparison

The conceptual foundation of a ratio is based on relative (multiplicative) reasoning, which involves making a comparison based on multiplication and scale factors (that is, 35 is 7 times bigger than 5, or 30 is $\frac{1}{2}$ of 60). The multiplicative comparison is also expressed in terms of percentage (that is, 9 is 50% more than 6). The bulk of students' elementary school experiences are based on absolute (additive) reasoning, which makes comparisons based strictly on how much more or less one number is than another (that is, 80 is 9 more than 71, or 67 is 3 less than 70).

Mathematics involves both types of comparison, but students must move beyond absolute comparisons and transition to relative reasoning, which is the foundation for proportional reasoning. As a starting point for examining this transition, refer to Box 11.10.

Box 11.10

You are an employee of Typical City ISD. The school district is considering a pay raise for all employees in the district. District leaders are considering two plans. Plan 1 is an annual increase of $1,000 across the board for all employees regardless of position. Plan 2 calls for a 4% pay increase for each employee. Disregarding income taxes, which plan is better and why?

Rather than rely on computation examples, teachers can use this type of contextual problem to bring the distinction between absolute and relative reasoning to the forefront.

Each plan exemplifies one of the two types of comparative reasoning. In addition, the problem presents a valuable real-life lesson on personal and public finance. The proper response to this quandary is "it depends." Employees making less than $25,000 a year would benefit more from a straight $1,000 raise because 4% of their individual salaries would be less than $1,000. In contrast, staff making more than $25,000 a year would benefit more from a raise based on relative reasoning (the 4% pay increase) because that method results in more money than the absolute increase of $1,000.

Laying the Early Foundations for Relative Reasoning

Because the transition from absolute reasoning to relative reasoning is so critical in mathematics, elementary and middle school teachers must establish proportional foundations, albeit covertly, by providing comparative experiences like the previous one. The task in Box 10.13 in Chapter Ten is an example of establishing early proportional reasoning through a conceptual understanding of multiplication. That early exposure to inverse variation is a starting point, but teachers also need to provide examples that more clearly emphasize the transition from absolute to relative reasoning.

Using Visuals. Visual representation is an excellent tool for helping students understand the difference between the two types of quantitative comparisons. Used appropriately, pictorial representation can deliver the message much more effectively than numerals. This fact provides another case for the need to emphasize the use of visuals in math classes. Refer to Box 11.11.

Box 11.11

A. Show me what "5 more" looks like. (Hint: Use vertical bar graphs.)

B. Show me what "twice as much" looks like. (Apply the same hint as above.)

The figures in Box 11.12 are possible examples of the set of graphs done by a student for the first task. The figures in Box 11.13 are examples of possible student work for the second task.

Tasks similar to those in Box 11.11 can be designed in context. Students could be asked to draw bar graphs to literally "get a better picture" of what it means to have $5 more (for example, Melissa has $6 dollars and Gabriel has $1; Robin has $20 dollars

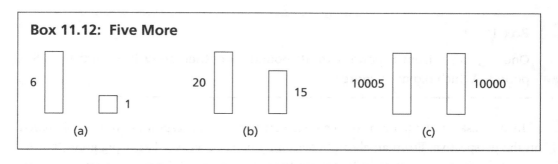

Box 11.12: Five More

6 | 1 | (a)

20 | 15 | (b)

10005 | 10000 | (c)

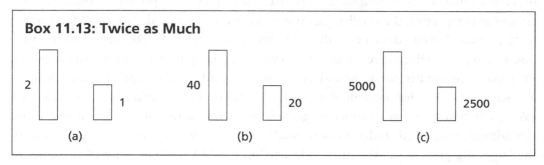

Box 11.13: Twice as Much

2 | 1 | (a)

40 | 20 | (b)

5000 | 2500 | (c)

and John has $15). Repeated tasks of this type that involve representation will enable students to see the patterns and distinctions between the two types of comparisons. With practice, students will begin to appreciate those differences and assimilate them into their long-term memories. Visuals that exhibit absolute differences can show that the size of the amounts being compared affects the relative degree of the comparison. For example, there is an obvious distinction in how the amounts differ in figures (a) versus (c) in Box 11.12. By examining such visual representations, students start to realize that the key advantage to relative comparison results in pairs of bar graphs that maintain the same visual relationship regardless of the size of the numbers. This consistency of course is the conceptual foundation for proportional reasoning—the ability to make comparisons in the same manner despite the size of the quantities.

Scaffolding Relative Reasoning. To provide students with a foundation in proportional reasoning, teachers can use scaffolding and gradually weave the concept into instruction as students mature. Once in middle school, students should be challenged with contexts similar to the one in Box 10.7 in Chapter Ten. With the proper foundation, students should be able to provide insightful responses to a task such as the one in Box 11.14 as the norm rather than the exception.

> **Box 11.14**
>
> One pig grew from 5 pounds to 10 pounds. Another grew from 100 to 108 pounds. Which pig grew more?

In this task, students need to recognize that two correct responses are possible based on the perspective. From an absolute reasoning perspective, the larger pig grew "more" because an increase of 8 pounds is more than an increase of 5 pounds. From a relative reasoning perspective, the smaller pig grew more because a growth rate of 100% (from 5 to 10 pounds) is more than a growth rate of 8% (from 100 to 108 pounds). And from an assessment perspective, there is tremendous value in asking this type of powerful question on a major concept in the same way across several grade levels. Repeating the question at each grade provides valuable data that truly informs instruction in comparison to asking different questions at different grade levels. For example, if the task in Box 11.14 was administered to all students across grades 5–8 and 90% of students responded that the larger pig grew more, the campus leadership would know that a lot of work needs to be done to transition students from absolute reasoning to relative reasoning. (Hint: Worksheets with the use of cross-multiplication to solve a proportion will not give students deep knowledge of proportional reasoning!)

RELATIONSHIPS: IMPORTANT CONSIDERATIONS

The transition from absolute to relative reasoning is but one component of recognizing and understanding relationships. Mathematical relationships, just like human relationships, involve multiple factors. Interestingly enough, those factors, which include assumptions, prior knowledge, perspective, and interpretation, parallel each other, although they manifest themselves quite differently.

Assumptions and Prerequisite Knowledge

Sometimes students struggle, not because of confusion with a new topic at hand, but because of a lack of understanding of prerequisite content for that topic. Teachers know not to make assumptions regarding student learning, but situations will occur where students have surprising difficulty with what might be considered well-grounded knowledge. As an example, an excellent contextual activity for illustrating proportion involves comparing one's height to one's total arm span. For most people, their "wingspan" is the same as or very close to their height. Classroom observation of such an activity revealed an interesting phenomenon to me. Student measurements produced height-to-arm-span data such as 98.9 cm to 99.3 cm, 112.1 cm to 110.9 cm, and so on. Surprisingly, students had a difficult time grasping that these comparisons approximated a 1-to-1 ratio. This difficulty may have been because of a lack of experience with ratios, but the root cause of not seeing the 98.9 to 99.3 comparison as approximating a 99 to 99 comparison may have been more about number sense than proportionality.

Multiple Perspectives

If the only tool you have is a hammer, you tend to see every problem as a nail.

—Abraham Maslow

Maslow's adage sums up a serious shortcoming of traditional math instruction in the United States. Too often, students are taught one specific process or algorithm and given little leeway for creative thinking and seeing things from multiple perspectives. This tendency, in many respects, also inhibits the ability to *discover relationships.* True, procedures and algorithms are usually more efficient and more universal in that they work despite the type of amounts or numbers involved. But by fostering creative thinking and the discovery of relationships, teachers provide students with a full toolbox rather than just a hammer. As an example, teachers can use the idea of density as an early illustration of a ratio because density is a comparison of some quantity to an amount of space or capacity. Refer to Box 11.15.

Box 11.15

Rancher Jones has 60 acres of land. He just purchased 20 cows at an auction, bringing the total size of his herd to 40 cows. However, it takes 2 acres to provide enough food to support 1 cow. What does Rancher Jones need to do?

The final question in this task is left ambiguous on purpose to encourage students to use logic in assessing the problem. The primary computation involved is to determine that

Rancher Jones' 60 acres can support only 30 cows. Although the main value of the lesson is experience with ratios using a density context, an additional value is that the reasoning does not require a numeric solution. Students need experience in the value of seeing a problem from different perspectives. In this scenario, logic shows that Farmer Jones must either obtain more land or get rid of at least 10 cows.

Box 11.16

Determine which is the better buy (left column versus right column) in each of the following. Explain your reasoning in each instance.

4 ounce can for 45 cents	10 ounce can for 90 cents
14 ounce can for 79 cents	18 ounce can for 81 cents
3 ounce can for 30 cents	4 ounce can for 44 cents

Examine the student thinking and relationships in Box 11.16. The preference in this task is that students base their choices on the relationships rather than on a formal algorithm for setting up a proportion. If focusing on relationships, in all likelihood, most students will look at the first pairing and see that the 10 ounce can is the better deal because 45 cents doubled is 90 cents and 4 ounces doubled is 8 ounces. This focus allows for an easy comparison because both choices now have 90 cents in common. For the second comparison, students should probably focus on cost again and see that the difference in cost is only 2 cents while the difference in size is 4 ounces, making the 18 ounce can the better deal. For the third comparison, a unit-rate strategy is sensible because the computation is relatively simple. The first unit rate is 10 cents per ounce and the second is 11 cents per ounce, making the 3 ounce can a better buy.

The instructional message in Box 11.16 is that the context *and* the amounts factored into the observed relationships, which in turn determined the best strategy to take. Note that even though the formal algorithm was not used, proportional reasoning was still involved. In addition, the focus was on the process used in reaching solutions rather than on getting "an answer." As an added benefit, tasks such as this one exemplify that processes can take different paths to arrive at the same place.

Translation Is Still a Key Ingredient

Even when using formal algorithms, uncovering the significant relationships in a problem is still vital. And a key ingredient of this process involves writing those relationships in plain English and then translating that version into a corresponding mathematical expression. Examine the problem in Box 11.17, which involves using the algorithm for a system of two equations.

Box 11.17

Sheila has a total of 32 nickels and dimes worth $2.15. How many nickels does she have?

This problem involves two basic relationships: one focused on the number of coins and the other on the monetary worth of those coins. The first primary task is to express the two relationships in plain English:

- *Relationship 1:* The total number of coins (nickels and dimes) is 32.
- *Relationship 2:* The value of the nickels plus the value of the dimes is the total monetary value of $2.15.

Next, we translate the English version into mathematics, ensuring that we include a translation key to explain what the symbols mean in English. For this problem, rather than use the typical x and y variables, let's use common sense and let N = number of nickels and D = number of dimes. Substituting those variables into the "coin" equation (Relationship 1), we transform the written version into its algebraic equivalent: $N + D = 32$. The "money" equation (Relationship 2) requires an intermediate step focused on how to express the *monetary value* of the coins as opposed to the *number* of coins. Once this step is completed, the money equation could appear as follows: $.05N + .10D = 2.15$. However, if teachers prefer to avoid decimals, the values can be expressed in terms of cents: $5N + 10D = 215$. Now, it is just a matter of doing the computation and solving the system of two equations in whatever method is preferred.

Although not always possible in every context, teachers should encourage the use of alternative approaches that utilize a unique interpretation of relationships. For example, the problem in Box 11.17 can be done informally without a system of equations. Suppose all the coins were dimes. You would have a total of $3.20, as each dime is worth 10 cents. However, that amount is $1.05 too much ($3.20 − $2.15). The relationship dictates a need to replace the extra number of dimes with nickels in such a way as to get $1.05 less. Dividing the $1.05 by .05 results in 21 nickels. Thus, the rest of the coins (32 − 21) would need to be dimes, which in this case would be 11. Using similar logic, we could also solve the problem by assuming that all the coins were nickels. Notice, this commonsense approach involves many of the same computations that would be done in solving the system of two equations. This parallel is not a coincidence, but rather indicates the similar reasoning used in each process.

RELATIONSHIPS: MAKING POWERFUL CONNECTIONS

Despite a knowledge of the factors that shape relationships in math, recognizing and understanding those relationships remains a daunting task that requires experience. Some of the most powerful examples of using relationships as the primary strategy are those where the insight to solve a seemingly complex problem is based on deep knowledge of fundamental concepts. This connects to the notion of *advanced fundamentals* where connecting back to fundamental concepts can provide insight into solving seemingly advanced problems. As the old adage goes, seeing is believing. With that principle in mind, the next step is to show advanced fundamentals and relationships in action. The following tasks illustrate the power of this convergence.

Box 11.18: A Farmer's Dilemma

A farmer has some pigs and some chickens. He sends his son and daughter to count how many of each he has. The two return with the following information: "I counted 70 heads," says the son. "I counted 200 legs," says the daughter. The farmer has never had any algebra or formal instruction in systems of equations. How can the farmer use his children's information to determine how many pigs and how many chickens he has?

For comparison purposes, the following would be the system of equations that would model this context:

$P + C = 70$ (number of animals: P = pigs, C = chickens)

$4P + 2C = 200$ (number of legs: 4P = pig legs, 2C = chicken legs)

However, the farmer's dilemma needs to be solved informally, without a system of equations. The problem in Box 11.18 is similar to the one in Box 11.17 and can be solved by using similar logic and relationships. Suppose that all the farmer's animals are chickens. This scenario results in a total of 70 heads and 140 legs, because each chicken has 2 legs. However, this result leaves a shortage of 60 legs. Because pigs have 4 legs, replacing each chicken with a pig yields an increase of 2 legs each. Thus, we need 30 pigs to make up the deficit of 60 legs. If there are 30 pigs, then the balance of the 70 heads must be composed of 40 chicken heads. Thus, there are 30 pigs and 40 chickens. As with the task in Box 11.17, this problem can also be solved by assuming that all the animals were pigs. And once again, the computation used in this commonsense approach aligns with that used in the computation used to solve the system of two equations.

Box 11.19: Not Another Age Problem!

Monte married a much younger woman. In fact, he is presently three times her age. He tries to divert attention from this fact by mentioning that in 20 years, he will only be twice her age. How old are Monte and his wife now?

Because of repeated experience with this type of scenario, many older adults wince at the thought of solving another age problem. That alone should be motivation to find an alternate and innovative approach. Because proportional reasoning is founded on comparison and ratio, could those relationships provide the vehicle to reach a solution? The answer is yes, with an assist from a visual representation.

Refer to the figures in Box 11.20. Each block in these diagrams represents a chunk of time to illustrate the age relationship between Monte and his wife now and in 20 years.

As given in the problem, the ratio of the couple's ages at the present time is 3 to 1. In 20 years, the ratio of their ages will be 2 to 1. Note the adjustment to the diagram in Box 11.20. An additional block was added to each spouse's age. Given that the difference in time is 20 years, the last block for each of their ages is 20. Thus, the ratio of the blocks in the right-hand figure in Box 11.20 is 4 blocks to 2. This ratio is equivalent to the mandated ratio of 2 to 1, so the diagram adheres to that required ratio. By definition, the parts in a fraction must all be of the same equal size. Thus, if one part of a fraction is 20, all the other parts must be as well. This requirement makes Monte's age in 20 years 80 and his wife's age 40. Substituting 20 for each block in the figure in Box 11.20 depicting their ages now enables the conclusion that he is currently 60 years old and his wife is currently 20. By using visual assistance coupled with the concept of a ratio, a unique strategy was used to solve an age-old type of problem.

Box 11.20

NOW

Given: 3-to-1 ratio in the ages

Husband's Age	Wife's Age

```
┌─────┐
│  ?  │
├─────┤
│  ?  │       ┌─────┐
├─────┤       │  ?  │
│  ?  │       └─────┘
└─────┘
```

20 YEARS FROM NOW

Given: 2-to-1 ratio in the ages

Husband's Age	Wife's Age

```
┌─────┐
│     │
├─────┤
│     │
├─────┤       ┌─────┐
│     │       │     │
├─────┤       ├─────┤
│ 20  │       │ 20  │
└─────┘       └─────┘
```

Box 11.21: Hammer and Lock Problem

Jose went to a hardware store and bought 2 hammers and 1 padlock for a total of $44. Later that day, Harvey went to the same store and bought the same type of items. He bought 1 hammer and 2 padlocks for $40. Find the price of each hammer and each lock. Explain your thinking and method of solution.

The approach to the problem in Box 11.21 is initially a visual representation of the system of two equations. In this format, the logic of the system of equations is better understood by younger students via pictures. In Box 11.22, the first equation visually represents Jose's purchase, and the second equation represents Harvey's purchase.

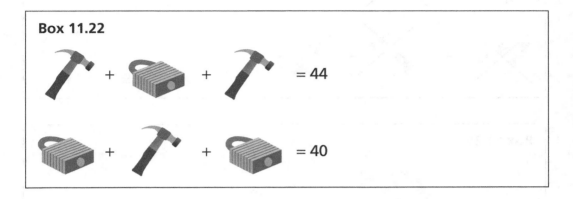

Box 11.22

Attention must now be paid to the next steps in the process and the rationale and justification for them. In Box 11.23 the equations depict that a hammer is removed from each. In Box 11.24, a lock is then removed from each of the two equations.

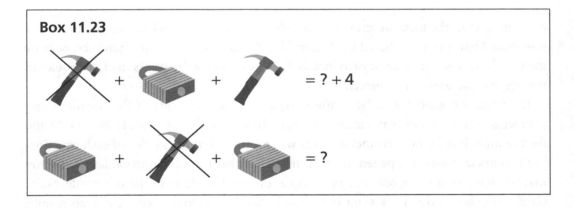

Box 11.23

As a result of these eliminations, we can see that only one hammer and one lock remain and the difference in the price of a hammer and a lock is $4, with the higher price being that of the hammer. Using this relationship, we can proceed. Examine Box 11.25. To transform the first equation to a statement with only one variable, we replace the lock with a hammer so that we have 3 hammers. However, because the price of the hammer

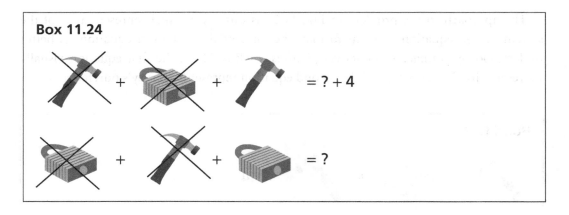

Box 11.24

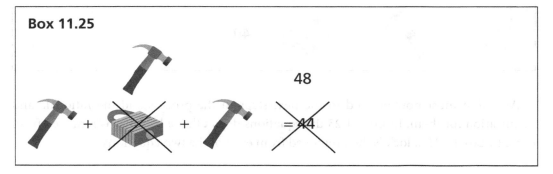

Box 11.25

is $4 more than the lock, we must increase the total cost from $44 to $48 as shown. We now have 3 hammers purchased for $48, making $16 the unit price for a hammer. Because the lock is $4 less, the price of each lock is $12. Substituting the prices in either equation verifies that the solution is correct.

Even astute readers might be confused regarding the right side of the equations and wonder if a basic law of mathematics has been broken in this process. In Box 11.23 and then again in Box 11.24, a distinct quantity was subtracted from one side of each equation, but it is unclear what happened on the other. There exists a fundamental law that states that whatever is done to one side of an equation must be done to the other side. Some clarification is in order. First, some of the work was not shown to keep the process simple. Second, and more important, change actually did occur to the right side of the equations, but the amount of that change was unknown. Refer to Box 11.26, which illustrates the two total costs of the purchases made by Jose and Harvey, $44 and $40 respectively. The focus here is on the *relationship* of the two numbers, one of which is $4 more than the other.

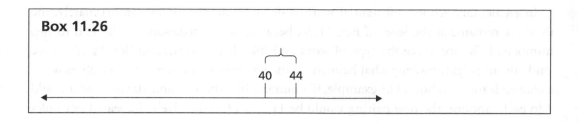

Box 11.26

Now, refer to Box 11.27. This box corresponds to Box 11.23 and Box 11.24 and illustrates what happened to the relationship of the two numbers when one hammer and then one lock were eliminated from each equation. By removing the hammers, the relationship shifted an unknown amount to the left because part of the cost was eliminated. A similar shift to the left also occurs with the removal of the locks. As a numeric example, if we start with the inequality $44 > 40$ and subtract 10 from each amount, the new inequality is $34 > 30$. Note that the entire relationship shifts to the left 10 spaces, but *the relationship remains the same* because the bigger number is still 4 larger than the smaller number. That observation is of huge significance!

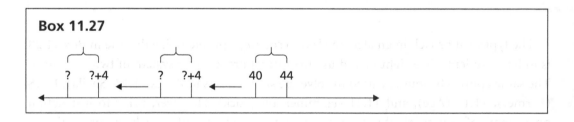

Box 11.27

In essence, what happens to the cost is a precursor to, and parallels, the law about doing the same thing to both sides of an equation. Expanded to a more general sense, this law can be thought of in terms of a *relationship*. If you have an established relationship, as long as you make equivalent changes to all of the components, the relationship remains unchanged. When we remove a hammer from each total (Box 11.23), we do not know the new numbers, but we do know that Jose's cost without the hammer is still 4 more than Harvey's cost without the hammer. In the next step, when the locks are removed, the relationship shifts yet again to the left an unknown amount. Once again, we do not know the new numbers, but we know the relationship remains the same. In Box 11.24, we see that only one hammer and one lock remain. Because the relationship between the two costs remains unchanged, we can deduce that the hammer costs $4 more than the lock. Problem solved.

In elementary school, substantial work is done on number lines. Unfortunately, the thinking remains at the level of Box 11.26, because the comparisons are limited to two numbers. It is rare to see the type of work and thinking illustrated in Box 11.27, where students investigate visually what happens to the relationship between two numbers when a change is made to both. For example, if a number line shows 7 and 10 and students add 4 to each amount, the new pairing would be 11 and 14, respectively. Repeated examples of this type would enable students to see that the entire relationship shifts left or right on the number line, but the relationship itself remained unchanged. This type of approach is advanced fundamentals in action. Such a foundation would leave students well prepared to internalize the algebraic equivalent that states what is done to one side of an equation must be done to the other.

Box 11.28: The Best Deal

Joe's Print Shop charges $.15 per picture and a $2.00 processing fee for developing prints. In contrast, Discount Printing charges a flat rate of $.20 per print. Which is the better rate? Solve and explain in detail.

The typical approach in an algebra class to solving a problem like the one in Box 11.28 is to have students dive right in and use the formal process of a system of two equations. The same approach would be used to solve the similar tasks in Boxes 11.17 (Sheila), 11.18 (Farmer), 11.19 (Age), and 11.21 (Hammer and Lock). However, prior to instruction on systems of equations, this type of contextual problem offers rich opportunities to help students recognize relationships and develop reasoning ability. The current problem incorporates the use of a graph, shown in Box 11.29. This graph carries the caveat that the domain (number of prints) must be limited to whole numbers and the range (cost) to decimals no more precise than the hundredths place to reflect our monetary system.

If students know how to "read" a graph and understand slope, Box 11.29 contains all the information needed to reason through to a solution. The intersection of the two lines (Point S) is where the cost is the same. For any number of prints less than Point S, Discount Printing is the better deal because the total cost is less than at Joe's. The reversal (Joe's is the better deal) is true for any number of prints larger than the intersection (S).

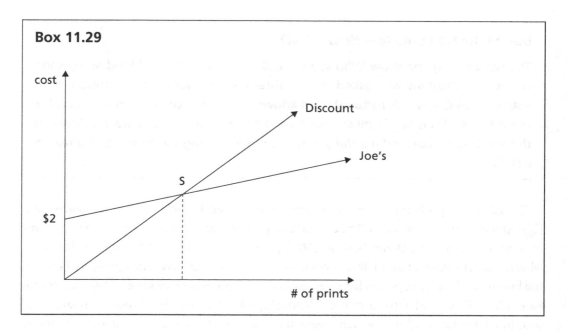

Box 11.29

cost

Discount

Joe's

S

$2

# of prints

Thus, the key is to find the number of prints where the cost is the same for both shops. This step is where the slope and the y-intercepts come into play. The slopes of the two graphs are actually the cost per print ($.15 for Joe's and $.20 for Discount). The $2 service charge is the y-intercept for Joe's Printing graph. The reason that Discount is the better deal initially is because of this $2 processing fee. Common sense informs us that the processing fee has been made up at the point of intersection (S). The key question, then, is how long does it take to make up the difference? Because the difference in the price is $.05 ($.20 – $.15), how many prints will it take to "catch up" at $.05 a print? There are 40 nickels in $2, so the price is the same at 40 prints. The "it depends" solution can now be fully described.

There are two interesting discoveries here. First, this "catch up" approach should work in similar contexts with two intersecting lines. One key is the difference in the y-intercepts, which gives the amount to be made up. The second key is the difference between the slopes, as that is the rate at which the difference is made up. The second discovery, which is similar to previous tasks, is that the computation done in this process is almost identical to the computation done in the system of equations. To math teachers and students alike, this parallel is a beautiful thing because it shows the power of reasoning!

The television game show *Who Wants to Be a Millionaire?* included an episode where a contestant was asked what Fahrenheit temperature is equivalent to −40 degrees Celsius. Unfortunately, a knowledge of the conversion formulas for these two scales is not in most adults' repertoires in the United States. How can this solution be reached *mentally* without remembering the formula? Explain in detail.

To solve the problem mentally requires some basic knowledge of the Celsius and Fahrenheit temperature scales. The critical comparisons are the boiling and freezing points of water on each scale. Water boils at 100 degrees Celsius and at 212 degrees Fahrenheit, whereas water freezes at 0 and 32 degrees on each scale, respectively. The difference between the boiling and freezing points for each scale is 100 degrees for Celsius and 180 degrees for Fahrenheit. Box 11.31 illustrates the relationship of the two scales. When compared and simplified, the ratio is 5 to 9, which means that 5 degrees Celsius is equivalent to 9 degrees Fahrenheit, as shown in Box 11.32.

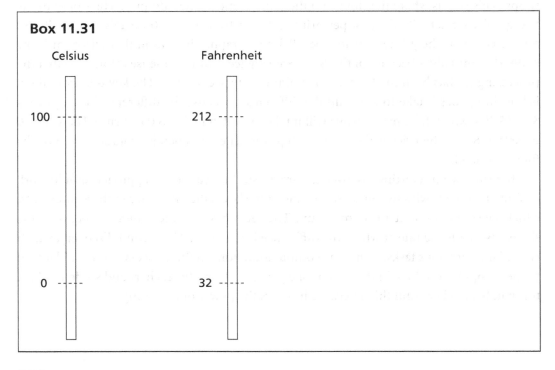

Box 11.31

Celsius   Fahrenheit

100   212

0   32

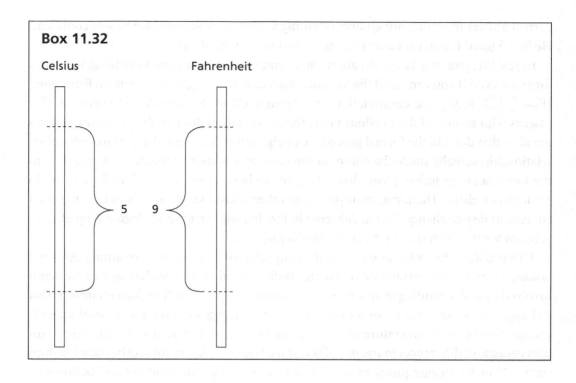

Box 11.32

Celsius   Fahrenheit

5   9

To continue the solution process, the focus must be on the equivalent amount of change in the two scales—the key relationship involved. Because the ratio 5 to 9 reflects this equivalent change, it is beneficial to think of Celsius in chunks of 5 compared to Fahrenheit in chunks of 9. The given temperature in Celsius was -40 degrees, which is equivalent to 8 groups of 5. A change of 5 degrees in Celsius must be accompanied by a change of 9 degrees in Fahrenheit. Thus, the equivalent degree change in Fahrenheit is 8 groups of 9, which is 72. The 40-degree drop in Celsius is equivalent to a 72-degree drop in Fahrenheit. However, the starting point for Fahrenheit is at 32 degrees (freezing point), not 0 degrees, as in Celsius. Thus, solving the problem requires starting at 32 degrees and dropping 72 degrees on the Fahrenheit scale (32 − 72), which is −40 degrees. Surprise, −40 degrees Celsius is equivalent to −40 degrees Fahrenheit! Who knew?!

The questions on *Who Wants to Be a Millionaire?* are often based on trivia. In all likelihood, the show's writers came across the bit of trivia that −40 degrees is the point on the two scales where the temperature is the same. However, the contestant who was asked this question on the show obviously did not know this fact. He took some time to respond, and viewers could see he was doing the problem mentally. But when he finally chose the correct answer from the four choices (winning $125,000), you could see he was confident. He had figured it out, probably in a manner similar to the above.

In real life, you may face a situation where you need to figure out something without a formula. Even if you can recall the formula, such as converting from Celsius to Fahrenheit $[F = \frac{9}{5} (C) + 32]$, the computation may be difficult to do mentally. However, in this case, as with several of the previous tasks, the computation done in the reasoning process parallels that done in the formal procedure or algorithm. Knowing the Celsius-Fahrenheit relationship actually made the computation simpler and more apparent. The parallels to the formula are as follows: You divide by 5 to see how many "chunks" of 5 there are in 40 degrees Celsius. Then, you multiply the number of chunks (8) in Celsius by 9 to get an equivalent degree change (72) in Fahrenheit. Finally, you start the 72-degree drop at 32 to account for the difference in the two scales' freezing points.

This problem shows the power, and the simplicity, of proportional reasoning. And as a bonus, the problem illustrates two examples, both focused on ratio and change, of the depth involved in understanding at an *advanced-fundamental* level. The first deep example is that a change can be equivalent, but the equal amount of change does not mean equal *numeric* change. For the two temperature scales, an equal amount of change involves different numbers because of differences in the size of the units. It is no different from other relationships such as 12 inches being equivalent to 1 foot or 1 gallon being equivalent to 4 quarts. Students need much more experience with those equivalencies being expressed as *ratios*. As was illustrated in this problem, a ratio in some cases can actually be an expression of equivalence.

The second, equally important example is that ratios can be associated with change. In mathematics, the delta symbol (Δ) indicates change. Thus, the ratio used in this problem is more accurately depicted in Box 11.33. In plain English, this expression states that "a change of 5 degrees in Celsius is accompanied by a change of 9 degrees in Fahrenheit." With repeated experience in this interpretation, students will learn that a ratio (in appropriate contexts) means a certain change in the numerator must be matched by a certain change in the denominator to maintain the relationship. This interpretation of a ratio as an expression of change is critical because it connects directly to the concept of slope in algebra and more advanced mathematics. And you never know when a solid understanding of ratios might pay off with a $125,000 prize.

Box 11.33

$$\frac{\Delta\ 5\ degrees\ C}{\Delta\ 9\ degrees\ F}$$

Box 11.35 provides a visual representation of the context described in Box 11.34, although not drawn exactly to scale. The distance BC is the diameter of the earth, and the distance AD is the distance of the concentric circle formed by the rope. To determine which animal form is the largest that can go under the rope, we must find the distance AB (or CD), which represents the distance the rope would be above the earth's surface.

Box 11.34: The Rope-Earth Problem

Assume the earth is a perfect sphere. The circumference at the equator is approximately 25,000 miles. You have a rope that is 6 *feet* longer than the earth's circumference. If you use this rope to form a concentric circle with the equator, which of the life forms below would be the largest that could walk, scurry, or crawl under the rope? If needed, 1 mile is 5,280 feet.

A. amoeba

B. ant

C. mouse

D. domestic cat

Box 11.35

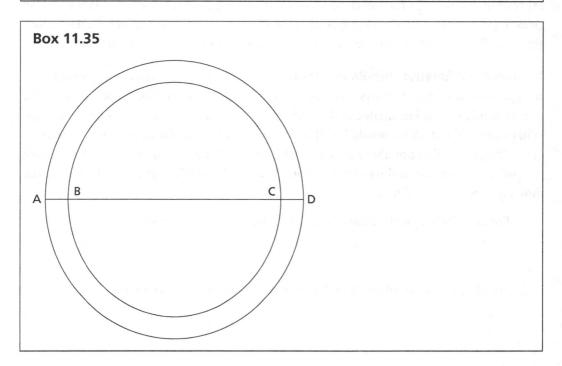

The "Jump Right In" Approach. I have presented this task at numerous professional development sessions. In most cases, high school teacher groups immediately go to the circumference formula for a circle (C = π · d). They then begin to labor through the inordinately complex calculations needed to convert feet to miles or miles to feet, depending on the approach. If done from a miles perspective, the earth's diameter is 7,957.747155 miles (25,000 ÷ π), and the rope-circle diameter is 7,957.747516 miles from $[25,000 + (\frac{6}{5,280})] \div \pi$. The difference of the two diameters is 0.000361 miles (7,957.747516 − 7,957.747155). This difference is actually the distances of AB and CD combined, so dividing by 2 gives results in AB = 0.953 feet. This amount is almost 1 foot, so the surprising response is (D) domestic cat!

A More Algebraic Approach. Some teacher groups attack the problem from a more algebraic perspective. This approach also uses the circumference formula (C = d π). In this context, let d = diameter of the earth. The circumference of the rope circle is 6 feet more than the earth's circumference. If C = the circumference of the earth, then the circumference of the rope circle is C + 6 feet. With substitution, C + 6 becomes (d π) + 6. The hidden difficulty in the next step is the need to factor out π, but to the untrained eye, π is not an apparent common factor in $[(d\,\pi) + 6]$. The result of this factoring is the expression $\pi\,(d + \frac{6}{\pi})$ for the circumference of the rope circle. Doing the computation gives $\pi\,(d + 1.906)$. The 1.906 represents the increase in diameter in feet. Dividing by 2 gives us AB = 0.953 feet, and we reach the same conclusion of (D) domestic cat!

A Conceptual Relationship-Based Approach. Whenever I watch a group of teachers struggle with this task, I always feel a bit guilty to reveal that middle schoolers, with the proper fundamental knowledge and focus, could do this problem in 2 minutes or less. What's more, the students would be off by less than one tenth of a foot in their estimation of the "height" of the rope above the earth. The foundation involved in this quick approach is a conceptual understanding of π (as more than 3.14) and of ratios as relationships. The thought process is as follows:

1. For any circle, π is the ratio of the circumference to the diameter:

$$\frac{C}{D}$$

2. For simplicity, round off the value of π pi to 3 and express as a ratio

$$\frac{3}{1}$$

3. Looking at this ratio from a change perspective (see Box 11.33), a change of 3 units in the circumference requires a change of 1 unit in the diameter to maintain the relationship:

$$\frac{\triangle 3 \text{ units in circumference}}{\triangle 1 \text{ unit in diameter}}$$

4. Again recalling Box 11.33, we know an equivalent change does not necessarily mean the change in the numerator will be the same amount as the change in the denominator. With this knowledge, we make the equivalent changes, ensuring to maintain a 3-to-1 circumference-to-diameter relationship:

$$\frac{3 \text{ add } 3}{1 \text{ add } 1}$$

5. The result is $\frac{6}{2}$. This ratio corresponds to the scenario because the length of the rope is 6 feet longer than the earth's circumference. Based on the above ratio, a change of 6 in the circumference results in a change of 2 in the diameter. As in the previous two approaches, the distance needed is AB, so we divide by 2. Thus, the "height" of the rope above the earth is about 1 foot, making the answer the, by now, not-so-surprising domestic cat.

The first solution approach is an example of the tendency to use a familiar process, formula, or algorithm to solve problems. In a way, this tendency inhibits learning and creative thinking. The second approach is insightful, but it entails a much more complex process than necessary. The last approach is definitely the winner. It provides another example of the power of deep yet simple reasoning resulting from the merger of a profound understanding of several fundamental concepts. For example, the reasoning process for the Rope-Earth task is connected to, and supported by, the conceptual understanding in the Celsius-to-Fahrenheit task (Box 11.30).

What makes the Rope-Earth task such a wonderful problem is the solution is so counterintuitive. The additional rope is merely 6 feet longer than the immense distance of 25,000 miles. Surely, only a minuscule "height" of rope would hover above the earth's surface. This faulty perception arises from the tendency to compare the 6-foot increase (new circumference) to the 25,000-mile length (original circumference). The change involves a comparison of circumference to diameter, not new circumference to original circumference.

Another insight provided by the Rope-Earth task is a new perspective of proportional reasoning as an additive process as well as a multiplicative one. When learning fractions, students are taught the following is the proper process to obtain an equivalent fraction:

$$\frac{1 \cdot 4}{2 \cdot 4} = \frac{4}{8}$$

Students are also taught, quite appropriately, that the following is not a viable procedure:

$$\frac{1+4}{2+4} = \frac{5}{6}$$

Examine the following two examples:

$$\frac{7+7}{4+4} = \frac{14}{8}$$

$$\frac{3+6}{5+10} = \frac{9}{15}$$

The above two processes yield correct equivalent fractions, but how can that be? They were obtained via addition, not multiplication. However, with some ingenuity, the addition in this type of context can be done so that the process is equivalent to multiplication. In the second example, if sets of 3 are continually added to the numerator, the addition is equivalent to multiplication. The same is true for the denominator, where adding sets of 5 would be equivalent to multiplication. As long as the *same number* of equivalent sets are added to *both* the numerator and the denominator, respectively, the original relationship is unchanged. Done in this way, addition is equivalent to multiplying the numerator and the denominator by the same factor.

The key to understanding equivalent fractions from a ratio perspective is knowing the relationship must remain unchanged. Revisit the incorrect example below:

$$\frac{1+4}{2+4} = \frac{5}{6}$$

This action is invalid because it does not maintain the integrity of the relationship. Unfortunately, this common error gives both teachers and students the misconception that addition (or subtraction) cannot be used to generate equivalent fractions. However, understanding how a relationship can be maintained results in an additive approach to equivalent fractions that expands the limits beyond multiplication. An important point to note is the critical difference between the two expressions below. This point has been made before, but bears repeating.

$$\frac{3+6}{5+10} = \frac{9}{15} \qquad \frac{3}{5} + \frac{6}{10} = \frac{12}{10}$$

Compare the fraction bars in the two equations. The left-hand equation involves addition in the numerator and the denominator of *one single* fraction. The right-hand equation involves adding *two different* fractions, a completely different operation. Teachers must provide repeated exposure to this distinction to instill it in students' long-term memories.

CONCLUSION

An intentional and substantive focus on relationships in math can provide students with new depths of understanding. As the tasks in this chapter show, understanding relationships enables students to tap into the remarkable power that comes from connecting fundamental concepts in mathematics. Naysayers could point out that the selected problems all lent themselves to a unique approach and discourage the use of universal and efficient procedures and algorithms. The chapter's message is by no means that algorithms are not useful or valuable. They have an important role in mathematics. The only caveat is that their overuse can squelch innovative and insightful reasoning and approaches, especially in students' quest to understand. Focusing on relationships gives students the opportunity to *think*. They will not become critical thinkers by observing teachers thinking at the front of a room any more than they will become good swimmers by watching someone else swim. Jump into the relationships waters with students and give them the chance to think about mathematics in new and powerful ways.

The Perfect Non-Storm: Understanding the Problem and Changing the System

The field of education has at its disposal a wealth of research to guide decisions. Such information has been used to develop a number of mathematics reforms in the United States, but student achievement still lags behind other nations. In the 2000 movie *The Perfect Storm,* a crew aboard a doomed fishing vessel is caught up in an unusually violent storm. The primary cause of the storm is a rare confluence of two vast weather fronts and a hurricane. Likewise, in K–12 math education, a combination of factors currently exists that seriously limits the effectiveness of the system. Yet, somehow, these major problems seem to fly under the radar, and the detrimental result is the perfect non-storm.

A SYSTEMIC ISSUE

The introduction to this book touched on some of the problems affecting K–12 math education in the United States. To tackle these problems and achieve change, math reforms must address the quality of learning at the classroom level. However, many classroom changes cannot occur without support from and change at the broader system level—the campus, district, state, and national levels. Chief among the issues mentioned in the introduction to this book is mathematics content and, in particular, the content expertise of the teaching force. This issue may seem like a classroom-level problem, but it is actually a system-level problem. Teachers can teach only what they know, and this knowledge is largely dependent on the content provided by the system itself at the K–12 and college levels and through professional development. Although the symptoms of this problem might be evident at the teacher or classroom level, the root causes are systemic.

Teacher Content Expertise

Of all the issues affecting K–12 math education, teacher content expertise best exemplifies the perfect non-storm. According to the National Research Council's publication *Adding It Up: Helping Children Learn Mathematics* (Kilpatrick et al., 2001), many elementary and middle school math teachers in the United States possess a limited knowledge of their subject matter. To clarify, these teachers usually do know the facts and procedures they teach; however, their understanding of the conceptual basis for that knowledge is often weak. My own research (Molina, 2004) and experiences support these findings.

As proposed earlier in this book, people tend to teach what they were taught and in the same way they were taught. In their own education, many teachers experienced traditional math instruction centered on isolated facts and procedures rather than on in-depth conceptual understanding. As products of the U.S. education system, these teachers may not even realize they do not know the content at a deep conceptual level. In fact, many math teachers rate themselves as competent in the content.

Adding to the problem, teacher evaluation and appraisal systems do not usually focus on mathematical content expertise. Perhaps evaluators do not think a content issue exists because many of them also experienced traditional math instruction. Another reason may be that people tend to assume college credentials are synonymous with content expertise. However, I found (Molina, 2004) that college teacher programs did not usually improve future teachers' mathematical knowledge. Although some progress has been made in this area, more is needed.

At the same time, school systems often assume the teachers they hire have a strong foundation in the content because they have completed teacher-training programs and passed certification examinations. High-performing countries such as Japan, however, do not make this type of assumption. They pattern their education systems to support ongoing learning across a teacher's profession. Many parents also assume their children's teachers know the content at a deep level, especially if students perform well on the state accountability exam. With all these factors at play, it is no wonder that math teachers' content expertise raises few concerns despite having serious repercussions in the classroom—the perfect non-storm.

Classroom-Level Issues

*Let me get this straight. We are behind the rest of the class,
and we are going to catch up to them by going slower?*

—Bart Simpson, upon being placed in the remedial "Leg-Up" program

Bart Simpson is a fictional underachieving child character on the animated television series *The Simpsons*. True to the character's nature, his statement is humorous but also points to a question faced in the classroom every day—what is the best way to help students learn?

Classroom Practices Within Teachers' Control. Math teachers have direct control over the instructional practices in their classrooms. Earlier chapters have addressed many common practices that may not support student learning. For example, methods and shortcuts that inhibit rather than spark student thinking are problematic. Another traditional practice that makes little sense is to stop teaching a fundamental property, such as the property of like items, only to have it resurface in formal algebra, then disconnected from its fundamental roots.

Classroom Practices Beyond Teachers' Control. Other classroom practices are beyond individual teachers' control. For example, when elementary teachers resort to shortcuts or acronyms to help students with whole-number computation or to solve word problems involving whole numbers, middle school teachers are challenged to help students "unlearn" them. The shortcoming of these practices is that more often than not, they do not apply to other sets of numbers, such as rational numbers. We should not instill math procedures that do not hold true for all sets of numbers (for example, teaching that when we multiply, the answer is larger or that we cannot "take" 6 from 2). In the long run, such practices end up doing more harm than good. Combined with careless language that has been part and parcel of traditional instruction for generations, practices regarding whole number computation become ingrained in students and make teaching computation with other number sets far more difficult than it should be.

Another area of concern across grade levels is the standard approach for teaching students how to solve word problems. As discussed in Chapter Ten, many teachers lament that students are not good problem solvers. Assuming this is not due to something in the water, shortcomings in math instruction are likely to blame, at least in part. In traditional problem-solving instruction, teachers lecture and demonstrate, showing students strategies for solving word problems of a certain type. Students then mimic the process with similar problems of that same type. Sometimes, the assigned problems are even accompanied with instructions such as, "Use multiplication to solve each problem." Through the use of such practices, students are not challenged to do any critical thinking or to develop any conceptual understanding, yet the system expects students to become problem solvers based on that experience.

The Bigger Picture

In mathematics, you don't understand things. You just get used to them.

—Johann von Neumann

Von Neumann's statement was introduced Chapter Ten, which presents instructional methods for addressing some of the classroom issues that often go unnoticed. Building on those recommendations, this chapter focuses on addressing classroom issues that go beyond teachers' scope of influence, those requiring action at a higher level of the system. As has been shown, many classroom issues are the result of more systemic problems. Only by focusing on these system-level problems can we hope to fully address issues regarding teacher content expertise and their instructional emphases and practices.

The actions suggested here will not eliminate all of the problems with the mathematics education system. However, these ideas may reduce the unnoticed blast and blow of the perfect non-storm besetting the system.

Teacher Content Expertise: Developing Math Specialists. A topic of significant attention has been math teachers' content expertise. Teachers have no control over the mathematical content the education system provided them as students and teachers-in-training; nor do they control what continuing education the system provides. True, teaching is a complex endeavor, and content expertise is only one component. Some empirical studies, such as that by Ahn and Choi (2004), indicate that the relationship between teachers' subject matter knowledge and student achievement is inconsistent. However, common sense suggests that teachers cannot teach what they do not know. Of course, one can be a mathematical genius and still be a terrible teacher, so *how* one teaches is also a critical factor. Nonetheless, a teacher using the most effective instructional strategies who has only a shallow understanding of the content can only provide the opportunity for students to learn shallow mathematics. The previous chapters illustrate that a deep knowledge of fundamental mathematics is critical to define and connect concepts, present multiple perspectives, and employ advanced fundamentals. Without this foundation, the instructional pyramid collapses.

The U.S. education system expects elementary teachers to cover all subjects equally well, but the feasibility of this approach is suspect. Part of this expectation may be due to the belief that elementary-level mathematics is relatively simple. As we have seen, however, fundamental mathematics is anything but simple.

In grades K–3 students are *learning to read*, but beyond those grades, students must transition to *reading to learn*. Part of this book's emphasis on language and symbolism is that reading in mathematics is just as important and difficult, if not more so, as in any other discipline. A transition at fourth grade from self-contained classrooms to departmentalized subjects could parallel the transition in reading for mathematics. Rather than elementary generalists, mathematics specialists with the necessary expertise and confidence could take over the responsibility for teaching fundamental mathematics from fourth grade onward.

Teacher Placement: Sensible Decisions for Obvious Priorities. Some educators have noted that teaching is a profession that "eats its young." This expression alludes to the fairly common practice of assigning beginning teachers to the least desirable, most challenging classes. Common sense says the best teachers should be assigned to the students who need the most help, especially in mathematics. Yet the tendency is to assign those students to the least experienced teachers, to the detriment of both struggling students and beginning teachers. The U.S. education system has a shortage of K–12 math teachers, yet the system drives away promising new educators through such practices. We must acknowledge this "elephant in the room" and make decisions on the basis of what is best for students, rather than on a misguided reward system for teachers.

One does not need to be an architect to understand that when building a house, the key is to have a strong foundation. Without it, no matter how elaborate or sophisticated the design, the house will crumble. In the same way, reforms aimed at improving middle school or high school math performance may be hindered unless students receive a strong foundation in mathematics in elementary school. Without this foundation, students will continue to enter middle school and high school with the same problems year after year.

A Call for Change: Time for Some Common Sense

A decision not to change means that what you are doing now is better than any alternative.

—Joseph Carroll

Possibly because of beliefs that there is nothing better to be done, a number of ineffective components of the U.S. education system continue. These practices and policies, many of which comprise the basic infrastructure of the system, often run counter to common sense. For example, the system still utilizes a school calendar based on an agricultural economy. Are young students still needed to work the fields in the summer? At the start of each school year, students are grouped into grades by age, placed at the same starting line, and expected to hit the finish line at the same time. Do all students learn at the same rate? Teacher workdays and class schedules typically support isolation rather than collaboration, even though some studies have shown that teachers who collaborate are more effective than those who work alone. Such entrenched policies have become revered educational traditions. Thus, these "sacred cows" remain in place to the detriment of student learning and achievement. These problems go beyond the mathematics classroom, but such general systemic issues must also be addressed for U.S. mathematics achievement to improve significantly.

Calls for educational reform in the United States, both in general K–12 education and in mathematics education, are nothing new. The following speech was delivered at an educational conference:

> By the old system, the learner was presented with a rule which told him how to perform certain operations on numbers; and when these were done, he would have the proper result. But no reason was given for a single step. His first application of the rule was on abstract numbers, and so large that he could not reason on them, if he had been disposed to do so. And when he had got through, and obtained the result, he understood neither what it was, nor the use of it. Neither did he know that it was the proper result, but was obliged to rely wholly on the book, or more frequently on the Teacher. As he began in the dark, so he continued; and the results of his calculation seemed to be

obtained by some magical operation, rather than by the inductions of reason. (Colburn, 1831, p. 282)

This speech was delivered in 1831. The issue in mathematics education that Colburn raised more than *180 years* ago remains a problem today! True, change sometimes occurs slowly, but this slowly? Surely, after almost two centuries, we should have successfully addressed this problem along with many others in math education. Although some progress has been made, the United States cannot remain globally competitive unless the shallow arithmetic and efficiency in math education is rapidly phased out and replaced by conceptual mathematics. At a minimum, the mathematics in our K–12 system needs an extensive makeover.

MATH MAKEOVER

Mathematics has an infamous reputation for being difficult to learn. This myth is being kept alive by the very system charged with disputing it. Primarily through the academic language and the language of instruction, the system mystifies mathematics and makes it more complex than it is.

Compounding these issues are traditional state assessments, which can hide rather than reveal weaknesses in students' understanding of mathematics. Because state math assessments traditionally measure procedural fluency rather than conceptual understanding, scores do not clearly indicate how well students have grasped fundamental concepts and big ideas. In effect, state assessments can be a double-edged sword because of false positives—students may perform exceptionally well on a topic, but this result indicates only a high degree of procedural knowledge; it is not an assurance of conceptual understanding. These factors suggest that perhaps an extensive makeover of math education should begin with the mathematics that we teach and test.

Content Standards: What Are We Teaching?

We should shift the primary focus from *how* teachers teach to *what* they are teaching. Many educators will be quick to point out that mathematics content has received substantial attention through the concerted efforts to develop and implement rigorous content standards. In fact, the phrase *standards-based reform* has been an approach for improving curriculum and instruction since the inception of standards. All states had adopted state content standards that detailed the mathematics students should learn by grade level and by secondary school course. Currently, the great majority of states have adopted the new

Common Core State Standards in mathematics and are phasing them in as the foundation for their math curricula and assessment programs.

A Wake-Up Call. If math instruction is truly based on the content standards, I propose we need a wake-up call. Some may argue otherwise, but many of the mathematics content standards I have reviewed focus on procedural fluency. A close examination of various content standards reveals objectives stating that students should know *how to* do this or *how to* do that, with a typical focus on procedure, computation, or a skill. These how-tos are examples of procedural fluency, not conceptual understanding. If a student can multiply 23 • 14, that skill does not mean the student understands what multiplication is or can connect that concept to other fundamental ideas, such as division. These additional abilities would indicate conceptual understanding. There is nothing wrong with stressing procedural fluency, but we should not stress it to the extent that conceptual understanding is slighted or omitted.

Standards-based education is a beneficial and sound approach, using content standards to guide content coverage, connect mathematics across grade levels, and ensure that the content being taught is uniform and consistent. Unfortunately, standards-based instruction is only as good as the quality of the content standards on which it is based. If the standards focus on superficial procedural knowledge, the instruction will follow suit. If crucial concepts are omitted in the content standards, then it is left to teachers to recognize the shortcomings or gaps and to fill them. Standards-based instruction will not do that for them.

A Closer Look. In a math education system without content standards, it might be understandable that secondary math teachers would have a limited understanding of π as 3.14. Likewise, teachers of fundamental math may have a limited understanding of fractions or be limited to the standard algorithm when multiplying mixed numbers. But the K–12 math education system in the United States—despite standards-based instruction—allows for the same limitations because the standards focus on procedural fluency over conceptual understanding. To illustrate this assertion, Box 12.1 provides examples from three sets of content standards: a state that did not adopt the Common Core State Standards (CCSS) in the first column, the CCSS in the second, and the previous standards for a state that did adopt the CCSS.

Box 12.1: Sampling of Content Standards

Topic	Non-Adopting State	CCSS	Previous Standards of Adopting State
Ratio	Not found until Grade 6.	Not found until Grade 6.	Not found until Grade 8.
Substitution	Not found in K–12.	Found in Grade 6.	Not found in K–12.
Angle	Grade 4 has a standard to identify and describe right, acute, and obtuse angles; no standards indicate when to teach an acceptable definition.	Grade 2 has a standard to identify the number of angles; Grade 4 standard expects students to know the concept of an angle.	Grades 3 and 4 have standards to identify the number of angles; Grade 4 standard expects students to identify and describe right, acute, and obtuse angles.
Equality	The term *equality* does not appear in Grades K–5; the term *equal* appears six times in K–5 standards, and in four of those cases, the reference is to equal parts of a whole.	Grade K covers equality in comparison of numbers; Grade 1 addresses the meaning of the equal sign.	Grade 3 covers the equality of the size of fractional parts and groups as well as equality in operations.

Topic	Non-Adopting State	CCSS	Previous Standards of Adopting State
Proportion	Proportional reasoning does not appear until Grade 6.	First appears in Grade 6.	First appears in Grade 8.
Distributive Property	Not found in Grades K–8; appears once in the Algebra 1 course in simplifying expressions.	Appears in Grade 3, again in Grades 6 and 7, and then in algebra.	Appears in Grade 5 only.
Change Slope	Change does not appear until Grade 6, with the exception of two K–5 references to a change in temperature; slope is not found until Algebra 1.	Change first appears in Grade 6 and later in algebra; slope first appears in algebra.	Change and slope first appear in algebra.
π	The concept of π is not found in K–12.	First found in Grade 8 as an example of an irrational number.	The concept of π is not found in K–12.

One may argue that broader interpretations of the standards allow for reading additional content into them and make it possible to infer concepts that are not explicitly mentioned. For example, the substitution principle is a critical idea stating that a number or expression can be replaced with another one as long as the two are of equal value. This basic principle, on which much of mathematics is founded, begins with contexts as simple as replacing $1 + 1$ with 2. If such a basic concept is never actually stated verbatim in the standards, then teachers might not realize the omission and never specifically teach the concept to their students. No matter how well a concept may be implied, there is no substitute for the real thing. Math content standards should include and describe all fundamental concepts that students need to learn. The math education system should not expect the teaching force to identify which critical and fundamental concepts are implied via a related idea or skill.

The Key Flaw.　Despite the good intentions and hard work that have gone into developing mathematics content standards, a critical flaw exists. The standards have become the basis for *high stakes assessments and accountability systems*. As a result, teachers must focus on what students will be able to *do* on examinations, not what students should *know*. Content standards *do* tell teachers what to teach, but the problem is that content standards *do not* tell teachers everything to teach. The content standards *do tell* teachers the *procedural fluency* to teach, but they *do not tell* teachers the *concepts* to teach. It is actually quite simple. If state mathematics content standards focus on teaching just skills, and state assessments focus on testing just skills, then teachers will only teach skills. You get what you asked for! We should not be surprised that the math education system is similar to what it was in 1831, when Colburn decried how a focus on procedural fluency was keeping students in the dark.

But Standards Go Beyond Content.　It is important to note that past and current standards do address far more than content. Important processes and reasoning that address Colburn's critiques are essential components of mathematics standards documents. For example, the National Council of Teachers of Mathematics (NCTM) included five Process Standards: problem solving, reasoning and proof, communication, connections, and representations. Another effort to develop higher-order thinking and reasoning in mathematics is the National Research Council's report (Kilpatrick et al., 2001), which proposes strands that together result in mathematical proficiency. These strands are adaptive reasoning, strategic competence, conceptual understanding, procedural fluency, and productive disposition.

　　The Common Core State Standards Initiative has developed the most recent mathematics content standards, which have been adopted by the majority of the states. Analogous to the five NCTM process standards, the Common Core State Standards include eight Standards for Mathematical Practice, which "describe varieties of expertise that mathematics educators at all levels should seek to develop in their students" (NGA Center & CCSSO, 2010). These standards state that all mathematically proficient students should be able to do the following:

1. Make sense of problems and persevere in solving them

2. Reason abstractly and quantitatively

3. Construct viable arguments and critique the reasoning of others

4. Model with mathematics

5. Use appropriate tools strategically

6. Attend to precision

7. Look for and make use of structure

8. Look for and express regularity in repeated reasoning

It Still Goes Back to Content. "What gets assessed, gets addressed." What is currently tested on state accountability exams reflects the objectives in the state's *content* standards, which do not necessarily include the NCTM Process Standards or the Common Core Standards for Mathematical Practice. In the current climate of school accountability, assessments are a major force in shaping the content teachers cover and emphasize. Current standardized tests are not designed to effectively measure the types of proficiencies and reasoning listed in the NCTM Process Standards or the Common Core Standards for Mathematical Practice.

A Possible Solution. Some educators describe the mathematics curriculum as "a mile wide and an inch deep." To improve student learning in K–12 mathematics, we need to rotate this image 90 degrees so that the content standards are much deeper than they are wide. If we expect students to learn mathematics at a conceptual level, then teachers will need *conceptual* standards to guide and inform them.

Conceptual Standards

What information should mathematics conceptual standards contain? First, what they should *not* contain is what students must do on a test! Those standards already exist. Instead, conceptual standards should parallel the idea of a simple yet deep definition as the basis of understanding a given concept or process. The importance of such definitions has been stressed repeatedly, particularly in Chapter Four. By nature, definitions explain what something is. Similarly, conceptual standards should delineate what students must know. The focus must truly be on what teachers should teach, the *what* and *why* of concepts. In that sense, to be an authoritative guide for teachers, conceptual standards must go beyond just definitions.

Inside the Classroom. Refer to Box 10.2, which provides a framework of the multifaceted knowledge students must possess to define and understand a fundamental concept on a deeper level. Applying a similar model and reasoning to conceptual standards, one result is the framework in Box 12.2. This framework goes far beyond the current skills-focused content standards, which center on what students should be able to do on a test. Using this framework, a conceptual standard would provide a much deeper approach, actually explaining what a teacher should teach and what a student should know about a fundamental concept, process, or big idea in mathematics. The expectation would be that the number of standards per grade level would parallel the smaller number of more in-depth mathematics standards that are taught in countries whose students excel on international assessments.

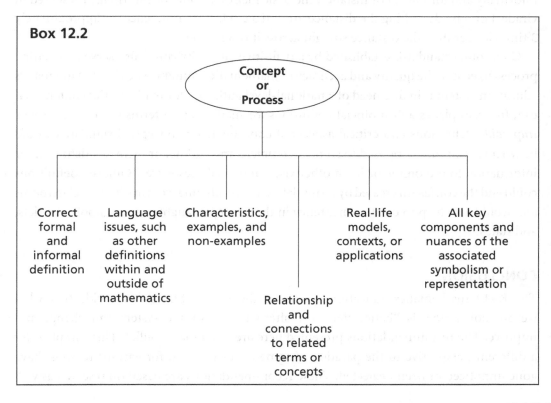

Box 12.2

Concept or Process

- Correct formal and informal definition
- Language issues, such as other definitions within and outside of mathematics
- Characteristics, examples, and non-examples
- Relationship and connections to related terms or concepts
- Real-life models, contexts, or applications
- All key components and nuances of the associated symbolism or representation

The elements of this framework reflect the various ideas emphasized throughout this book. Each standard should have a conceptual definition as its foundation and building block. The establishment of such definitions should be guided and facilitated by a linked framework, such as the one in Box 10.2. Each standard should also include a focus on the historically neglected language, symbolism, and visual representations that relate to the concept. Next, a focus on a concept's relationships and connections is critical to a deeper understanding. And last, because relevance is important to students, the framework suggests the inclusion of real-life models, contexts, or applications.

Beyond the Classroom. The development of conceptual content standards would have additional benefits as well. The standards could serve as a guidance document for college teacher preparation programs. What better place to ensure that future teachers of mathematics have the content expertise and understanding they need than the college programs that certify them? Conceptual standards could provide a means for better vertical alignment of concepts. Instead of organizing concepts by grade level, standards could group concepts into larger time windows, including time frames for presenting concepts both informally and formally. For instance, the basic idea of π could be informally presented in Grade 4 or 5 by describing the distance around a circle (circumference) as approximately 3 times longer than the distance straight across it (diameter).

Conceptual standards established by a definitive authority could also serve as a vetting process to ensure the quality and accuracy of mathematics content. The K–12 mathematics education system is in dire need of a national-level authority for mathematics content that can, for example, establish official definitions for mathematical terms such as *average* or *trapezoid*. Definitions and critical aspects of concepts from conceptual standards would be what is utilized, as opposed to some incomplete, misleading, or incorrect definition or information found online or in an otherwise "unofficial" resource. "Official" definitions could end the confusion created by terms defined in conflicting ways in different classrooms and would also help to create consistency in the concepts taught across schools, districts, and states.

CONCLUSION

The K–12 mathematics education system in the United States can decide that what we are doing now is "better than any alternative"—or the system can change and improve. The recommendations presented here are not a magic bullet. They simply offer a different perspective to the paradox of some problems that, for various reasons, have gone unnoticed or been neglected. These recommendations are based on research as well as real-life experience and, for lack of a more sophisticated term, common sense. Looking at student performance in mathematics, something needs to change if the United States is to compete globally and maintain a workforce with the math skills necessary for progress and innovation in STEM fields.

One solution is to shift mathematics education from the historical emphasis on procedural skills to a focus on language, concepts, relationships, and advanced fundamentals. Without such a change, the conventions, procedures, and algorithms of traditional mathematics instruction will continue to trump conceptual learning. However, I am confident that the system I experienced as a student and classroom teacher will adapt and the beneficiaries will be the next generations of teachers and students.

BIBLIOGRAPHY

Ahn, S., and Choi, J. "A Synthesis of the Quantitative Literature on Students' Mathematics Achievement." Paper presented at the American Educational Research Association, San Diego, 2004.

Colburn, W. "Lecture XI: On the Teaching of Arithmetic." In *The Introductory Discourse and Lectures Delivered in Boston, Before the Convention of Teachers, and Other Friends of Education, Assembled to Form the American Institute of Instruction. August 1830.* Boston: Hilliard, Gray, Little and Wilkins, 1831, p. 282.

Conference Board of the Mathematical Sciences. *The Mathematical Education of Teachers.* Providence, RI: American Mathematical Society, 2001.

Falkner, K., Levi, L., and Carpenter, T. 1999. "Children's Understanding of Equality: A Foundation for Algebra.". *Teaching Children Mathematics,* 6(4), 232–236.

Kilpatrick, J., Swafford, J., and Findell, B. Mathematics Learning Study Committee, National Research Council (U.S.). *Adding It Up: Helping Children Learn Mathematics.* Washington, DC: National Academy Press, 2001.

Molina, C. *A Qualitative Case Study of the Subject Matter Knowledge of Central Texas Middle School Mathematics Teachers* [Unpublished doctoral dissertation.]. Corpus Christi: Texas A&M University–Corpus Christi, 2004.

National Governors Association Center for Best Practices (NGA Center), and Council of Chief State School Officers (CCSSO). "Standards for Mathematical Practice," Common Core State Standards Initiative. 2010. Available from http://www.corestandards.org/the-standards/mathematics/introduction/standards-for-mathematical-practice/

INDEX

Classroom practices: beyond teachers' control, 253–254; within teachers' control, 253

Clue words, 194–195

Colburn, W., 256–257, 261

Combined units, and multiplication, 102

Common Core State Standards Initiative, 261–262

commutative, 37

Comparison, 223

Conceptual connections, and symbolism, 163–166

Conceptual definition, use of term, 48

Conceptual standards, 262–263; beyond the classroom, 264; inside the classroom, 263–264

Conceptual understanding, 28, 41–62; bad habits, 59–61; defined, 41; definitions of key concepts, 42–51; distinguishing between concepts and how-to procedures, 47–48; naked numbers, repeated use of, 61; power and value of, 41–42

Conference Board of the Mathematical Sciences, 22

Connect the dots, 51–54; poor connection vs. strong connection, 52

connect the dots, 51

Content standards, 257–258, 262; education systems without, 258; sampling of, 259–260

Context, 55–57

continuous, 44

Covert distributive property, 53

D

Definitions: need for, 4–5; summary, 50–51; words used in, 46

degree, 14

denominator, 149, 157

difference, 13

digit, 19, 48, 52

discrete, 44

Distributive property, 91, 103, 260; applied to division, 53; covert, 53; with division,

subtraction perspective, 54; with division using factorable chunks, 54; with mixed numbers, 142–143; power of, 54; with whole numbers, 142

Dividing fractions, 150–159, *See also* Fractions; division contexts, 151; hypothesis testing, 153–154; pattern approach, 152–153; quotative model of, 159; reciprocal, 154–157

Division: algorithm, 28; defined, 83; and distributive property, 92–93; equal-sized groups, 83; partitive, 151, 157–158; as a proportion, 206–207; quotative, 151, 159; wholes in, 123–124

divisor, 12

Drifting, 50, 60, 200–201

E

Educational reform, calls for, 256–257

English language: abstract terms, 13; ambiguous and idiomatic expressions, 14–15; compounded ambiguity, 15–16; convergence of mathematics and, 11–13; homonyms, 14–15; polysemous terms, 13–14; problems based on, 13–16; similar spellings, 14–15

Equal distribution, 83

Equal redistribution, 84–85

Equal sign, 165–166

Equal-sized groups, 205; average, 84; multiplication/division, 83

Equality, 259

Equations, 165–166

Equivalent fractions, 208–210; chart, 209–210

expand, 15

exponent, 45–46

F

factor, 13, 21

Falkner, K., 22, 60

Farmer's dilemma problem, 234–235

figure, 19

Figures, using to interpret formulas, 177–178

Findell, B., xxi, 25, 261

"Fluid" math terms, 36

FOIL method, 37, 93–94

Formulas, using figures to interpret, 177–178

Foundation of learning, developing, 9

Fraction Kingdom, 107–114; notion of the whole, 122–124

Fractions, 105–125, *See also* Adding fractions; Dividing fractions; Multiplying fractions; Subtracting fractions; adding, 26–27, 127–131; defined, 108; defining, 105–107; dividing, 127–131, 150–159; as division, 114; Fraction Kingdom, 107–114; interpreting, 116–117; multiplying, 131–150; operations with, 127–159; probability, 110–111; as quantities, 111–114; quantities, contexts involving, 117–122; ratio, 109; as rational numbers, 115; relationship, 113–114; as relationships, 109; and relationships, 224–226; simplifying, 25–26; slope, 110–111; subtracting, 127–131

Frayer Model, 190–191

functions, 44

G

Geometric figures, interpreting, 175–177

goes into, 24–25, 83

graph, 43–44

Graphing: real-life contexts, 168–171; in reverse, 172–175

Graphs, interpreting, 168

Grouping symbols, 72–74

Grouping table, 86

H

Hammer and lock problem, 236–239

High stakes assessments and accountability systems, standards as basis for, 261

Homonyms, 14–15

I

Idiomatic expressions, 14–15

Instruction shortcomings, *See* Tradition instruction shortcomings

Interpretation: of geometric figures, 168–171; power of, 178–187; and symbolism, 166–167

Intersecting-lines method, multiplication, 97–99

inverse relationship, 205

inverse, 38

K

Kilpatrick, J., xxi, 25, 261

L

Language and symbolism in math, 1–6, 78, *See also* Symbolism; as bridge to relationship recognition, 222–223; importance of, in mathematics, 9; logic schematic for emphasis of, 39; mathematics vocabulary, limited use of, 12–13; as vehicles for relationship recognition, 220–224; vocabulary, 12; vocabulary instruction, 12

Language focus in mathematics, 11–20, 38–39

Language-focused conceptual instruction, 6, 189–217; addition facts chart, 210–214; advanced fundamentals, teaching, 204–205; ambiguity task 1, 198; ambiguity task 2, 198–199; ambiguity task 3, 199–200; ambiguous statements/terms, 197–200; clue words, 194–195; determining operations to use, 194; division as a proportion, 206–207; drifting, 200–201; equivalent fraction chart, 209–210; Frayer Model, 190–191; instructional strategies, 197–216; manipulatives, 57, 102, 145, 189, 202, 215–216, 222; mathematics definition framework, 191; merge and connect, 207; multiplication and inverse proportion,

Language-focused conceptual instruction, *(continued)* 205–206; multiplication chart, 207–208; place value, 201; problem-solving strategies, common threads running through, 192; repeated patterns, 201; thinking, promoting/visualizing, 196–197; transitioning from single-step to multistep problems, 196; translation into mathematics, 195; word-problem interpretation process, 192–193; word-problem road map, 192; word problems, solving, 192; world of Transportia, 202–204

Language, precision in, 220–221

Lattice method, multiplication, 94–97

Levi, L., 22, 60

logarithm: defining, 44–45; use of term, 14

M

Manipulatives, 57, 102, 145, 189, 202, 215–216, 222

Math specialists, developing, 254–255

Mathematical proficiency, competencies required to attain, 41

Mathematics: context, 55–57; convergence of English language and, 11–13; failure to provide sufficient instruction, 59–60; "fluid" math terms, 36; FOIL method, 37; in-depth knowledge of concepts, legend as, 187; inadequate definitions of, 38; interpretation/translation of, 55–61; invention of terminology to make mathematics "fun," 37; key symbols, failure to review, 59–60; language focus, 11–20, 38–39; language of, 33; makeover, 257–264; meaning, 55–57; multiple meanings, 38; negative sign, 57–59; new terminology, 36–37; nuance, 55–57; reading, 33; reading like English, 59; redundant terms, 38; and relationships, 8–9, 219–249; symbolism of, 2; symbols, 35; taking liberties with

mathematical language, 37; unintended consequences, 34–35

Mathematics definition framework, 191

Mathematics instruction: as complex enterprise with multiple interrelated factors, 6; focus on procedural fluency, 42; language of, 3

Mathematics Learning Study Committee (Kilpatrick), xxi, 25, 261

Mathematics makeover, 257–264; concept or process framework, 263–264; conceptual standards, 262–264; content standards, 257–258, 262; education systems without content standards, 258; key flaw, 261; standards addressing more than content, 261–262

Mathematics vocabulary, 12–13

Meaning, 55–57

Memory aids, 93–94

Mismatched symbolism, 28–29

Misunderstanding, patterns of, 5–6

Mixed numbers, 140–141; distributive property with, 142–143

Molina, C., xxi, 25, 252

more, 198–199

multiple, 13

Multiplication, 93–94; algorithm, 28, 70–71, 89–92; area, 102; combined units, 102; defined, 82; distributive property, using the power of, 88–100; and division, 82–83; division and distributive property, 92–93; equal-sized groups, 83; FOIL method, 93–94; *groups of*, 86; interpretation of first factor and second factor, 87; interpretation of symbolism, 87; interpreting, 86–88; intersecting-lines method, 97–99; and inverse proportion, 205–206; key definitions and connections, understanding, 81–86; lattice method, 94–97; multiplication algorithm, 89–92; problematic with respect to resulting units of, 101; *sets of*,

86; *times*, 88; units in, 100–102; using as a critical knowledge base, 81–103

Multiplication algorithm, 28, 70–71, 89–92

Multiplication chart, 207–208

Multiplying fractions, 131–150, *See also* Fractions; algebraic approach, 142–143; connecting the dots, 150; context, 133; geometric approach, 143–144; mixed numbers, 140–141; numeracy approach, 141–142, 145–146; by one, 131–133; standard algorithm, 146–149; unit conversion in an area context, 149–150; whole as a set, 135–136; whole of 1, 134–135; wholes, 136–140

N

Naked numbers, 31–32, 61

National Council of Teachers of Mathematics (NCTM), 76, 261–262

National Governors Association Center for Best Practices (NGA Center), 262

National Research Council, 261

nearby, 47

Negative sign, 57–59

neighbor digit, 48

neighbor number, 48–49

New terminology, 36–37

No formula problem, 242–245

Nuance, 55–57

number: associated terms, 19; nonmathematical meanings, 19–20; use of term, 16–19, 48, 52

numeral, 17, 48, 52

numerator, 149, 157

numero, 20

O

Order of operations, 63–79; agreement, 64–65; built into standard multiplication algorithm, 70–71; communicating, 75–76; distributive property connection, 71–72; grouping symbols, 72–74; multiplication

and division before addition and subtraction, 67–69; natural order, 65–78; prerequisite knowledge, 66; rationale for, 75; relevance, 66; rules, 64–65; standard method for teaching, 63; teaching, 76–78; underlying principles, discovering, 67

order, 37

ounce, 38

P

pair, 15

paradigm, 14

Parallelograms, 179–183; area formula for, 179

Partitive division, 151

PEMDAS, 63, 65, 72, 75, 79

Perfect Storm, The (film), 251

perpendicular, 12

Perspective, and symbolism, 167–168

Pi, 163–165

place value, 19, 201

Polysemous terms, 13–14

power, 46

Probability, 110–111

Procedural fluency, 103, 261; defined, 41; as sole focus of instruction, 42

product, 13, 223

Productive disposition, defined, 41

Proper fraction, 157

Proportion, 260

Proportional reasoning, 227–230; absolute reasoning, transitioning to relative comparison, 227–228

Pythagorean theorem, 163

Q

quantitative computation, 149

Quantities, contexts involving, 117–122

Quantity contexts, wholes in, 123

Quotative division, 151

quotient, 12, 13

R

Radicals, 29–30
Rate, 111
Ratio, 109–110, 259; defined, 109
Real-life contexts, graphing, 168–171
reduce, 15, 24
regrouping, 23
Relationships: advanced fundamentals, 234–246; age problem, 235; best deal problem, 240–241; farmer's dilemma problem, 234–235; and fractions, 224–226; hammer and lock problem, 236–239; important considerations, 230–234; interpreting, 113–114; and language, 222–223; and mathematics, 219–249; no formula problem, 242–245; powerful connections, making, 234–246; proportional reasoning, 227–230; relative reasoning, scaffolding, 229–230; rope-earth problem, 245–249; and symbolism, 221–222; visual representations, 228–229; wholes in, 123
Relative comparison, transitioning from absolute reasoning to, 227–228
Relative reasoning: laying early foundations for, 228; scaffolding, 229–230
Repeated patterns, 201
resulting unit, 149
rise over run definition of slope., 49
Rope-earth problem, 245–249
round/rounding, 46–47, 52

S

Sampling of approaches, 6–8
Scale factor, 156–157
scale, 13
second, 14
Shallow definitions, complexity of, 43
Shortcuts, 25, 91, 100
similar, 198
Simple yet deep definitions, 43
simplest form, 29

Simplifying fractions, 24, 25–26; long method, 26; short method, 25
Slope, 110–111; defining, 49
Southwest Educational Development Laboratory (SEDL), 64
Standard algorithm, 146–149
Standards-based reform/education, 257–258
Standards for Mathematical Practice, Common Core State Standards Initiative, 261
Strategic competence, defined, 41
Substitution, 259
Subtracting fractions, 127–131, *See also* Fractions; incorporating the property of like items, 128–129; reinforcing like items in elementary school, 130–131; solutions and benefits, 128; with unlike denominators, 128
sum, 13, 14, 55, 195
Swafford, J., xxi, 25, 261
Symbolism, 161–168; and assumptions, 113; and conceptual connections, 163–166; equal sign, 165–166; and interpretation, 166–167; and K-12 instruction, 162; and perspective, 167–168; pi, 163–165; and relationships, 221–222; weak, 162–163
Symbols, 61
Systemic issue, 251–257; call for change, 256; classroom practices, 253–254; math specialists, developing, 254–255; teacher content expertise, 252–255; teacher placement, 255–256

T

Teacher content expertise, 252–255
Teacher placement, 255–256
Thinking, promoting/visualizing, 196–197
times, 30–31, 88
to a nearby number, 47

Traditional instruction shortcomings, 22–28; adding fractions, 26–27; *bigger half*, 23; *borrow*, 23; *cancel*, 24, 26, 131; careless vocabulary, 22–25; *carry*, 23; division, 27–28; *goes into*, 24–25, 83; illogical obstacles, 28–29; mismatched symbolism, 28–29; multiplication, 27–28; multiplication mysteries, 30–31; naked numbers, 31–32; number values, 29; radicals, 29–30; *reduce*, 24; shortcuts, 25; *simplest form*, 29; simplifying fractions, 25–26

Trapezoids: area formula for, 179; connecting parallelogram area formulas and, 185–186; definitions of, 36; perspective I, 179–181; perspective II, 181–183; perspective III, 183; summary, 186–187

twice as big, 199

V

Vague meaning, 199–200

Visual representations, 168–178; formulas, using figures to interpret, 177–178; geometric figures, interpreting, 175–177; graphing in reverse, 172–175; graphs, interpreting, 168; real-life contexts, graphing, 168–171; and relationships, 228–229

Vocabulary: careless, 22–25; historically limited focus on, 12; mathematics, 12–13

Vocabulary instruction, 12

volume, 13

von Neumann, J., 254

W

Weak symbolism, 162–163

Whole numbers, distributive property with, 142

Wholes: in division, 123–124; in quantity contexts, 123; in relationships, 123

Word problems: solving, 193; interpretation process, 192–193; road map, 192

Words, clue, 195; used in definitions, 46

World of Transportia, 202–204